JANE AUSTEN
AND THE FICTION OF HER

This book presents Jane Austen as a radical innovator. It explores the nature of her confrontation with the popular novelists of her time, and demonstrates how her challenge to them transformed fiction. It is evident from letters and other sources, as well as the novels themselves, that the Austen family developed a strong scepticism about contemporary notions of the proper content and purpose of fiction. Austen's own writing can be seen as a conscious demonstration of these disagreements. In thus identifying her literary motivation, this book (moving away from the questions of ideology which have so dominated Austen studies in this century) offers a unifying critique of the novels and helps to explain their unequalled durability with the reading public.

Mary Waldron is the author of *Lactilla: The Life and Writings of Ann Yearsley, 1753–1806* (1996) and has taught on the continuing education programme at the University of Essex. She has published articles on women's writing and eighteenth-century literature in a number of scholarly books and journals.

JANE AUSTEN AND THE FICTION OF HER TIME

MARY WALDRON

CAMBRIDGE
UNIVERSITY PRESS

PUBLISHED BY THE PRESS SYNDICATE OF THE UNIVERSITY OF CAMBRIDGE
The Pitt Building, Trumpington Street, Cambridge, United Kingdom

CAMBRIDGE UNIVERSITY PRESS
The Edinburgh Building, Cambridge, CB2 2RU, UK
40 West 20th Street, New York, NY 10011–4211, USA
10 Stamford Road, Oakleigh, VIC 3166, Australia
Ruiz de Alarcón 13, 28014 Madrid, Spain
Dock House, The Waterfront, Cape Town 8001, South Africa

http://www.cambridge.org

© Mary Waldron 1999

First published 1999
Reprinted 2000 (twice)
First paperback edition 2001

Printed in the United Kingdom at the University Press, Cambridge

Typeset in Baskerville 11/12.5pt   [CE]

A catalogue record for this book is available from the British Library

Library of Congress Cataloguing in Publication data applied for

ISBN 0 521 65130 1 hardback
ISBN 0 521 00388 1 paperback

To Daniel, Rachel, Adam, Anna, Marion and Alice

– pictures of perfection as you know make me sick & wicked

(Letter to Fanny Knight, 23 March [1817])

Contents

Acknowledgements

Chapters 4 and 5 of this study are based on articles which previously appeared in two journals; 'The Frailties of Fanny: *Mansfield Park* and the Evangelical Movement' was published in *Eighteenth-Century Fiction* 6, April 1994, and 'Men of Sense and Silly Wives: the Confusions of Mr Knightley' in *Studies in the Novel* 28, 1996. I am grateful to the editors of these publications for permission to use this material.

I am grateful also to Josie Dixon of the Cambridge University Press for her knowledgeable interest and for her encouragement throughout the writing process; and to the Press's two readers, whose criticisms and suggestions have so much improved the early drafts.

My thanks are also due to members of the London Women's Studies Group 1500-1825 for listening to some of the original ideas. Special appreciation should go to Linda Bree for reading part of the manuscript and to Lois A. Chaber for sharing her Richardson expertise.

Finally, I must thank my son Tom Waldron, who first believed that I was right about *Mansfield Park*, and my husband Ronald Waldron for his unfailing encouragement over a long period, and his invaluable help in the preparation of the manuscript.

Texts and abbreviations

References to Jane Austen's works are to the following editions:

The Novels of Jane Austen, ed. R. W. Chapman, 5 vols., 3rd edition (London; Oxford University Press, 1933), reprinted 1960
Minor Works, ed. R. W. Chapman (London; Oxford University Press, 1954), reprinted with revisions, 1963
Jane Austen's Letters, collected and edited by R. W. Chapman, 2nd edition (London; Oxford University Press, 1952), reprinted with corrections, 1964

ABBREVIATIONS

E	*Emma*
MP	*Mansfield Park*
MW	*Minor Works*
NA	*Northanger Abbey*
P	*Persuasion*
PP	*Pride and Prejudice*
SS	*Sense and Sensibility*

Introduction

> I do not write for such dull elves
> As have not a great deal of ingenuity themselves
> *(Letters,* 29 January, 1813, p. 298).[1]

' "It is really very well for a novel." – Such is the common cant.'
Jane Austen's defence of the novel in *Northanger Abbey* brings together
her abiding obsession with fiction and her deep dislike of the
expression of unexamined fashionable opinion. But despite her
spirited support of her fellow-novelists here, her letters and other
family documents show that she by no means considered them
innocent of certain kinds of 'cant' themselves; her trenchant criticisms of the novels that she discusses with Cassandra and other
members of her family often identify stereotypical characters and
events which she considered had no credible existence outside the
accepted world of the contemporary novel; the denunciations 'unnatural', 'improbable', even 'absurd', appear frequently, occasionally
applied even to novels she enjoyed. 'I do not like a Lover's speaking
in the 3d person; – it is too much like the formal part of Lord Orville
[the hero of Burney's *Evelina*], and I think it is not natural', she
writes to her niece Anna in 1814, giving her advice on the writing of
her own novel.[2] Other contemporary writers come in for stronger
castigation. In Mary Brunton's *Self-control*, the heroine, a young lady
of great strength of mind and unassailable virtue, is abducted by her
dissolute lover and taken to Canada, where she only escapes his
attentions by floating alone down a river in a convenient canoe.
Austen sums it up thus: 'an excellently-meant, elegantly-written
Work, without anything of Nature or Probability in it. I declare I do
not know whether Laura's passage down the American River, is not
the most natural, possible, everyday thing she ever does'.[3] Of Sarah
Burney's *Clarentine*, a very popular and morally improving work, she

I

says: 'It is full of unnatural conduct & forced difficulties, without striking merit of any kind.'[4] 'Unnatural conduct' in a novel, especially if it was used to support the moral tendency of the work, she found deeply unsatisfying; she appears to have judged that writers of fiction had a duty to keep faith with readers – invention must tie in with what she thought they would recognise and to some extent share. This appears to have been her interpretation of that rather slippery eighteenth-century concept, 'nature' – that which is common to all human beings – which was closely related to her second stated requirement, 'probability'. There had been vigorous debate about fictional probability from the early years of the eighteenth century – the consensus from such theoretical studies as had taken place was that a work of fiction ought to combine a moral tendency with a credible scenario.[5] Without the moral the credibility might be dangerous, especially to young readers. They might want to imitate the 'bad' characters if they were not given clear guidance. Austen was surely aware of the currency of these ideas through her reading of Dr Johnson, especially of *Rambler* 4, but felt that the balance had been disastrously disturbed; she appears to have concluded that fiction was beginning to sell out to polemic; to prioritise didacticism of one kind or another; in short, to give way to 'cant'. This may have seemed particularly evident in the 1790s as the novel became the focus of a radical–conservative debate about morality in the wake of the French Revolution. What has been called 'the novel of crisis' developed, in which fiction was used as a site for moral and social debate.[6] As extreme examples of a numerous genre we might mention Mary Hays at the radical end of the scale, with her novel *The Memoirs of Emma Courtney* (1796) in which she presents a woman attempting to take charge of her sexual destiny, and at the same time opens up current Godwinian theories of anarchism and the perfectibility of man; and at the conservative end, Maria Edge-worth and Jane West, who both denounced the fashionable doctrines of high sensibility and radical politics (which nearly always went together) in *Letters for Literary Ladies* (1795) and in *A Tale of the Times* (1799).[7] The polarisation of aims led to a hardening of novelistic formulae. Certain stereotypes were collecting around the reading public's idea of the novel – the deluded female who reads too many novels, the model girl, the female rebel, the hero/guardian who has all the right answers, contrasting pairs of heroines, one right, the other disastrously wrong; most novels, whether politically conservative or radical, made use of some or all of these. Many conservative novels were strongly influenced by popular conduct manuals, such as Dr Gregory's *A Father's Legacy to his Daughters* (1774). Jane West herself published two conduct books;[8] her novels are to a great extent fictional versions of these. Internal evidence from the novels makes clear that Austen knew the Gregory treatise, and she mentions Gisborne's *Enquiry into the Duties of the Female Sex* (1797) in one of her letters to Cassandra.[9] We also know a certain amount about the novels Jane and Cassandra read, but the comments which survive do not include allusion to radical writers like Wollstonecraft and Hays – perhaps Cassandra saw fit to exclude such comment in the reaction against late eighteenth-century feminism which gathered momentum in the first decades of the nineteenth. But it seems reasonably safe to assume that the whole Austen family, assiduous novel-readers as they were, were well acquainted with the literary scene in general. We know how Austen reacted to the more conservative writers like Mary Brunton; it is likely that fiction with the opposite purpose would have struck her very similarly. She set about a challenge to contemporary assumptions, attempting to free fiction from elements which she thought hampered its relationship with its readers – perhaps broke the illusion which she supposed a fiction-writer was trying to create. In making this effort she created a new kind of novel which put all her predecessors and contemporaries more or less in the shade and ensured that her work outlived theirs. The exact nature of this achievement and the reasons for it have been the subject of continuous debate for nearly two centuries.

From the first her apparent narrowness of range was regarded with somewhat surprised approval. Readers of the early nineteenth century were used to novels that offered them adventure of some kind – fictional experience of broad scenes and/or exciting events which were outside their personal knowledge but made plausible by the persuasive skill of the writer. Though Richardson is ostensibly writing about life below stairs, he does not pretend that Pamela's trials are what any maidservant might expect in the course of her duties, and his later imitators often vied with each other in the production of situations of intense misery and terror which few readers could expect to experience. The picaresque novel, including *Tom Jones*, is by definition full of action and intrigue. Novels of sensibility on the Mackenzie model existed to provoke pleasurable and often exaggerated anguish in their readers. Austen's scenes of (apparent) unrelieved domestic triviality were new, but they were also thought safe. Her earliest critics regarded with condescending favour her ability to be interesting without the artificial excitements and sensationalism that they associated with the novel of the period, and to be morally 'unexceptionable' into the bargain. This kind of novel, they thought, was unlikely to lead to enervating emotionalism and Lydia Languish-like fantasies among the 'fair readers' – thus far, Austen seemed to be conforming with received opinion. She had managed to exclude the moral dangers which Johnson had associated with excessive realism. 'We will detain our female friends no longer than to assure them', says the anonymous reviewer of *Sense and Sensibility* in 1812, after pronouncing favourably on the work in comparison with others of the genre, 'that they may peruse these volumes not only with satisfaction but with real benefits, for they may learn from them, if they please, many sober and salutary maxims for the conduct of life'.[10] Even Walter Scott, justifiably admired for his early and intelligent enthusiasm for Austen, from the first assumes the essential triviality of the genre itself – 'these light volumes', he says of novels in general, may 'beguile ... hours of languor and anxiety, of deserted age and solitary celibacy'. The sum of his encomium is that Austen beguiled her readers in a less harmful way than some of her more sensational and fantastic fellow-novelists. '... the youthful wanderer,' he adds, 'may return from his promenade to the ordinary business of life, without any chance of having his head turned by the recollection of the scene through which he has been wandering'. Though he clearly perceived that Austen had effected some significant change – 'she has produced sketches of such spirit and originality', he says, 'that we never miss the excitation which depends on a narrative of uncommon events' – he fails to identify it with any exactness.[11] Her fidelity to 'real life' and 'knowledge of the human heart' were consolations for the absence of the exalted models of human character which the century continued in theory to require from novels. Sometimes, though, the sober tranquillity and low-key humour failed to satisfy; a Mrs Guiton, or Guitton, possibly of Little Park Place, near Fareham, when asked for an opinion of *Emma*, responded succinctly: 'too natural to be interesting' (*MW* 437); and according to Mary Russell Mitford '[Austen] wants nothing but the *beau-idéal* of the female character to be a perfect novel-writer'.[12] For many of her admirers her excellence lay in the wisdom of her restriction of her fictional range to those scenes likely to be familiar to a polite maiden lady without experience of the wider world – they were happy to dispense with the elevation of mankind in favour of the everyday-life moral which is always mentioned as an essential ingredient. Archbishop Whately can only justify the popularity of the novel at all in terms of its power to instruct, and admires Austen most for making her morality palatable, in contrast to Maria Edgeworth and Hannah More: 'The moral lessons of this lady's novels, though clearly and impressively conveyed, are not offensively put forward ... they are not forced upon the reader'.[13]

The nineteenth century on the whole preferred this image, and it was given a good deal of authority by members of Austen's family. The 'Biographical Notice of the Author' by her brother, added to the posthumous edition of *Northanger Abbey* and *Persuasion* in 1817 and revised in 1833, established the picture of the Christian authoress, 'gentle Aunt Jane', which became so comfortingly familiar, and the quotation of her estimate of her own work in a letter to her nephew, James Edward, the 'little bit (two Inches wide) of Ivory, on which I work with so fine a Brush, as produces little effect after much labour',[14] helped to consolidate an impression of a writer who had no strong views on anything above the petty doings of rather insignificant people. Occasional outbreaks of a more energetic engagement with the riddle of her popularity, such as George Henry Lewes's comments in the critical press and his full-length essay in 1859, did little to dissipate the impression of an acceptable, undisturbing lady author, whose work was exquisite and true to life, but – well – not quite, unfortunately, in the first rank. Lewes insisted on her artistic achievement, and begins his 1859 essay by describing her as 'an artist of the highest rank' but talks himself into innumerable qualifications, until he concludes with what must be the ultimate in faint praise: 'But, after all, miniatures are not frescoes, and her works are miniatures. Her place is among the Immortals; but the pedestal is erected in a quiet niche of the great temple.'[15] This hardly solved the problem of why she continued to be read when so many other eighteenth- and early nineteenth-century writers were falling out of favour. The publication of the *Memoir* in 1870[16] reinforced earlier estimates, and Richard Simpson's really appreciative essay of that year is riddled with apologies for her limitations and actually concludes with the words 'dear aunt Jane'.[17] This was more or less the critical position at the beginning of the twentieth century. So far her apparent avoidance of the great serious issues of humanity had gained her work qualified approval. Simpson sets the tone with a Latin tag, 'Ne gladium tollas mulier' – 'Woman, bear not the sword.' The inference is that she very properly avoided the tumult of controversy and stayed in her correct sphere. The moral tendency of her work was taken for granted – it was conservative, single-minded and safe. Her only fault – if it could indeed be rated a fault – was the restriction of the range of her attention.

The twentieth century was to uncover difference excellences and a wider selection of faults and failings. 'Gentle Aunt Jane' disappeared from serious criticism (though she surfaces from time to time in the media), first of all in Reginald Farrer's ground-breaking estimate in 1917.[18] He was the first to see her as essentially an iconoclast: 'standing aloof from the world, she sees it, on the whole, as silly. She has no animosity for it; but she has no affection.' He sweeps away the earlier complaint that she ignored the 'vast anguish of her time' with the assertion that 'she was concerned only with the universal' and 'is coextensive with human nature', 'preaches no gospel, grinds no axe'. Such insights were startling and revealing, but they are accompanied by a new set of reservations. Farrer's assessment will not contain the whole *œuvre*; he has doubts about *Sense and Sensibility*, and dismisses *Mansfield Park* as an out-and-out fall from grace: '*Mansfield Park* is vitiated throughout by a radical dishonesty...Jane Austen is torn between the theory of what she ought to see, and the fact of what she does see.' His perception of Austen as somehow unable to sustain her own fictional principles was to become a typical feature of twentieth-century criticism which it is part of the aim of the present study to challenge. However, at this early date, Farrer's more open-minded approach to what he saw as Austen's somewhat distant and critical relationship with her society, combined with the close and sensitive reading of text later recommended by I. A. Richards and the 'New Critics', whose work became increasingly influential from the thirties onwards,[19] certainly encouraged new, more searching appraisal of the novels. These approaches, together with the publication and consequent increased accessibility of most of the surviving letters in 1932, made possible a rather less bland version of Austen – she began to present an altogether more serious problem for critics.

Austen studies became particularly central to a fresh critical approach associated with F. R. Leavis and his followers.[20] In their general attack on what they saw as outmoded academic gentility, they sought to introduce greater rigour into the study of literature; their aims were not identical to those of the New Critics, though there was a similar emphasis on the importance of close reading. Leavis's main concerns were, however, historical and social. His formulation of the 'great tradition' excluded writing which did not, in his opinion, convey a sense of a continuing 'vigorous humane culture'. Jane Austen was one among the very few novelists of the past considered worthy of serious attention on these grounds. It was under his aegis, in the periodical *Scrutiny*, that the Austen of the *Memoir* received her *coup de grâce* in D. W. Harding's 'Regulated Hatred' (1940) which replaced the kindly if not quite elegant lady-writer with a sharply intelligent woman writing against the grain of the narrow society within which she was inevitably confined. His estimate includes much of the ironic humour in the texts of the novels which earlier critics had often touched upon, but dismissed as mere fun, wit, or whatever did not interfere too much with the overall picture. But he is quite clear that the ridicule to which Austen holds up establishment figures like clergymen does not constitute satire – 'She has none of the underlying didactic intention ordinarily attributed to the satirist. Her object is not missionary.'[21] Harding's essay was certainly a new departure, but his arrival is more in doubt. Rejecting satire he identifies Austen's acerbic humour as a kind of personal therapy: 'she was sensitive to [her society's] crudenesses and complacencies and knew that her real existence depended on resisting many of the values they implied. The novels gave her a way out of this dilemma.' This hardly engages in any positive way with what the novels *did* achieve. Other *Scrutiny* articles by Q. D. Leavis and her survey of fiction emphasise Austen's basic detachment from her society, but insist upon her continuing cultural relevance; they come to more constructive conclusions.[22]

Meanwhile the first really searching, thorough and immensely influential literary biography of Austen had appeared, that of Mary Lascelles, who, working at Oxford, was not part of the *Scrutiny* group.[23] Her critical aims and her strong reservations about nine-teenth-century critics are summed up in her Preface: 'Is this perhaps a characteristic of that generation of critics, that they exclaim, with Jonson, "By God, 'tis good, and if you like't, you may", and carry entire conviction – but leave us at the exciting "how?" and "why?" of analysis?'

It was inevitable that the overall approval of critics such as the Leavises and Lascelles would produce a reaction. A substantial number of commentators in the forties saw Austen's novels as less than relevant to anything in modern life – indeed tied securely to the ethos of her times.[24] To some of these her novels were simply didactic, rather elaborate courtesy-books which partook of the Anglican Evangelical morality which was at its strongest during her writing life. Their moral purpose might be obliquely stated, but it was, many critics asserted, as present as in any of the more moralistic fiction of her time. They could perceive little of the challenge to contemporary mores identified by Harding.[25] This strain of criticism naturally centred upon *Mansfield Park*, but a certain reading of the other novels based on twentieth-century ideas of personal freedom seemed to these critics to reveal a recommendation of differing degrees of decorum and submission to the young female protagonists and to come to rather moralistic conclusions. The spell of the novels was often seen as nostalgia for a more settled and reliable moral and social scene thought to have existed during Austen's writing life. For some, especially Marxist critics seeking politically acceptable values from literature, the nostalgia was rather discreditable, based on what Arnold Kettle saw as her 'unquestioning acceptance of class society'; her failure to include the lower reaches of that society and its contemporary problems was seen by him and many others as restricting her moral vision.[26] This dismissal produced its own reaction – the emergence of what has been called the 'subversive' school of Austen criticism – studies which, building on Harding's in 1940, exposed a greater or lesser challenge to the values of her society. Almost invariably these analyses result in adverse criticism, particularly of the resolutions of the novels, which are often perceived as failures on the part of the novelist to face up to the implications of her irony in an accommodation to the moral and social status quo. In the criticism of the fifties, Marvin Mudrick's *Jane Austen: Irony as Defense and Discovery* stands out not only as a refreshing and astringent corrective to gentle-Janeism that is much more deeply analytical than Harding's, but also as a specific challenge to Q. D. Leavis's view of Austen as a universally involved but free spirit.[27] Mudrick's alternative picture of a writer constantly resorting to a defensive irony as an escape from confrontation with what she perceived as real evils is fascinating; but it is also curiously destructive. Every commentary, as he charts the development and refinement of the irony, identifies flaws and failures; one finishes the book with the perception that, in Mudrick's eyes at least, Austen never quite made it. The conclusion of *Sense and Sensibility* is 'too abrupt and half-hearted to convince' (p. 92); *Pride and Prejudice* is more successful, but only insofar as 'the flaw of an irrelevant defensiveness has almost vanished' (p. 126); 'the world of *Mansfield Park* fails to convince' (p. 180); *Persuasion* is in need of revision; only in *Sanditon* is her irony 'dynamic, changing or expanding *at last* [my italics] into an authentically unrestricted point of view'. In a swing away from the 'subversive' school A. Walton Litz in *Jane Austen: A Study of her Artistic Development* (1965) perceives Jane Austen as 'assum[ing] a universal and traditional moral standard' which was conventional and unsensational, and which her narratives uphold.[28] His chief interest lies in the way in which he sees her as developing the power to reconcile this standard with individual freedom. With this approach it is easier for him to admire the novels, but its developmental schema necessarily implies the presence of many 'flaws' – and in any case, he is unable to demonstrate that the development was even. He speaks of *Pride and Prejudice*, only the second novel to be published, as in a crucial way the peak of her achievement, 'a triumph not to be repeated', because it bears out his view of her objectives as a writer; *Mansfield Park* is a comparative failure because, he asserts, it does not produce the required synthesis of feeling and conventional morality. One is left with the inescapable suspicion that both Mudrick and Litz feel that Austen was capable of writing much better novels than she actually did; Mudrick seems almost to be suggesting that Austen's work would have been more effective *without* the irony; Litz blames her for falling short of a set of aims which were not necessarily hers. This latter approach became a dominating tendency in the criticism of the next decades. Its tone is indulgent but oddly patronising – yes, we all enjoy reading Jane Austen, but here are the reasons why she doesn't altogether deserve our praise. Academia needed to find seriousness in Austen's work; when they found it, they tended to find failure too. Survival, according to such critics, is not necessarily the same as success.

Litz's view was upheld and extended during the seventies at a time of much ideological confrontation which affected criticism generally and revived doubts such as those earlier voiced by Arnold Kettle. Post-structuralist critics particularly argued strongly that all engagement with literature involves some political attitude on the part of writer and reader. Q. D. Leavis's view of Austen as a universal free spirit, and indeed all New Critical and Leavisite interpretations based on close textual examination, were rejected by those following the most up-to-date critical directions, on the grounds that the exponents had utterly failed to free themselves of the academic and political narrowness that they had tried so hard to escape. But on the whole, Austen studies remained curiously unaffected by the abstractions of new theory; major Austen critics of the seventies began to take a different, though still historical, line from that of Leavis, mainly by confronting the very political bias that postmodern theorists found so objectionable. Acceptance of the essentially conservative nature of Austen's reaction to the world in which she found herself had its best-known expression in Alistair Duckworth's *The Improvement of the Estate* in 1971 and Marilyn Butler's *Jane Austen and the War of Ideas*, published in 1975.[29] Again, having postulated an overarching tendency in the novels, these critics, particularly the latter, identify as failure the exceptions and departures from that tendency – in *Sense and Sensibility* Austen fails 'to get us to read her story with the necessary ethical detachment' because we tend to sympathise with Marianne, who is rebelling against the ethical system; and *Mansfield Park* is 'an artistic failure' because, in Fanny, Austen tries to merge the 'exemplary' with the 'suffering' heroine and does not, in Butler's view, succeed.

The 'conservative' picture presented by these critics, of Austen as the upholder of tradition at a time of great ideological ferment, did not satisfy certain feminists, who perceived a distinctly subversive vein in Austen's treatment of her male characters. However, a good deal of feminist criticism of the eighties reaches the conclusion that women novelists of the eighteenth century were by and large forced into acceptance of the literary and social norms of their society by a dominating and powerful patriarchy which would only tolerate them if they upheld the standards of the establishment. Austen's often ironic slant on male–female relations, and the undeniable shortcomings of male characters, did not seem to critics like Mary Poovey, in *The Proper Lady and the Woman Writer*, and Nancy Armstrong, in *Desire and Domestic Fiction*, to go far enough to demonstrate her independence.[30] Two other feminist critics took up a very different position, one which has had a strong influence on the present study.[31] Margaret Kirkham, in *Jane Austen: Feminism and Fiction*, successfully and most interestingly places Jane Austen in the context of her contemporaries and of Enlightenment feminism, showing her to be much more positively engaged with the problems of being a woman at the turn of the eighteenth century than anyone had previously perceived, and much more effectively than Poovey and Armstrong were prepared to admit. The thesis of the book is very persuasive, and its revelations of Austen's continual reference in the novels to contemporary writers and to her experience of the theatre are extraordinarily valuable. But, once again, the old problem arises: there are points where the thesis won't quite stick, especially in the commentary on the novel texts, and we are left with the impression that Austen had not quite achieved what Kirkham sees as her aim – to make the heroine's moral consciousness the motivating principle of each novel. It doesn't seem quite satisfactory to say, for instance, about Anne Elliot's defence of Lady Russell: 'In the end, we are not quite so sure *as we ought to be* [my italics] that Anne's regard for her is wholly justified.' The obligation is laid upon us by Kirkham, not Austen, and to say, as she does in the next paragraph, that our doubts are due to the imperfect revisions of the novel further begs the question.[32] Points like this one will be taken up later in this book, as Austen's undoubted feminism is slotted into what can be perceived as a much wider objective on her part. The second work, Claudia L. Johnson's *Jane Austen: Women, Politics and the Novel*, builds on Kirkham's, but is much more searching in its analysis of the novels and gives a very lucid and detailed account of the effect of the French Revolution on contemporary woman writers. Some of my readings of the novels are similar to hers; but again, Austen's feminist slant seems only one component of the broader issues I wish to explore.

Other preoccupations besides feminism have surfaced in the blurring of the boundaries between literature and history. New Historicist criticism has insisted on the consideration of context in all literary comment. This is a very productive process and has provided a corrective to what became a rather sterile concentration on the 'words on the page' among later adherents to the New Criticism, and also to the often unspecific abstractions of other brands of modern literary theory. But it has its dangers. Given that the impact of a novel can never be exclusively the product of an author's intention and may allow for many readings, we should surely not stray so far from the text in uncovering implied meanings that we ignore what the *action* of an episode is telling us. A tendency to prioritise what *we* think was important over the perceptions of the author working within the cultural parameters of his/her time can damage the coherence of a novel and alter its dynamics. Arnold Kettle and cultural historians like Raymond Williams [33] may be right *in their terms* to see Austen's fictional world as essentially class-based, but 'class' in the Marxist sense that they use did not exist in Austen's lifetime; her society was only just emerging from a semi-feudal situation. It is interesting to identify foreshadowings in the novels of what were to become elements in the adversarial world of Marx – bourgeois versus proletarian – but they tell us nothing about the world within which Austen's characters interact, the world which she and they assume. By historicising in this way we run the risk of losing the novel. An example of the sort of historical criticism I should wish to avoid in this study is contained in recent discussions of *Mansfield Park*. The lack of response to Fanny Price's question about the slave trade which is referred to in a conversation between her and Edmund (*MP* 198) has been seen as a crucial reference to the collective guilt of the Bertram family about their economic reliance on the Antigua plantation. There seems to be no room in the novel for such elements and nothing to support the idea that Sir Thomas goes to Antigua to save Mansfield from financial collapse. Coming back to the text and what can be perceived in a reading based on narrative coherence, 'the silence of the Bertrams' can be seen to stem from the indifference and shallowness of some members of the family group now left by themselves at Mansfield and the deep personal preoccupations of others. In the scene in question we can infer from the slight information given, that Lady Bertram is thinking about nothing, in her habitual way; Tom probably chafing at the loss of his sophisticated amusements and dying to get away; Maria and Julia thinking in one way or another about young men, and Mrs Norris fussing about domestic trivia. Edmund is preoccupied with the absent Mary Crawford, as he makes clear in this very conversation, though he speaks with comic indirectness: ' "Dr. and Mrs. Grant would enliven us, and make our evenings pass away with more enjoyment even to my father" ' (*MP* 196). Fanny, unlike most of her cousins, is a serious-minded girl with pious Evangelical leanings (and consequently with an interest in the Abolition), and no place in the marriage market as far as she knows, who would in any case probably feel some duty to save Sir Thomas from talking entirely to himself. So she asks a question (unspecified) 'about the slave trade' which interests only Sir Thomas. She aims to please, but can't please everybody, and gives Edmund very adequate reasons for with-drawing when she gets no help – ' "I thought it would appear as if I wanted to set myself off at their expense." ' While such richness of perception is available from this short dialogue alone, there seems no good critical reason for swinging attention away from it towards commercial (or possibly, it has been suggested, marginally illegal) activities in which Sir Thomas may or may not be engaged.[34]

While historicising, as I believe, sufficiently, I shall show in this study that it is possible to construct a unifying critique of the novels based on Austen's own view of what she was about and her knowledge of the society in which she found herself, without either straying inappropriately into peripheral historical–cultural detail or insisting on single authoritative readings. Plenty of evidence is available in the texts of the novels and in the letters to identify what drove Austen to write. Though securely contained within the particular section of English society of her birth and upbringing, Austen was acutely aware of its snobberies and hypocrisies. But with Elizabeth Bennet, she 'delighted in everything ridiculous' and like all ironists, wanted, not to change things, but to write about them. There can be no doubt about her discontent with the fiction that already existed; letters to Cassandra and her nieces, especially Anna, and the 1816 *Plan of a Novel*, show that the enjoyment in novels that she shared with her sister and nieces consisted largely in poking fun at what she and they regarded as absurdities. Her sense of the ludicrous even extends to Richardson and Burney (when James Austen-Leigh wrote his *Memoir* he perhaps conveniently forgot that her 'living friends' were not exempt from Aunt Jane's biting sarcasm).[35] Part of the absurdity lay, in her view, in the fixed moral programme which justified the existence of many a contemporary novel; when this led to the interpolation of passages of 'solemn specious nonsense ... about something unconnected with the story' she felt that the fiction was damaged thereby; her pretended criticism of *Pride and Prejudice* and her mischievous suggestion that it should be 'stretched out here and there with a long chapter of sense' should by no means be taken seriously.[36] Her aim was to dispense with the fixed programme, at the same time using the assumption that it would be present in order to splinter the reader's allegiances, putting the locus of moral approval in continual doubt. This was made more effective by the reduction of setting to a certain kind of commonplace domestic scene. In adhering to what she thought of as

'Nature' and 'Probability' Austen did more than she perhaps intended. Because we are not aghast at the predicaments of Austen's central characters (as we must be with Clarissa, Cecilia, Camilla, Ellis–Juliet, for instance) we can be more open to the intricacies of their minds, which always betray more weaknesses than they initially appear to have. All Austen's major characters – yes, even Fanny Price and Mr Knightley – are morally inconsistent, threading their way through conflicting courses for which there proves to be no systematic guide. Though they are recognisably related to the great figures of earlier fiction, they differ from them in fundamental ways.

Austen's disagreement with contemporary assumptions about fiction, then, resulted in a demonstration that the novel form was capable of containing more uncertainties and unanswered questions than had before been thought, and that it could still identify issues of principle without dealing in extremes of 'guilt and misery'. We do not know what she thought of *Pamela* and *Clarissa* (*Sir Charles Grandison* is the only novel of Richardson that she actually refers to) but if the *Memoir* is correct she did think they were works of 'striking merit'; however, she had all the confidence – even arrogance – of an innovator and felt that the Richardsonian tradition had begun to peter out in 'absurdities'. Beginning with burlesque, her fiction is gradually transmuted into an infinitely subtle and detailed exploration of the largely unsuccessful human effort to achieve a satisfactory self-image. As she refines dialogue and free indirect style, her fictional world becomes so extraordinarily complex that there is no room and no need for interpolations of 'solemn, specious nonsense' to 'stretch out' the story. The stories speak for themselves and take care to impose no perfect solution. Readers are always left with the possibility of choice in their response to the actions and thoughts of the main characters. But Austen refers constantly, implicitly or explicitly, to novels which, in contrast, do not offer this choice. Much of her fiction, then, is about fiction itself, its parameters and possibilities – as Rachel M. Brownstein has said, she 'wrote to criticize and perfect the form'.[37] Because Austen wrote consciously against the grain of contemporary didacticism but within a familiar fictional framework, her narratives become not only ironic but richly contrapuntal; we are conscious of the presence of a number of points of view at every turn. It is perhaps this special narrative complexity that has proved so permanently satisfying even to readers with little or no knowledge of the literary matrix which gave it birth. But an appreciation of the ways in which her immediate predecessors and contemporaries impinged upon her writing adds immeasurably to that pleasure. The following chapters will re-examine her work, dwelling on key passages from the juvenilia and early unfinished narratives and the six completed novels to *Sanditon*, with this in view, referring appropriately to some of the novelists and other writers of her time whose work, from the evidence of the letters and other references, we can be sure she knew, and which offered her an irresistible challenge.

The juvenilia, the early unfinished novels and 'Northanger Abbey'

Early in her reading experience Jane Austen became obsessively interested in the form and language of the novel, and in its relationship with its readers; her first experimental writing was dominated by attempts to refashion fiction as she knew it. With merciless disrespect she isolated elements which were at best formulaic, at worst perfunctory. Early burlesque shows Austen identifying popular narrative forms as hypnotic and thought-denying. She was moved to make hilarious fun of the wilder examples of the novel of sensibility, and some even wilder interpretations of the liberation ideologies of the French *philosophes*; but ordinary received moral wisdom was not exempt from her youthful scorn. Her earliest writing puts a number of fashionable fictional stereotypes, often derived from the pomposities of conduct-literature as well as from fashionable progressive ideas, into a domestic frame which renders them ludicrous and, more importantly, shows them to be repetitious and stultifying. From the start she set out to put forms and theories to the test of the everyday, without which they were, as she saw it, merely substitutes for coherent and rational deliberation.

The language of contemporary moral discourse fascinated her. She perceived very early that formulaic phrase-building can acquire the ring of truth, and she often parodies the typical Johnsonian antithetical maxim – for example, in the description of Lady Williams in *Jack and Alice* we are informed that: 'Tho' Benevolent & Candid, she was Generous & sincere; Tho' Pious & Good, she was Religious & amiable, and Tho' Elegant and Agreable, she was Polished & Entertaining.' Common sentence patterns are constantly used either to create nonsense or to turn conventional moral expectation on its head; also in *Jack and Alice* we read: 'The Johnsons were a family of Love, & though a little addicted to the Bottle & the Dice, had many good Qualities' (*MW* 13). The joke is clear enough, but its implication is less so – mouthing phrases can be a substitute for thought, language can be used as a soporific.

The parodic experimental novels in *Volume the Second, Love and Freindship* and *Lesley Castle* are also concerned with the effects of a conventional, formulaic language. Expected elements of the Mackenzie style of epistolary narrative unroll on the page, producing a comic double-take – for example, this from *Lesley Castle*:

Perhaps you may flatter me so far as to be surprised that one of whom I speak with so little affection should be my particular freind; but to tell you the truth, our freindship arose rather from Caprice on her side than Esteem on mine. We spent two or three days together with a Lady in Berkshire with whom we both happened to be connected – . During our visit, the Weather being remarkably bad, and our party particularly stupid, she was so good as to conceive a violent partiality for me, which very soon settled in a downright Freindship and ended in an established correspondence. She is probably by this time as tired of me, as I am of her; but as she is too polite and I am too civil to say so, our letters are still as frequent and affectionate as ever, and our Attachment as firm and sincere as when it first commenced. (*MW* 120)

The sober balance of the initial phrasing and sententious vocabulary for a moment conceal the outright nonsense of the sentiments. Both *Love and Freindship* and *Lesley Castle* are full of similar deliciously ludicrous moments. But there is more to this than mere burlesque of a style. As her experiments continue Austen engages also with the increasingly stereotyped fictional concepts of human relationships and motives which she observed in sentimental novels and edges into a challenge to fashionable moral and social trends. Popular reversals of current convention, such as contempt for the practicalities of life, for parental guidance and the ordinary demands of family and society, are thrown into ridicule more for their lack of pragmatic applicability than for their moral implications. She invents characters who are virtually dead to all common sense. In *Love and Freindship* Edward's ritual defiance of his father takes precedence over his real desires – he is hamstrung by 'common cant':

'My Father, seduced by the false glare of Fortune and the Deluding Pomp of Title, insisted on my giving my hand to Lady Dorothea. No never exclaimed I. Lady Dorothea is lovely and Engaging; I prefer no woman to her; but know Sir, that I scorn to marry her in compliance with your Wishes. No! Never shall it be said that I obliged my Father.' (*MW* 81)

Having married Laura after less than half-an-hour's acquaintance he pours scorn on his sensible sister's concern for the couple's means of livelihood: ' "Victuals and Drink! ... and dost thou then imagine that there is no other support for an exalted Mind (such as is my Laura's) than the mean and indelicate employment of Eating and Drinking?" '(*MW* 83).

Such broadly comic treatment of fashionable sentiment gives way to something more serious in the more extended but ultimately abortive novels, *Catharine or The Bower* (1792), *Lady Susan* (1793–4) and *The Watsons* (1804–5) (*MW* 193–363). The reasons why these attempts were abandoned may hold some clues to the gradual development of Austen's fictional aims. I include *Catharine* among the unfinished novels rather than as part of the juvenilia as defined by R. W. Chapman (*MW* vii) on the grounds that it is a far more complex fiction than the other fragmentary narratives and marks a turning-point. All three abortive novels move away from burlesque; though they are still on the attack, often through derision, they have a largely different target. Austen does not take contemporary attempts to overturn traditional moral conventions too seriously – for her, trendy radical ideas were easy objects of ridicule. The acid test of the day-to-day was enough. Not for her the solemnities of Maria Edgeworth in 'Letters of Julia and Caroline' or Jane West in *A Tale of the Times,* for instance, where misery or death lie in wait for those too easily persuaded to adopt fashionably extreme notions.[1] But this did not mean that she accepted the currently respectable moral and social precepts without reservation, and in *Catharine* some of these are also held up not so much to ridicule as to ironic examination. In 1790, at the beginning of the period when most of the juvenilia and fragmentary novels were being written, *The Young Lady's Pocket Library, or Parental Monitor,* a compilation of conduct books dating from 1727 to 1774 was published.[2] This work, like many others produced at the time, proved a profitable investment for the publisher – such was the nervousness, particularly about the education of young women, which had been engendered by current events in France, and by a long superficial acquaintance with egalitarian 'philosophies', associated mainly with Rousseau and Voltaire, who were supposed to be attacking all traditional standards, especially of sexual morality. A salutary dose of old-fashioned notions of feminine compliance to duty and submission was thought appropriate reading for girls – not least as an antidote to novel-reading. One of the works contained in the compilation was Dr John Gregory's *A Father's Legacy to his Daughters.* Jane Austen had certainly read this, for she refers to it in *Northanger Abbey*.[3] The character 'Catharine', or 'Kitty' as she is called through much of her short fictional life in Austen's unfinished story, is a direct negative response to the sort of pontification about the proper behaviour of young girls which is to be found in this treatise, and which the young Austen clearly saw as mindless and irrelevant. Typical of Gregory's pronouncements is the following:

One of the chief beauties in a female character, is that modest reserve, that retiring delicacy, which avoids the public eye, and is disconcerted even at the gaze of admiration ... This modesty, which I think so essential in your sex, will naturally dispose you to be rather silent in company ... There is a native dignity in ingenuous modesty to be expected in your sex, which is your natural protection from the familiarities of men, and which you should feel previous to the reflection that it is your interest to keep yourselves sacred from all personal freedoms.[4]

Mary Wollstonecraft was shortly to point out how much this sort of thing pandered to the desires of men rather than the well-being of women,[5] but Austen is more interested in what she saw as its irrelevance to social realities. Modest reserve is not a feature of Catharine's persona; although she is aware that she perhaps ought to be less forthcoming, her native warmth and friendliness usually supervene. Catharine's guardian, Mrs Percival, is well acquainted with conduct literature, but bringing up a girl has been made to appear so complicated that she has been forced to reduce the whole gamut to a single precept – let not your daughter *meet a man* and you will be safe. Mrs Percival is not at all clear whether she is worried about Catharine's morals or her money, whether she may be prey to a seducer or a fortune-hunter. She clings to a single, unvarying, second-hand prohibition because she has become incapable of thinking. The consequence is that Catharine, a cheerful, intelligent girl, has no real respect for her aunt, and is thrown back on her own resources when, alone in the house, she has to receive an unknown young man whose charming indifference to decorum she is unable to combat without seeming prudish and over-refined; ordinary good humour and congeniality predominate over propriety as she is persuaded to go alone with him to join her family at a ball and enters the room in company with him – both cardinal sins in her aunt's eyes:

There was such an air of good humour and Gaiety in Stanley, that Kitty, tho' perhaps not authorized to address him with so much familiarity on so

short an acquaintance, could not forbear indulging the natural Unreserve
& Vivacity of her own Disposition, in speaking to him, as he spoke to her.
She was intimately acquainted too with his Family who were her relations,
and she chose to consider herself entitled by the connexion to forget how
little a while they had known each other. (*MW* 216)

Catharine tries, somewhat ineffectively, to persuade Stanley to adopt
a conventional attitude on their arrival, and when he accuses her of
prudery points out that she has already offended against decorum by
coming alone in the carriage with him. He says:

'Do not you think your Aunt will be as much offended with you for one, as
for the other of these mighty crimes.'
    'Why really said Catherine, I do not know but that she may; however, it
is no reason that I should offend against Decorum a second time, because I
have already done it once.'
    'On the contrary, that is the very reason which makes it impossible for
you to prevent it, since you cannot offend for the *first time* again.' (*MW* 219)

Catharine chooses not to appear 'missish' on the Gregory model and
answers in the same kind – ' "You are very ridiculous, said she
laughing, but I am afraid your arguments divert me too much to
convince me" ' (*MW* 219) – and subsequently appears before her
outraged aunt 'with a smile on her Countenance, and a glow of
mingled Chearfulness & Confusion on her Cheeks, attended by a
young Man uncommonly handsome, and who without any of her
Confusion, appeared to have all her vivacity' (*MW* 220).
    When she is subsequently found in her 'bower' with him, Mrs
Percival is overwhelmed with despair at the depravity of her ward,
although the reader is aware that Catharine had initiated none of
these transgressions, but is unable to escape them except by downright bad manners. She is rushed into submitting to 'freedoms'
(Edward Stanley kisses her hand with the deliberate intention of
shocking Mrs Percival), which she could only have avoided by being
permanently and obsessively mindful of strictures such as Dr
Gregory's, and investing the situation with more significance than it
really has. This clash of two or three imperatives confusing the
actions and thoughts of protagonists was to become typical of the
development of an Austen novel, and is helped on by the '*style
indirecte libre*' which Austen did not perhaps invent, but which reaches
a very high degree of sophistication in her hands even in this piece of
a novel. By this method Catharine is perceived by the reader to be

toying with ideas inadmissible by such as Dr Gregory; she would like Edward to be in love with her:

The more she had seen of him, the more inclined was she to like him, & the more desirous that he should like *her*. She was convinced of his being naturally very clever and very well disposed, and that his thoughtlessness & negligence, which tho' they appeared to *her* as very becoming in *him*, she was aware would by many people be considered as defects in his Character, merely proceeded from a vivacity always pleasing in Young Men, & were far from testifying a weak or vacant Understanding. Having settled this point within herself, and being perfectly convinced by her own arguments of it's truth, she went to bed in high Spirits, determined to study his Character, and watch his Behaviour still more the next day. (*MW* 235)

Catharine, we perceive, is in a muddle, and could be fooled. But, also like her, we are not altogether sure; the only thing that is certain is that Mrs Percival's vacuous bleating of conduct-book platitudes has been and will be useless in helping her niece to deal with real-life situations:

'This is beyond any thing you ever did *before*; beyond any thing I ever heard of in my Life! Such Impudence, I never witnessed before in such a Girl! And this is the reward for all the cares I have taken in your Education; for all my troubles & Anxieties! and Heaven knows how many they have been! All I wished for, was to breed you up virtuously; I never wanted you to play upon the Harpsichord, or draw better than any one else; but I had hoped to see you respectable and good; to see you able & willing to give an example of Modesty and Virtue to the Young people here abouts. I bought you Blair's Sermons, and Cœlebs in Search of a Wife, gave you the key to my own Library, and borrowed a great many good books of my Neighbours for you, all to this purpose. But I might have spared myself the trouble – Oh! Catherine, you are an abandoned Creature, and I do not know what will become of you.' (*MW* 232)

All this is grossly out of keeping with the offence in question and, it should be noted, is second-hand wisdom. Mrs Percival has never done anything to assist Catharine through the moral maze of life but give her books to read. It is clear that Austen had strong views on the inefficacy of popular conduct-works, for in 1809, seventeen years after first writing this story, she substituted Hannah More's *Cœlebs in Search of a Wife*,[6] the current book of guidance for pattern females, for the older explanation of the catechism by Thomas Secker.[7] In bringing Mrs Percival up to date Austen demonstrates her continuing consciousness of the absurdity of model heroines such as More's Lucilla Stanley. In Catharine we have the first early glimpse of the typical Austen heroine wandering virtually pilotless among a number of moral and social paradigms designed to guide her but, from their unpractical nature, incapable of doing any such thing. Catharine's intelligence is insulted by Mrs Percival's mindless parroting of the current belief that in the modesty of females lies the safety of the nation (received wisdom from 1791 and Burke's *Reflections on the Revolution in France*):

'But I plainly see that every thing is going to sixes & sevens and all order will soon be at an end throughout the Kingdom.'

'Not however Ma'am the sooner, I hope, from any conduct of mine, said Catherine in a tone of great humility, for upon my honour I have done nothing this evening that can contribute to overthrow the establishment of the kingdom.'

'You are Mistaken Child, replied she; the welfare of every Nation depends upon the virtue of it's individuals, and any one who offends in so gross a manner against decorum & propriety is certainly hastening it's ruin. You have been giving a bad example to the World, and the World is but too well disposed to receive such.' (*MW* 232–3)

Catharine now offends in another way – she fails in proper respect for her elders: ' "Pardon me Madam ... but I *can* have given an Example only to *You*, for You alone have seen the offence" ' (*MW* 233). She then contrives to distract her aunt from her diatribe and escapes further castigation. But contemporary readers would have a problem – Mrs Percival may be stupid, but is Catharine justified in being pert? Does Mrs Percival's stupidity invalidate the Burkean doctrine she is spouting? No rule of thumb could provide the answer, and neither narrator nor character directs the reader.

Why did Austen not go on with this novel? It is in many ways the best of the fragments, especially in its feisty central character, and we are disappointed to lose her so soon. She promises to be at least as delightful as Elizabeth Bennet, and is perhaps her forerunner. Brian Southam suggests that Austen lost control of the character, who failed to become a 'single, unified personality', but an uneasy amalgam of the mocked sentimental heroine, 'a lively young woman of keen intelligence' and 'an *ingénue* of foolish simplicity'.[8] I would suggest rather that the contradictions are deliberate. Elizabeth Bennet is all of these things at different times; Jane Austen was not in the business of creating 'unified' heroines – or heroes, for that matter. Indeed, it may have been the very fact of Catharine's complexity in contrast with the more obviously 'unified' characters that caused Austen to abandon the project – the Edward Stanley/ Catharine/Mrs Percival triangle seems too tight at the outset for fictional manoeuvre. No one in the story except Catharine seems likely to develop in any unforeseen way. Mrs Percival's single moral obsession does not promise to be anything like as productive of incident for the heroine as Mrs Bennet's and could become tedious. It is perhaps significant that the fragment ends with her pondering with growing anxiety 'the necessity of having some Gentleman to attend them' to the play. *Some* social life is necessary for a heroine, however unsentimental, to operate. Mrs Percival begins here to look like an insuperable obstacle (*MW* 240).

But *Catharine* provides plenty of indications of the way in which Austen's fiction was developing. The daughter of the Stanley family, Camilla, is given a mode of speech brilliantly exposing fashionable cant. As often as Catharine tries to persuade her into some sensible comment about the banishment of her friend Cecilia Wynne to Bengal in search of a husband, Camilla returns with a stock utterance, to the purport of which she has clearly given no thought whatever:

'But as to the Wynnes; do you really think them very fortunate?'
'Do I? Why, does not every body? Miss Halifax & Caroline & Maria all say they are the luckiest Creatures in the World. So does Sir George Fitzgibbon and so do Every body.'
'That is, Every body who have themselves conferred an obligation on them. But do you call it lucky, for a Girl of Genius & Feeling to be sent in quest of a Husband to Bengal, to be married there to a Man of whose Disposition she has no opportunity of judging till her Judgement is of no use to her, who may be a Tyrant, or a Fool or both for what she knows to the Contrary. Do you call *that* fortunate?'
'I know nothing of all that; I only know that it was extremely good in Sir George to fit her out and pay her Passage, and that she would not have found Many who would have done the same.' (*MW* 204–5)

The phrase 'in the world' is a particular favourite – the whole creation is brought into play for Camilla's expression of her supposed loves and hates; its emptiness of meaning is highlighted by Catharine's sardonic response:

'You cannot think how fond I am of him! By the bye are not you in love with him yourself?'
'To be sure I am replied Kitty laughing, I am in love with every handsome Man I see.'

'That is just like me – *I* am always in love with every handsome Man in the World.'

'There you outdo me replied Catherine for I am only in love with those I *do* see.' (*MW* 222–3)

This is typical of Camilla, who is quite unable to sustain any rational dialogue; she is the forerunner of Mrs Palmer in *Sense and Sensibility*; and her conversational style is related to that of Lady Bertram's letters – all surface and no substance, except that the latter comes alive at the onset of real feeling about the danger threatening her elder son (*MP* 427). Camilla, we see, cannot experience real feeling; though she sometimes gives way to emotion, it is all expressed through meaningless formulae and empty hyperbole: ' "Well, I must say *this*, that I never was at a stupider Ball in my Life! But it always is so; I am always disappointed in them for some reason or other. I wish there were no such things" ', and, when she is jealous of Catharine's success at the ball , ' "I wish with all my heart that he [her brother Edward] had never come to England! I hope she may fall down & break her neck, or sprain her Ancle" ' (*MW* 225–6, 224). Moreover, and perhaps most damning, she pretends to judge books without reading them, as part of a general presentation of herself as fashionably in the swim. Eagerly questioned by Catharine about ' "Mrs. Smith's Novels" ' she replies, ' "I am quite delighted with them – They are the sweetest things in the world – " ', and proceeds to reveal that she knows nothing about *Emmeline,* and has found *Ethelinde* too long to be read in its entirety (*MW* 199).[9]

It may be that Austen became so fascinated with the reproduction of this sort of vacuous chatter that she overdoes Camilla; in the later novels this comic mode is used more sparingly and to greater effect. Neither John Thorpe nor Isabella's invisible friend, Miss Andrews, has any staying power in the completion of standard popular works of fiction, but Catherine Morland is a far less knowing witness of their shortcomings and the interaction is more satisfying. Mrs Palmer and Robert Ferrars are minor irritants for Elinor Dashwood – she accepts them resignedly as a normal part of social life. Unlike Catharine, she concludes that such people do not deserve 'the compliment of rational opposition' (*SS* 252). As with other characters in *Catharine,* Camilla's idiosyncrasies have too much space given them and Catharine's reactions become too predictable. It is difficult to see how the narrative can develop. What is clear is Austen's interest in the hollow cant of social exchange, which goes along with her impatience with fashionable fictional forms. Here we have both set in a scene of domestic realism with devastating effect, a formula which she will refine and perfect in the major novels.

Lady Susan is a very different matter. Many problems surround the dating of the manuscript, which survives as a fair copy on paper with an 1805 watermark. That its composition cannot be as late as this has been well established, and it is now usually thought to have been written in 1793–4, immediately after *Catharine* and before the first draft of *Sense and Sensibility*, 'Elinor and Marianne'. Both *Lady Susan* and 'Elinor and Marianne' were composed in the popular epistolary form, which Austen eventually abandoned. There have been many speculations as to the reasons for this change. However, if we accept that Austen's drive was towards complexity of character and an escape from moral paradigms, it is easy to see why the novel-in-letters did not suit her. In *Catharine* she had discovered free indirect style, which allowed the character to speculate about her own motives, to deceive herself and enlighten the reader through irony. When Lady Susan presents her motives differently to different correspondents, the deception is clear, but unsubtle – Lady Susan is unadulteratedly wicked, whereas Catharine is revealed as self-deceived, reacting ad hoc to situations as they arise and she leaves far more room for the reader to identify with her, to sympathise and sometimes condemn. It must have struck Austen that the possibilities in her kind of straight narrative for the manipulation of the reader's attention and allegiance are infinitely greater and require much less space than the exchange of letters. 'Elinor and Marianne', composed in this way, probably wrenched the central characters too close to moral stereotypes and left the reader with no doubts to resolve. Whatever the case, she put both *Lady Susan* and 'Elinor and Marianne' aside and began another novel in about 1796. 'First Impressions', the early draft of *Pride and Prejudice*, was probably not composed as letters, though this has been suggested.[10] It must have been different from and in some way more impressive than the earlier work, for it was this manuscript which Jane Austen's father offered Cadell for publication in 1797. It was rejected and put aside, though it was still read aloud and enjoyed within the family. A version of *Northanger Abbey* called 'Susan', completed (according to Cassandra Austen) in 1798, was accepted by Crosby in 1803, but not published. Between that year and 1811, Austen recast 'Elinor and Marianne', tinkered with 'Susan' and wrote the fragment *The*

Watsons. We must now consider why, when, with one work rejected, one inexplicably shelved, she had had little encouragement from outside the family to believe that she would ever get a novel published, she decided to drop *The Watsons* (written circa 1804) in favour of 'Susan' and of *Sense and Sensibility*, which became the focus of her attention until 1811, when it was published.

This time the solution probably *does* lie with the conception of the heroine. The reader knows exactly where moral approval must be located – with Emma Watson herself, who, typically, finds herself surrounded by unscrupulous venality and cold egotism, but has no difficulty in sorting the good from the bad. Without being in the least like Gregory's ideal girl, she was too much in danger of becoming one of those 'pictures of perfection' which Austen later told Fanny Knight, made her 'sick & wicked'.[11] A heroine who consistently got things right would not do for the mature Austen. That this limitation could have been attended to there is no doubt, but it may be that much of *The Watsons* was incorporated into the eventual revision of 'First Impressions' that became *Pride and Prejudice*. This possibility will be explored in a later chapter. 'Elinor and Marianne' seems to have offered greater possibilities, once the epistolary form was abandoned, for double and treble reader-perception, for moral doubt and relativity.

'Susan' meanwhile was mouldering on Crosby's shelf. But Austen had another copy[12] and probably revised it between 1803 and 1816 when the copyright was bought back by 'one of her brothers'[13] – possibly she began the revision around 1809 when there seem to have been new plans for its publication. Certainly the heroine's name was changed before 1817;[14] R. W. Chapman conjectures 1809, from there having been another *Susan* published anonymously in that year (*NA* xii). The original conception of the novel may have been very early – close to *Catharine* – for even in its final form it is more schematic in its engagement with popular fiction than any of the other completed novels and is much closer to burlesque (though it is clear even from this novel that Austen has moved on to a more complex kind of fiction). Catherine Morland is set up from the outset as an anti-heroine. She has none of the characteristics of novel-heroines; she is not an orphan, but somewhat over-provided with near relations; she is not beautiful but 'very plain', only rising by fifteen to 'almost pretty'; nor is she clever – 'she never could learn or understand any thing before she was taught' (*NA* 13–15). Of the contemporary novels which Austen knew, Charlotte Smith's *Emmeline* is the most obvious target. Emmeline, despite being brought up parentless in a half-ruined castle, has somehow acquired both dignity and accomplishments. She has 'a kind of intuitive knowledge; and comprehended every thing with a facility that soon left her instructors [the old steward and the semi-literate housekeeper] behind'; 'she endeavoured to cultivate a genius for drawing' – it will be recalled that Catherine's 'greatest deficiency was in the pencil' (*NA* 16) – and secretly makes a sketch of Delamere, her importunate lover, which he discovers.[15] Catherine, on the other hand, 'fell miserably short of the true heroic height ... for she had no lover to pourtray' (*NA* 16). Scenes of abduction, including Delamere's of Emmeline, are parodied in the efforts of John Thorpe to force Catherine into an expedition to Blaize Castle. Thus Emmeline:

'No! No!' cried she – 'never! never! I have passed my honour to Lord Montreville. It is sacred – I cannot, I will not forfeit it! ... Let me go back to the house, Mr. Delamere; or from this moment I shall consider you as having taken advantage of my unprotected state ... to offer me the grossest outrage.'[16]

And Catherine:

'Stop, stop, Mr. Thorpe ... it is Miss Tilney; it is indeed. How could you tell me they were gone? – Stop, stop, I will get out this moment and go to them ... How could you deceive me so Mr. Thorpe? – How could you say, that you saw them driving up the Landsdown-road? ... You do not know how vexed I am. – ' (*NA* 87)

But the critique of popular fiction (there are many similarly talented heroines and dramatic abductions) here moves on to a different level, for it not only ridicules novelistic stereotypical characters and situations, but defeats the reader's expectation of a burlesque on the style of Charlotte Lennox's *The Female Quixote*, or Sheridan's *The Rivals*,[17] by making Catherine, at least at first, very sensible and quite unaware of any parallel with her reading in the rather low-key excitements of her social life or the bullying be- haviour of the Thorpes and her brother. In Lennox's novel, Arabella, having been totally isolated from the world, has read nothing but 'bad translations' of seventeenth-century French romances, chiefly originating from the pen of Madeleine de Scudéry.[18] She finally emerges to engage with mid-eighteenth society in the manner of a romance heroine, whose lovers must either earn her regard by suffering in various ways or be categorised as potential 'Ravishers'. The resulting high comedy, combined with exposure of the shallow artificiality of fashionable social life in the 1750s, was relished by Austen; she read the novel more than once.[19] But she herself aimed to do more than confront the banal with the fantastic; Arabella's fantasies and Lydia Languish's dreams of a romance-style elopement are amusing, but relatively straightforward – Austen was intent on complicating the fictional message, and in *Northanger Abbey* she does it very thoroughly. Catherine is, at the opening of the novel, a burlesque of a burlesque – the diametric opposite of Arabella, for *her* minimal education and uncomplicated family situation have made romantic dreams unnecessary. Life is quite exciting enough and her pleasures are simple. But she is nevertheless in danger, not from unruly lovers or delusions of high romance, but from other people's reconstructions of everyday life. Apparently *in statu pupillari* she has in fact no effective adviser. Henry Tilney cannot function as the good Doctor does for Arabella, for he has too many problems of his own. At the end of the novel Catherine still has her best guide in her own naive reactions, which at various times in her story have *appeared* quite indefensible, but are revealed to be nearer the actuality than anything indicated by those who might be supposed to be capable of advising her.

Instead of caricaturing inadequate guardians as she had done in *Catharine*, Austen produces parents for her heroine who are super-ficially ideal but in practice unhelpful. They are neither cruel, neglectful nor venal, but dutiful and caring, comfortably provided with the necessities of life. They have no problems. But underneath the cheerfully reassuring description of the down-to-earth rational family that appears in the first chapter there is an ironic critique. Catherine's education has been conventional and not very thorough or effective, consisting chiefly in learning improving texts and bits of English literature by heart. Mrs Morland 'wished to see her children every thing they ought to be' (*NA* 15) but her bustling, energetic life leaves no room for subtleties or what she would regard as romantic nonsense. It is difficult to imagine any of her children consulting her about anything more complicated than clean underwear. When Catherine leaves for Bath she confines her advice to care for her health and her money; she assumes that the ordinary habits and regulations of society will take care of everything else. She has no time for details. But her bluff optimism is called in question, if only by implication; she cheerfully hands over Catherine to begin her adult life with Mrs Allen, a woman who she must know is quite outstandingly stupid and will be no help whatever to Catherine, even in the most ordinary decisions of everyday life. Somehow, she seems to be thinking, things will sort themselves out; her daughter will pick up the information she needs. Like many parents, she chooses to forget the problems of her own youth and pretends to herself that everything is simple. Like Mrs Percival, when the going gets rough she looks for a book which will, she fondly imagines, put her daughter back on the rational track, though she quite mistakes the cause of Catherine's unease on her return from Northanger, thinking, according to the stereotype, that she has been 'spoilt for home by great acquaintance' (*NA* 241). She is, in fact, very ordinary, but in an Austen novel, plain common sense is not always an inevitable route to rational action.

Initially, Mrs Morland's brisk inattention to the things outside the family which will shape Catherine's life has produced a quite untroubled young woman, for Catherine, never having been forced with any great vigour to do what she did not like – she shirks her lessons, and is allowed to give up music after a year's struggle – has no perception that life may produce difficulties, and has no thoughts which she could not reveal to her mother, until her collision with the Tilney family. At the beginning of her story she is totally unaffected by her reading of novels, which she has enjoyed, 'provided they were all story and no reflection' (*NA*, 15), and has no expectation that her life will mirror fiction. As she sets out for what turns out to be a boring and frustrating evening at the Upper Rooms, she only 'hoped at least to pass uncensured through the crowd. As for admiration, it was always very welcome when it came, but she did not depend on it' and 'her humble vanity was contented' when 'two gentlemen pronounced her to be a pretty girl' (*NA* 20–4). Delamere, on the other hand, when he first sees Emmeline, 'fixing his eyes on her face with a look of admiration and enquiry that extremely abashed her ... seemed to be examining the beauties of that lovely and interesting countenance which had so immediately dazzled and surprised him'.[20] Echoes of *The Female Quixote* are also detectable in Austen's Bath episodes. The stir of Arabella's arrival is in sharp contrast to the invisibility of Catherine. Unlike Arabella, Catherine is in no wise brought to suspect her two low-key admirers of plans to 'carry her off'; nor has she any propensity to impose tasks on her lovers in the

manner of the heroines of Mlle de Scudéry.[21] For a large part of the
novel she is in grave doubt as to whether she has a lover at all; she
never for a moment takes John Thorpe's pretensions seriously, and
Henry keeps her guessing until the very end.

So Catherine is, on her first introduction to the world, neither like
Emmeline, who knows the right moves by instinct, nor Arabella, so
bemused by her reading that she cannot tell reality from fiction.
When Henry Tilney parodies the fashionable preoccupations of the
average novel-heroine, she reacts in amused disbelief because so far
she thinks of such behaviour as occurring only between the covers of
a book (*NA* 26–7). She is unable to join in Isabella's pseudo-romantic
prattle – 'she was not experienced enough in the finesse of love, or
the duties of friendship, to know when delicate raillery was properly
called for, or when a confidence should be forced' (*NA* 36). Isabella
is, but Catherine cannot rise to the occasion. Isabella effuses in the
sentimental novel style but Catherine can produce nothing but
common sense:

'Where the heart is really attached, I know very well how little one can be
pleased with the attention of any body else. Every thing is so insipid, so
uninteresting, that does not relate to the beloved object! I can perfectly
comprehend your feelings.'

'But you should not persuade me that I think so very much about Mr.
Tilney, for perhaps I may never see him again.'

'Not see him again! My dearest creature, do not talk of it. I am sure you
would be miserable if you thought so.'

'No, indeed, I should not . . .' (*NA* 41)

Catherine is safe at least from the excesses of sensibility. But the
reader has a double perception, and it is this layering of the reader's
response that is the innovative aspect of this novel. The heroine's
down-to-earth reactions are at one and the same time sensible and
impossibly naive. By failing to interpret the codes of other people's
discourse Catherine is made resistant to cant, because it makes no
sort of sense to her, and at the same time extremely vulnerable, not
to seducers and robbers, but to persons living according to a fiction
which she does not understand and which she is not able to share.
She is reasonably proof against Isabella's mixture of sentimental
claptrap and selfish ambition, which does not damage her although
she is so slow to recognise it; she is not long deceived by John
Thorpe's vision of himself as a dashing man-about-town. But she is
seriously taken in by the Tilney family, for the internal dynamics of

which she has received no sort of model in her own life. It is here that Gothic fantasy and real life mesh for Catherine; for the first time her reading is her only guide.

General Tilney is as immediately recognisable to the modern reader as he must have been at the turn of the nineteenth century as the archetypal domestic tyrant. But nothing in Catherine's experience could have prepared her for him, and recognition of the reality comes to her much more slowly than it does in the case of Isabella and her dreadful brother. Mr Allen, who fills the space usually occupied in novels by a sensible and reliable male guide, has only the duty to discover that the Tilneys are 'a very respectable family'; it would not be his business, even if he knew all about it, to warn Catherine that General Tilney was grasping, irrascible, overbearing, insincere and despotic; such things were by no means incompatible with respectability and were irrelevant to his enquiry. With the introduction of the General, Austen engages with a third fictional mode, already part of Catherine's experience, but not so far of the action of the novel – Radcliffean Gothic. General Tilney is capable, not of sensational betrayals on the grand scale, but of petty domestic cruelty. Later, for Catherine, he acquires 'the air and attitude of a Montoni', and she is sure that he must have a guilty secret (*NA* 187); but he operates in the open – he is socially acceptable; he walks the streets in daylight and has no need to hide. Mr Allen of course does not recognise him. He therefore retreats to the card-room and pays little more attention. The only time he advises Catherine is in the matter of the impropriety of young ladies driving with young men in open carriages – when she has in fact already refused to go. For the rest of the time she is left to the stupidities of his wife. Whereas Emily in *The Mysteries of Udolpho* is isolated from the everyday world among people with mysterious and terrifying purposes, Catherine, in a typical Austen subversion, moves about among a perfectly ordinary crowd of companions who have no apparently nefarious agendas, but are only selfish, ignorant, obtuse or, to her (but not to the reader), impenetrable. No 'blood glare[s] upon the stairs',[22] but Austen's readers are rendered almost as uneasy for Catherine as Radcliffe's are for Emily as soon as General Tilney appears on the scene.

As the friendship between Catherine, Henry and Eleanor develops, the reader is increasingly aware of what Catherine fails to understand, that the young Tilneys are in a state of unusual

subjection to their father. Henry will not, until his treatment of
Catherine precipitates a quarrel, fall out with his father – apparently
on principle, for he proves to be financially independent; Eleanor
has no choice. Both tolerate their situation and repress their
reactions; their superior education and cultivated habits impress
Catherine, who mistakes their sophisticated demeanour for happiness. Even Frederick, though his absence from home leaves him
more freedom, and he is less unwilling to offend him, feels the
weight of the authority exercised by the General over his family.
Catherine is intermittently puzzled by the effect that he has on his
children's spirits, and cannot account for her own discomfort in his
presence. Isabella's melodramatic reconstruction of Catherine's
description of her first visit to their lodgings (' "Such insolence of
behaviour as Miss Tilney's she had never heard of in her life! Not to
do the honours of her house with common good-breeding! – To
behave to her guest with such superciliousness! – Hardly even to
speak to her!" '), based as it is on the stereotypes of sentimental
fiction, 'did not influence her friend' (*NA* 129–31) – she does not
connect her own experience with her reading in this particular way,
because she is conscious of genuine regard in Henry and Eleanor.
But she cannot explain the General, and gradually comes to connect
him in her mind with her most recent reading – *The Mysteries of
Udolpho* and the 'horrid' novels mentioned in chapter six of the first
volume.[23] There she finds male tyrants and helpless female victims
in plenty. Although at the time Catherine appears undisturbed by
Henry Tilney's melodramatic construction of a Gothic romance –
her reactions evince relish rather than anxiety (' "I am sure your
housekeeper is not really Dorothy. – Well, what then?" ' ' "Oh! no,
no – do not say so. Well, go on" ' (*NA* 159–60)) – his teasing and
Northanger Abbey itself ultimately work upon her imagination.
Impressions of horror rush in to fill the vacuum left by her education;
because she cannot find any other explanation for the behaviour of
General Tilney, she interprets the evidence as proof that he is guilty
of an unspeakable crime, which weighs upon his conscience and
renders him irritable and anti-social. The reader is made well aware
that the General's chief preoccupation as he introduces Catherine to
the Abbey is the best way to display his wealth. But to Catherine,
unacquainted as she is with acquisitiveness on this scale, his manoeuvrings inevitably appear sinister. Her internal monologue, as she
works herself up into a state of luxurious apprehension in chapters 6

to 9 of the second volume, has much to do with her obscure sense of exclusion in a family grappling with its own tensions. The behaviour of Henry and Eleanor in the presence of their father still puzzles her, as does his own. She tries to convince herself that all is well:

'In a house so furnished and so guarded, she could have nothing to explore or to suffer . . . How glad I am that Northanger is what it is! If it had been like some other places, I do not know that, in such a night as this, I could have answered for my courage: – but now, to be sure, there is nothing to alarm one.' (*NA* 167)

In a sense, throughout this episode Catherine knows at one level that her alarms are ridiculous; but Austen's subversion of the Gothic plot has far more complexity than the usual burlesque of it (for instance, in Barrett's *The Heroine*).[24] Catherine's problems are real. All is not well in that house, as she is acutely aware. Gothic fantasy displaces more tangible worries and eventually focuses on the General himself. Patrolling the house in secret in search of evidence for her sensational suspicions, Catherine finds nothing to add to the know-ledge that she already has, if she would only recognise it – that General Tilney is addicted to power and can do without love. When she discovers nothing but 'an handsome dimity bed, arranged as unoccupied with an housemaid's care' (*NA* 193) – surely the most succinct and complete expression of solid domestic comfort imagin-able – and is herself discovered by Henry, he clearly knows quite well what is troubling Catherine. But he cannot enlighten her. He cannot, because of current standards of filial respect, say, 'My father is a cruel and hateful man and that is why you feel as you do.' But what he does say only acquits the General of the worst of Catherine's suspicions. Of his father's treatment of his wife he has this to say:

'He loved her, I am persuaded, as well as it was possible for him to – We have not all, you know, the same tenderness of disposition – and I will not pretend to say that while she lived, she might not often have had much to bear, but though his temper injured her, his judgment never did. His value of her was sincere; and, if not permanently, he was truly afflicted by her death.' (*NA* 197)

This hardly exonerates him altogether, for it is clear that being judged of value by someone is no consolation for being injured by his temper. But Henry proceeds to fudge any admission he has made by insisting on the way in which Catherine appears to have subverted the Gothic-novel scenario:

'If I understand you rightly, you had formed a surmise of such horror as I have hardly words to – Dear Miss Morland, consider the dreadful nature of the suspicions you have entertained. What have you been judging from? Remember the country and the age in which we live. Remember that we are English, that we are Christians. Consult your own understanding, your own sense of the probable, your own observation of what is passing around you – Does our education prepare us for such atrocities? Do our laws connive at them? Could they be perpetrated without being known, in a country like this, where social and literary intercourse is on such a footing; where every man is surrounded by a neighbourhood of voluntary spies, and where roads and newspapers lay every thing open? Dearest Miss Morland, what ideas have you been admitting?' (*NA* 197–8)

But none of these things has prevented General Tilney, by his own son's admission, from being the apparently unrepentant source of great unhappiness. In her self-castigation in the next chapter, Catherine forgets this, and, condemning herself for Arabella-like delusions, concludes only that General Tilney is 'not perfectly amiable' – a profound understatement so long as we are not judging him upon the standards of the Gothic novel. She is ultimately to discover that he is at the mercy of his ambition and pride to the exclusion of all feeling either for his children or for her, and when he throws her out of his house reflects 'that in suspecting General Tilney of either murdering or shutting up his wife, she had scarcely sinned against his character, or magnified his cruelty' (*NA* 247). Catherine's education is complete – she has always been proof against the codes of sentimental fiction; having now recognised the existence of real everyday inhumanity, she no longer needs the tropes of Gothic romance to explain it. It is, after all, only too common, and the General is clearly not regarded as a villain by anyone else. He continues to be as 'respectable' as Mr Allen's enquiries found him to be. But it is ultimately her own experience which enlightens Catherine – no one has been free to help her. Arabella was more fortunate. Henry is too personally involved to function as the good doctor does at the end of *The Female Quixote*, though his arguments are somewhat similar. Arabella's adviser urges her to test her perceptions against everyday observation, much as Henry does for Catherine; but the shadow of the tyrannical husband and father will not thereby be dissipated.

Thus Austen complicates the interplay of fictional forms and leaves the reader unsure whether to approve or disapprove of the heroine, who has been both eminently sagacious and egregiously silly; and we might be equally ambivalent about the hero, whom we could accuse of pusillanimous subjection to his father's commands at the expense of Catherine, though he finally makes up for his shortcomings. Well-meaning minor characters like Mrs Morland and Mr Allen fail to save the heroine from her unpleasant adventures, though there is nothing in their behaviour for which they can be exactly blamed. This blurring of the moral focus was new in fiction – so new that it was almost universally ignored in the initial reception of the novels. But to Austen it became almost an addiction, and in the revisions of her early drafts she increasingly undermines expectation of coherent, consistent action among her cast of characters. The one or two thoroughgoing villains are vastly outnumbered by the morally ambivalent, the dubious, the obtuse. This novel produces one of Austen's equivocal closures, which, chiming ironically with the last paragraph but one of *Udolpho*, makes a clear statement of Austen's fictional policy of leaving the reader to work things out. Ann Radcliffe thus sums up the purport of her work, leaving no room for argument:

O! useful may it be to have shewn, that, though the vicious can sometimes pour affliction upon the good, their power is transient and their punishment certain; and that innocence, though oppressed by injustice, shall, supported by patience, finally triumph over misfortune![25]

That Austen thought this more than a touch simplistic is clear from her alternative, which is a bundle of oblique and uncommitted comment on the unstable nature of accepted social mores and their treatment in fiction:

professing myself ... convinced that the General's unjust interference, so far from being really injurious to their felicity, was perhaps rather conducive to it, by improving their knowledge of each other, and adding strength to their attachment, I leave it to be settled by whomsoever it may concern, whether the tendency of this work be altogether to recommend parental tyranny, or reward filial disobedience. (*NA* 252)

The closure also presents readers with a conventional happy ending which is calculated to remind them that the domestic life of Henry and Catherine, unlike that of Emily and Valancourt, will be fraught with family tensions.[26] The meeting of Mrs Morland and General Tilney is awful to contemplate. In addition, Catherine will have to cope with the undying hostility between James and her new brother-in-law, Captain Tilney; and the mind boggles at the impact of Catherine's eight other siblings on General Tilney's network of aristocratic connections. But Austen has worse in store – already Mrs Bennet exists in draft to plague Darcy and infuriate Lady Catherine de Bourgh.

CHAPTER 2

The non-heiresses: 'The Watsons' and 'Pride and Prejudice'

Jane Austen's continuous consciousness of the fictional tradition within which she worked has frequently been discussed by scholars and critics. In *Pride and Prejudice* there is a strong structural and thematic connection with the novels of Fanny Burney, especially with *Cecilia* (1782), but also with *Camilla*, published in 1796[1] when Austen was reportedly engaged with the first draft of the novel, entitled 'First Impressions'.[2] My own analysis of the interaction between Burney and Austen between 1796 and the final publication of *Pride and Prejudice* differs somewhat from that of others, as will become evident in what follows. Too often the search for a consistent set of moral objectives has led critics to conclude that Austen has failed in her attempts to subvert Burney, suggesting, as Marilyn Butler has done, that she has 'badly fudged the moral issue' and left the reader in a 'moral limbo'. 'Confusion enters', she writes, 'because *as a whole* intelligence is represented as faulty in the novel.'[3] Examining *Pride and Prejudice*'s probable genesis and some of its crucial episodes will strongly suggest that the 'confusion' is intended, and is itself part of the challenge to Austen's contemporaries.

In contrast to the novels of sensibility in the Mackenzie manner, Fanny Burney's fiction seems almost obsessively concerned with money. Sentimental heroes and heroines often seem to be able to do without the vulgar necessities of life – indeed, Austen herself caricatures this attitude in *Love and Freindship*, as we have seen, and comments more seriously on it in *Sense and Sensibility*, when Marianne dismisses money ' "beyond a competence" ' as irrelevant (*SS* 91). Burney also clearly intended to cut through this high-minded contempt for the practicalities of life by showing how very necessary, particularly to women, was the certainty of a 'provision'; in *Cecilia*, the heroine's great inheritance is dependent on her marrying a man who will take her name instead of giving her his; dissolute and grasping guardians, as well as the intransigence of the family of the man she loves, reduce her to near penury and the brink of death before she is forced to compromise and give up all her ambitions to use her money to live according to her own ethical standards, and accept the reluctant support of her husband's family. It is a fine and gripping story, but we are compassionate witnesses rather than sharers of Cecilia's distress; her experiences are too extraordinary for the reader absolutely to identify with her. *Camilla* also has inheritance as a major defining theme, but the problems the heroine faces are not those of what Austen called 'common life'.

There is no doubt that Austen very much admired Burney, but it is also clear that she wanted to bring fiction closer to the experience of her readers in order to press home what Burney had begun to identify – that in life there are neither ideal people nor perfect solutions to their problems. Burney stepped back from creating a morally chequered heroine; Cecilia never strays from the standards of female obedience and submission still *de rigueur* in fiction in 1782. She often has difficulty in deciding on the right course of action, but is never guilty of petulance or rebellious thoughts. The character of Camilla is more daring; she persists in contacts with dubious characters out of kindness and spontaneous generosity, but although she often appears to Edgar to be straying from grace, he is mistaken. She remains all that Dr Gregory would have wished.

In her unfinished novel *The Watsons* (*MW* 314–63), first published in the *Memoir*, 1871, Austen attempts a modification of the Burney model, and produces a heroine who is very much like Cecilia. Emma Watson also loses an inheritance and suffers the tribulations of a girl who has assumed she was safely provided for but is suddenly exposed to the sordid machinations of the marriage market and the narrow-minded speculations of her illiberal relations. But the resemblance is purely structural; within the recognisable narrative Austen was concerned with a much more intricate range of human reactions than was possible in *Cecilia*; because the scenario is less grandiose the focus is closer, we have a much more intimate insight into the pain Emma feels as she tries to do right by her family at the same time as maintaining her own identity. The petty rivalries of her sisters, the snobbery of her sister-in-law, the obsequious deference paid to the local aristocrat and his family, all jar on the reader as they do upon Emma and we approve as she strives to keep herself aloof. But the story did not satisfy Austen, and she abandoned it sometime between 1803 and 1807.[4]

·'First Impressions', the original draft of *Pride and Prejudice*, had existed since 1797 (according to Cassandra, it was begun in 1796).[5] It was put aside after that date, when Thomas Cadell the bookseller declined even to read it.[6] After *Sense and Sensibility* was accepted for publication in 1811, Austen went back to the earlier work and revised it. It was probably originally much longer than the final version (George Austen described it to Cadell as 'about the length of Miss Burney's *Evelina*' and Jane Austen herself says she 'lop't and crop't' it), but we really know nothing about it apart from that.[7] However, there are certain faint intimations of *Pride and Prejudice* in both *Catharine* and *The Watsons* which suggest that Austen combined elements from them with 'First Impressions' in her efforts to produce a work which satisfied her. There is much less evidence of these connections with *Sense and Sensibility*, which in the main seems to have sprung more from an engagement with sentimental fiction and the moralistic stories of Jane West and Maria Edgeworth than with Burney or the two unfinished works. The parallels of *The Watsons* with *Cecilia* are also present in *Pride and Prejudice*: the inheritance problem is reduced to the entail of the Longbourn estate away from the female line – less sensational than the terms of Dean Beverley's will in *Cecilia*, but nevertheless as troubling for the heroine; though, unlike Emma Watson, Elizabeth Bennet cannot apportion any blame for her predicament (Emma's aunt has made an injudicious second marriage, which cuts her niece off from the expected 'provision'). The use of inheritance as a motivating force is, of course, also present in *Sense and Sensibility*, but it impinges less unpleasantly on Elinor and Marianne. Both Emma Watson and Elizabeth Bennet are caught up in strong and overt pressures to find husbands in order to solve the problems of their maintenance. Emma's sisters are actively and outspokenly manoeuvring among the men of their acquaintance, and Mrs Bennet has very few other thoughts in her head. Further reminders of *Pride and Prejudice* are perceptible in at least one of the male characters in *The Watsons*: Lord Osborne, Emma's snooty aristocratic admirer, foreshadows Darcy. There are distinct whispers of the Meryton Assembly collision between him and Elizabeth at the 'first winter assembly in the Town of D. in Surry' where Emma first comes across Osborne:

Ld. Osborne was a very fine young man; but there was an air of Coldness, of Carelessness, even of Awkwardness about him, which seemed to speak him out of his Element in a Ball room. He came in fact only because it was judged expedient for him to please the Borough – he was not fond of Women's company, & he never danced. (*MW* 329–30)

The considerable difference is that Osborne is immediately, if rather boorishly, attracted to Emma, and tries to get himself introduced without the bother of having to dance; but Darcy's opposite behaviour rather confirms his literary kinship with Lord Osborne than otherwise. His disdain of Elizabeth is a new manifestation of an old fictional stereotype, in which the rich man is so often the potential seducer of the poor but pretty girl.

There are other vital differences, especially in the personality of the heroine. Emma Watson is much closer to Cecilia in her responses; she is, unlike Elizabeth Bennet but like Cecilia, newly beset by previously unknown problems, and she meets them with unfailing dignity and cheerful tolerance, though we are conscious of her inward criticism; her honest answers to her sister's enquiries make clear her dislike of what is going on. During the ball, we perceive the snobbish and egocentric manoeuvring of the local very eligible young man, Tom Musgrave, entirely from her deprecatory point of view, and she afterwards tells her sister:

'I do *not* like him, Eliz: -. I allow his person & air to be good – & that his manners to a certain point – his address rather – is pleasing. But I see nothing else to admire in him. On the contrary, he seems very vain, very conceited, absurdly anxious for Distinction, & absolutely contemptible in some of the measures he takes for becoming so. – There is a ridiculousness about him that entertains me – but his company gives me no other agreable Emotion.' (*MW* 342)

Her sister Elizabeth is incredulous (' "My dearest Emma! – You are like nobody else in the World" ' (*MW* 342)). The reader shares her incredulity, and so, we suspect, did the author. No other heroine, however sensible, in Austen's fiction is so completely proof against a plausible young man who makes himself 'agreable' to all and sundry; doubtless this was a descent into the 'unnatural' and 'improbable' which Austen finally felt obliged to reject. Emma is perhaps 'too good' for Austen, more so even than Anne Elliot.[8] Catharine, her other short-lived heroine, in her rejection of the Gregory ideal of female retiring modesty, in her willingness to be seen to like a young man who seems to like her, and her propensity to challenge authority (see chapter 1), was more what Austen required for the new version of her novel, especially if it was to break with the Burney tradition of vulnerable but noble-minded heroines. So Emma Watson disappears (though one might perceive vestiges of her in Elinor Dashwood), and Catharine, with modifications, lives on in Elizabeth Bennet.

Elizabeth departs quite startlingly from the Gregory – and the Burney – ideal. She is far from silent, frequently pert (at least by contemporary fictional standards) openly challenging to accepted authority, and contemptuous of current decorums (her wild and muddy walk to Netherfield has often been commented on). But we do not have to believe that there were no girls like Elizabeth between 1796 and 1813, when the novel was written, revised and published. They were probably all too common for the taste of the older generation, and themselves generated the improving works designed more or less to turn back the clock in manners and behaviour to something which may or may not have existed in the past. Every generation has its illusions of lost innocence. So far, it seems, novelists had largely felt it incumbent upon them to support the conduct-book standard – the success of a heroine most often lay in her efforts to do right, usually in opposition to traditional authority figures, at the same time as endorsing supposed external norms of proper submission. (This often agonising conflict goes straight back to Richardson and was itself a reaction against the amoral heroines of Defoe.) Radical novelists of the eighties and nineties like Mary Hays and Mary Wollstonecraft for the most part produced heroines like Emma Courtney (1796) or Maria (1798), rebellious and often outspoken, but so seriously concerned with their confrontation with society that pertness and challenges to pettier forms of tyranny are out of the question.[9] As a central female character Elizabeth is quite new. She may not, for instance, wish to usurp any male prerogatives, like Emma Courtney, or countenance the initiation by the woman of divorce, like Maria, but she does wish to subject current shibboleths to intelligent examination instead of accepting them blindly, and, extraordinarily for the fiction of the time, she is encouraged in her behaviour by her father. This comes out clearly in an early conversation she has with Bingley in the presence of Mrs Bennet, when she is visiting Jane at Netherfield during the illness which keeps both girls there for a few days. Bingley comments on his own character:

'Whatever I do is done in a hurry,' replied he; 'and therefore if I should decide to quit Netherfield, I should probably be off in five minutes. At present, however, I consider myself as quite fixed here.'

'That is exactly what I should have supposed of you,' said Eizabeth.

'You begin to comprehend me, do you?' cried he, turning towards her.

'Oh! yes – I understand you perfectly.'

'I wish I might take this for a compliment; but to be so easily seen through I am afraid is pitiful.'

'That is as it happens. It does not necessarily follow that a deep, intricate character is more or less estimable than such a one as yours.'

'Lizzy,' cried her mother, 'remember where you are, and do not run on in the wild manner that you are suffered to do at home.'

'I did not know before,' continued Bingley immediately, 'that you were a studier of character. It must be an amusing study.'

'Yes; but intricate characters are the *most* amusing. They have at least that advantage.' (*PP* 42)

Elizabeth's challenge to Bingley is mainly an intellectual one, and it is expressed without deference to him as a man, entitled to automatic respect. It is impossible to imagine any of Burney's heroines behaving in this way, and it is interesting to remember that Charlotte Grandison's confrontational manners are presented as unwomanly and in need of reform. Mrs Bennet pays lip-service to a standard which she imagines will be required by these great people from London, but she clearly expects little else from Elizabeth, and has no means of controlling her. Neither Bingley nor Elizabeth takes the slightest notice – Bingley continues 'immediately', and Darcy, clearly the object of her last remark, joins in by suggesting that a country neighbourhood could provide little enough for her entertainment. But Elizabeth gets her comeuppance when Mrs Bennet interrupts in her inimitable manner, bringing the conversation down to her own naive and vulgar level. Elizabeth finds herself 'blushing for her mother' (*PP* 43) and defending Darcy – not at this time a favourite with her. There is a sense in which the immediate reaction of the reader – even of a modern reader, such is the compelling nature of the dialogue – is to say 'Serve her right!' and laugh at what is, after all, high comedy. But several other responses come rushing in to complicate the issue and produce sympathy for Elizabeth in the many problems which beset her: her concern for Jane's prospects; the necessity to soften the impact of Mrs Bennet's manners while keeping up an entirely spurious appearance of respect for a parent; *and* her own compelling reasons for not wishing to defer in any way to Mr Darcy. The reader is conscious, too, of Darcy's growing interest in her, his undoubted and increasing reservations, and Bingley's two sisters looking down their noses in the background, not to mention Elizabeth's two silly sisters deciding to confront Bingley about a possible ball at Netherfield. It is a brilliantly successful exercise in the fragmentation of attention, which continues with Mrs Bennet further embarrassing Elizabeth by her all-too-obvious hints about her hopes for Jane, until every pause in the conversation, which she tries to direct, makes 'Elizabeth tremble lest her mother should be exposing herself again' (*PP* 45). This dispersal of reader-perception involves an authorial detachment about the heroine which is new. We do not have a focus for approval or disapproval, as we always have, for instance, in *Camilla*. Mrs Bennet's remonstrance, here as elsewhere, is a dead letter.

The episode at Netherfield nicely sets up the interplay of emotion in all the characters there displayed – including Caroline Bingley's anxiety to marry Darcy and the sisters' ambitions for a marriage between Darcy's sister and their brother. A dialogue about marriage in general has already begun. Because the question does not revolve around enormous inheritances and eccentric wills, but the ordinary prosaic decisions of the gentry families, the exploration can be much more detailed and complex than in Burney and leave the girls, particularly, with a far more convoluted set of options. The debate centres upon Charlotte Lucas, whose voice and actions expose a fundamental contradiction in received doctrine which is revealed through the shocked protestations of Elizabeth – how is a girl to retain what Gregory and others call her 'delicacy' and get herself decently off her family's hands? The agonisings of Evelina, Cecilia and Camilla seem grand and remote by comparison, and are eventually solved much more easily.

Austen clearly wanted to explore this contradiction at a different level from Burney. In *The Watsons* the debate is almost crude. Emma listens to her sister Elizabeth's statement of their sister Penelope's desperate search for a husband in growing horror; having been disappointed in the local male coquet:

'since then, she has been trying to make some match at Chichester; she wont tell us with whom, but I beleive it is a rich old Dr. Harding, Uncle to the friend she goes to see; – & she has taken a vast deal of trouble about him & given up a great deal of Time to no purpose as yet.' (*MW* 317)

Emma then states her reaction:

'I am sorry for her anxieties, said Emma, – but I do not like her plans or her opinions. I shall be afraid of her. – She must have too masculine & bold a temper. – To be so bent on Marriage – to pursue a Man merely for the sake of situation – is a sort of thing that shocks me; I cannot understand it. Poverty is a great Evil, but to a woman of Education & feeling it ought not, it cannot be the greatest. – I would rather be a Teacher at a school (and I can think of nothing worse) than marry a Man I did not like.' (*MW* 318)

Elizabeth then shows how her life has deprived her of the luxury of discrimination: '"I should not like marrying a disagreable Man any more than yourself, – but I do not think there *are* many very disagreable Men; – I think I could like any good humoured Man with a comfortable Income"' (*MW* 318). She goes on to suggest that Emma has been brought up to a 'refinement' which she now can't afford. Nor can she afford the luxury of conforming to current standards of femininity. She must find a way of being both feminine *and* predatory. This exchange represents the nub of an important theme in *Pride and Prejudice* which perhaps proved fictionally unwieldy in *The Watsons* – the polarisation of attitude is too absolute and Emma clearly has the author's support. When Austen takes up this theme again, the issues are much less clear but the atmosphere less darkly agonised. Charlotte's brisk common-sense has none of the sordidness of Penelope's machinations or Elizabeth Watson's fretful whimperings, and almost convinces the reader that she (Charlotte) is in the right. Her first pronouncements concern Jane Bennet. Jane is a Dr Gregory girl with this difference – though she can *appear* to have no thoughts of marrying Bingley, she cannot be expected to prevent herself from *feeling*, a distinction which the conduct-books rarely make. Anybody who knows Jane well knows that she is falling in love. Charlotte states the real problem – supposing she conceals this also from her potential suitor and he then loses heart? The conduct-books, often following Rousseau, assume the universal pleasure of the male in the chase, in overcoming reluctance. This is the kind of generalisation which Austen subtly exposes – Bingley is not that sort of man. Charlotte already perceives this; Elizabeth has yet to learn it. Charlotte's advice is hard-headed – Jane had better make things clear to Bingley, or she will '"lose the opportunity of fixing him"'; but let her keep her feelings under control: '"When she is secure of him, there will be leisure for falling in love as much as she chuses"' (*PP* 21–2). Charlotte advances a detailed battle-plan which is infinitely subtler and, moreover, more cynical, than anything adduced by Rousseau. Elizabeth will have none of it; she insists on a combination of romance and rationality – Jane must be sure '"of the degree of her own regard"' and its ' "reasonableness"'; she must get to know Bingley better (*PP* 22). Stuff and nonsense, returns Charlotte, in effect:

'Happiness in marriage is entirely a matter of chance. If the dispositions of the parties are ever so well known to each other, or ever so similar before-hand, it does not advance their felicity in the least. They always continue to grow sufficiently unlike afterwards to have their share of vexation; and it is better to know as little as possible of the defects of the person with whom you are to pass your life.' (*PP* 23)

Charlotte's views must at one level sound safe and sensible. The reader is far more confused by them than by the attitudes of Penelope and Eizabeth Watson, unsure whether to gasp in horror at such cynicism or nod sagely at such worldly wisdom. Elizabeth, in her inexperience (Charlotte is seven years older), *is* sure – ' "Your plan is a good one ... where nothing is in question but the desire of being well married; and if I were determined to get a rich husband, or any husband, I dare say I should adopt it ... but it is not sound. You know it is not sound, and that you would never act in this way yourself"' (*PP* 22–3). But when Charlotte 'fixes' Mr Collins, we remember Elizabeth's touching faith in her friend.

Though it covers much the same ground as *The Watsons*, this episode has that complexity and depth – what I have called counter-point – which is typical of Austen's mature fiction; the narrator leaves readers alone with the evidence and presents no conclusion. Their attention is engaged, not by terrific events and dilemmas, but by the ordinary decisions of ordinary people, so often presented in the fiction and conduct literature of the time as soluble by rule of thumb. This lack of authorial direction and sense of choice had not so far been reckoned appropriate to fiction, and is effective in increasing involvement by allowing the reader to recognise and share in the doubts and dilemmas of the protagonists, and, with them, come to no effective conclusion.

Elizabeth is far from clear – though at this moment she may think she is – about what is a 'sound' attitude to these matters. Her collision with Mr Collins does not enlighten her (*PP* 105–9), and the division between her and Charlotte deepens as a result of the latter's engagement. The attentive reader who also knows Dr Gregory's treatise will note that, somewhat unexpectedly in view of her departure from his standards in behaviour, Elizabeth replicates some of his opinions on marriage. Elizabeth's assertions about Jane are very close to his. In his chapter on 'Friendship, Love and Marriage' he says:

I know nothing that renders a woman more despicable, than her thinking it essential to happiness to be married. Besides the gross indelicacy of the sentiment, it is a false one, as thousands of women have experienced. (42)

Better, he thinks, not to marry at all than marry for an establishment. He pays little attention to the alternative, for he is careful to point out that his daughters will be left with ample financial provision. He is particularly insistent that no daughter of his should 'marry a fool'; women, he thinks, should not land themselves with husbands 'for whom you have reason to blush and tremble every time they open their lips' – a pretty accurate description of Charlotte's later situation at Hunsford ('When Mr. Collins said any thing of which his wife might reasonably be ashamed ... [Elizabeth] involuntarily turned her eye on Charlotte. Once or twice she could discern a faint blush' (*PP* 156)). And yet, accepting it as she does ('in general Charlotte wisely did not hear') as a fair payment for security, she is reasonably happy. But 'delicacy'? Of course not. Charlotte the sensible is in fact defying conventional pieties; Elizabeth, apparently much less willing to obey Gregory's dicta in other ways, is still locked into this one, revolted by the idea of marrying merely to survive economically. Austen is playing fast and loose with contemporary received opinion here, and with the stereotypes of fiction.

But Elizabeth is not unreservedly willing to accept such opinion on other aspects of courtship and marriage, and proves herself quite able to slide into all kinds of inconsistent views. What would be perceived in 1813 as her somewhat reprehensible tendency to argue with her elders emerges when her aunt Gardiner warns her against falling in love with Wickham, who has not 'the fortune he ought to have' (that is, in order to be fit to marry a penniless girl). Elizabeth by no means promises anything:

'In short, my dear aunt, I should be very sorry to be the means of making any of you unhappy; but since we see every day that where there is affection, young people are seldom withheld by immediate want of fortune, from entering into engagements with each other, how can I promise to be wiser than so many of my fellow creatures if I am tempted, or how am I even to know that it would be wisdom to resist? All that I can promise you, therefore, is not to be in a hurry. I will not be in a hurry to believe myself his first object. When I am in company with him, I will not be wishing. In short, I will do my best.' (*PP* 144–5)

Mrs Gardiner appears to be satisfied with this crisp and trenchant reply; she knows Elizabeth well enough to realise that it is all she will get. Elizabeth is challenging contemporary mechanical judgements which she sees have little bearing on the actualities of life as she has to live it. Later, still on the subject of Wickham, and still in conversation with her aunt, Elizabeth's comments become really combative and sarcastic. Wickham's 'attentions were over, he was the admirer of some one else' – Miss King, with ten thousand pounds. Elizabeth is not deeply concerned, and writes cheerfully to her aunt that she understands that '"handsome young men must have something to live on, as well as the plain"' (PP 149–50); but face to face with her she is tempted into an exposure of the lack of logic in conventional expectations of courtship. Mrs Gardiner would be, she says, '"sorry to think our friend mercenary"'. Elizabeth ripostes:

'Pray, my dear aunt, what is the difference in matrimonial affairs, between the mercenary and the prudent motive? Where does discretion end, and avarice begin? Last Christmas you were afraid of his marrying me, because it would be imprudent; and now, because he is trying to get a girl with only ten thousand pounds, you want to find out that he is mercenary.'

Mrs Gardiner has no real answer to this except to assert that to prove that he is prudent and not mercenary, he must show himself to be really in love with the girl:

'If you will only tell me what sort of a girl Miss King is, I shall know what to think.'

Now Mary King is later described by Lydia as 'a nasty little freckled thing' at whom no self-respecting handsome officer would look twice, and Elizabeth is ashamed *then* of her similar thoughts at the time. But on this occasion she says in reply to her aunt:

'She is a very good kind of a girl, I believe. I know no harm of her.'
'But he paid her not the smallest attention, till her grandfather's death made her mistress of this fortune.'

A man, then, has to be wary indeed if he is looking for a rich wife. Elizabeth sharply cuts through this with some inelegant but apposite observations:

'No – why should he? If it was not allowable for him to gain *my* affections, because I had no money, what occasion could there be for making love to a girl whom he did not care about, and who was equally poor?'

'But there seems indelicacy in directing his attentions towards her, so soon after this event.'

'A man in distressed circumstances has not time for all those elegant decorums which other people may observe. If *she* does not object to it, why should *we*?'

'*Her* not objecting, does not justify *him*. It only shews her being deficient in something herself – sense or feeling.' (*PP* 153)

Mrs Gardiner's use of the words 'delicacy' and 'feeling' points up the contradictions evident in the situation and shows her to be mouthing the Gregory dicta to which Elizabeth herself had paid allegiance not long ago. Again the reader has multiple references to attend to. Elizabeth may be exposing confusions in received doctrines, but she is far from consistent herself. We are aware that disillusion with Charlotte has injected a certain cynicism into her thinking since her earlier comments about Jane. The defection of Bingley has also had its effect. The rather crude analysis she has just uttered is the result of impatience with the bland assumption that moral attitudes are simple either to acquire or to recognise, and this from one of the few of her elders whom she both loves and respects. But when she wishes to reject all attractive young men and says, ' "Stupid men are the only ones worth knowing, after all" ' – referring to Mr Collins – we are quite aware that no Burney heroine could be guilty of such a petulant speech, and possibly agree with Mrs Gardiner that she should ' "Take care – ... that speech savours strongly of disappointment" ' (*PP* 154). Contemporary readers were often disconcerted by this aspect of Austen's heroines – like Miss Mitford, they missed the 'beau-idéal of the female character' – but most of all they missed being told what to think. Elizabeth is disturbing comfortable norms – is she good, or isn't she? Though it is very similar in its structure and also aims to emphasise the irrationality of popular moral currency, this episode is a world away from the similar scene in *Catharine* (see chapter 1 above) where the older authority figure is a caricature. Mrs Gardiner is *not* stupid, but she is no practical help to Elizabeth, and Austen has thereby successfully blurred the issue in a way which immeasurably increases reader involvement.

So Elizabeth's position as an anti-Burney heroine is more complex than is usually supposed; in following her thoughts we come much closer to a confrontation with some contemporary taboos than Burney ever does. But it is up to us, the readers, to make of it what we will.

Darcy presents much the same kind of complexity; it is no news to see him as a subversion of the 'patrician hero' of so much eighteenth-century fiction; but he is much more than a Grandison/Orville/Mandlebert figure plus a few venial faults.[10]

To begin with, as a patrician, his choice of close friends is peculiar. Austen goes to some trouble to establish the Bingleys as *nouveaux riches* (*PP* 15), and Darcy as the representative of old money, with aristocratic connections. But he does not seem quite sure of himself. For a rich and handsome man of twenty-eight he seems curiously inexperienced. His behaviour at the Meryton assembly is described by the locals as 'proud ... above his company' (*PP* 10), but could also be accounted – if it were not for the ten thousand a year – more gauche than anything. His determination there not to unbend is very quickly shaken as his attraction to Elizabeth takes hold. This is amply demonstrated in the text by the contrast in his reactions to her and to one of his supposedly destined brides, Caroline Bingley (the other being Miss de Bourgh). He is clearly fed up with Miss Bingley's mixture of deference and amorous advance, and it becomes difficult to understand why he spends so much of his time with the Bingleys. The question of an alliance with them through his sister is aired, but never really surfaces – though he does seem in a sense to be grooming his friend for stardom as his possible brother-in-law. This would account for his reluctant presence at a provincial assembly which his friend is obliged, as a local worthy, to attend. Such obligations are taken for granted in the society within which the novel is operating. But Bingley is a touch too sociable for purely practical purposes (the Osbornes, in *The Watsons* make clear their kind condescension in mixing with local tradesmen and impoverished gentry), and perhaps needs an eye kept on him.

Darcy's unsociable behaviour is not, like Lord Osborne's, presented as normal for a man in his position – we find out later that his cousin, Colonel Fitzwilliam, at least equal in rank, though not so rich, regards it as aberrant (*PP* 175). He is an oddity. It is perfectly open to the reader to see him as insecure. He is young for the amount of responsibility he has. We learn later that, his father having died 'about five years ago' (*PP* 200), he has been head of his family and proprietor of a great estate since the age of twenty-three, besides being responsible, with his cousin Colonel Fitzwilliam, for the upbringing of his sister from the age of eleven. Shortly before his meeting with Elizabeth he has had proof that his arrangements for the safety of this sister and the neutralisation of Wickham have almost failed.[11] He needs to feel in control, and Bingley is eminently controllable. Safely married to Bingley, Georgiana would also remain under his surveillance.

However, on their all coming into Hertfordshire the whole safety network starts to disintegrate; Bingley, in his interest in Jane, shows himself oblivious to any plans for himself and Georgiana, and Darcy himself gradually realises that his own feelings cannot be denied in his imagined future. Complicating all this is his anxiety not to betray his caste. The Bingleys are just about acceptable – their money plus his own countenance will 'bleach' their mercantile origins. But the Bennets are carefully portrayed as very dubious indeed by his standards – a dreadful mixture of gentry misalliance (Mr Bennet), country law-practice (the Phillipses), and mercantile commerce (the Gardiners). The Bennet girls have not even been properly educated, unlike Mrs Hurst and Miss Bingley ('in one of the first private seminaries in town' (*PP* 15)).

We are not given very much of the internal discourse of Darcy, but there is enough (*PP* 23–4 and 52) to show that he is thrown into terrible doubt and dismay when he realises that what he has regarded as social imperatives start to lose their force when he finds Elizabeth far more to his taste in every possible way than any woman in his previous experience. Later in the Netherfield episode during Jane's illness, at which we have noted Mrs Bennet's regrettable display of vulgarity, he is seen strongly resisting the ideas which have assailed him since their first meeting, though he is quite prepared to tease Miss Bingley by insisting on Elizabeth's attractiveness (*PP* 27). His demeanour at this time is typical of a young man so determined on managing his own reactions and creating the right impression that he is unable to relax and becomes pompous. It is not perfectly aristocratic in its usual fictional manifestation of careless confidence. He is too anxious to put people right. Bingley, unburdened by proprietorship, adolescent sisters and recalcitrant dependants, is able to brush aside problems of rank and position: ' "If they had uncles enough to fill *all* Cheapside" ', he says in answer to his sisters' jibes about the Bennets, ' "it would not make them one jot less agreeable." ' Darcy's solemn answer is significant in view of our knowledge, and his, of the fact that there is little to choose between him and Bingley in their respective little weaknesses: ' "But it must very materially lessen their chance of marrying men of any consideration in the world" '(*PP* 37). His answers are all solemn. Alistair Duckworth maintains that Austen gives him this 'humorless formality' so that it can both modify and be modified by Elizabeth's spontaneity, thus conveying the author's 'serious concern over the proper relation of the individual to society'. Naturally Duckworth's analysis depends upon his conviction of Austen's essentially didactic purpose and support for the dominance of such as Darcy. But if we look carefully at the outcome of this conversation, in which Darcy expounds his essentially distant and controlled attitudes, we find that far from modifying Elizabeth's spontaneity he renders himself extremely vulnerable to it, ending by informing the company of his faults in a way he has seen fit to reprove Bingley about earlier – ' "Nothing is more deceitful . . . than the appearance of humility. It is often only carelessness of opinion, and sometimes an indirect boast" ' (*PP* 48). In his conversation with Elizabeth at the end of chapter 11 he has to resort to the indirect boast himself, after Elizabeth has expressed herself ' "perfectly convinced that Mr. Darcy has no defect. He owns it himself without disguise" ':

> 'No' – said Darcy, 'I have made no such pretension. I have faults enough, but they are not, I hope, of understanding. My temper I dare not vouch for. – It is I believe too little yielding – certainly too little for the convenience of the world. I cannot forget the follies and vices of others as soon as I ought, nor their offences against myself. My feelings are not puffed about with every attempt to move them. My temper would perhaps be called resentful. – My good opinion once lost is lost for ever.' (*PP* 57–8)

There is a sense here of self-defence – Darcy has been boxed into a corner, and he is right to feel, as he does in the last lines 'the danger of paying Elizabeth too much attention'. His defences are in fact weak; his unsociableness is not really the 'grand and careless' attitude of a Sir Thomas Bertram, but a rather small-minded caution born of insecurity. His remarks are not, as Marilyn Butler has described them, 'careful, scrupulous, truthful',[12] but pretentious and intended to inhibit discussion which might put him at a disadvantage. His notions of how he should behave and how people should behave to him are shown to be based on assumptions about rank and status which are under vigorous attack. The direct interaction between confident heroine and insecure hero is new in fiction.

There is what has been reckoned a sole reference to Chesterfield's *Letters to his Son*, first published in 1774, in one of Austen's letters.[13]

Though direct allusion may be hard to find, there are enough indirect references to the work in *Pride and Prejudice* to suggest that she knew it and had it in mind when creating the characters of both Mr Collins and Darcy. It is also clear that, like Johnson and Cowper, she held the work in no charitable estimation. Mr Collins is obviously a devotee of conduct books – he recommends James Fordyce's *Sermons to Young Women* to the Bennet girls, and almost quotes him in his estimate of the behaviour of 'elegant females' during his proposal to Elizabeth. He has also paid some attention to Chesterfield. In chapter 14 of the first volume he describes his relationship with Lady Catherine de Bourgh, much to Mr Bennet's sardonic amusement:

'I have more than once observed to Lady Catherine, that her charming daughter seemed born to be a duchess, and that the most elevated rank, instead of giving her consequence, would be adorned by her. – These are the kind of little things which please her ladyship, and it is a sort of attention which I conceive myself peculiarly bound to pay.'
'You judge very properly,' said Mr. Bennet, 'and it is happy for you that you possess the talent of flattering with delicacy. May I ask whether these pleasing attentions proceed from the impulse of the moment, or are the result of previous study?'
'They arise chiefly from what is passing at the time, and though I sometimes amuse myself with suggesting and arranging such little elegant compliments as may be adapted to ordinary occasions, I always wish to give them as unstudied an air as possible.' (*PP* 67–8)

In the letter of 16 October 1747, Chesterfield writes to his son of the 'art of pleasing'. It is fair to say that all this instruction was designed to produce a diplomat and courtier and to inculcate a necessary, if somewhat hypocritical, ability to be all things to all men. Later use of the work tended to take the advice out of context – not surprisingly, since alphabetised extracts were produced in their hundreds for the use of the parents of sons and the socially inept. It is impossible not to perceive Mr Collins's reliance on Chesterfield in the following:

There are little attentions, likewise, which are infinitely engaging, and which sensibly affect that degree of pride and self-love, which is inseparable from human nature; as they are unquestionable proofs of the regard and consideration which we have for the persons to whom we pay them. As for example: to observe the little habits, the likings, the antipathies, and the tastes of those whom we would gain; and then take care to provide them with the one, and to secure them from the other.[14]

It will be perceived that Mr Collins bases most of his life-decisions on this small extract, turning himself into an intolerable sycophant, fit only for the ironic jibes of a cynic like Mr Bennet, instead of the the urbane and graceful gentleman at which Chesterfield, and presumably Collins himself, aims.

Austen's use of Chesterfield in her concept of Darcy is much less obvious and very much more complex. Echoes of Chesterfield abound in the early episodes – his dislike of dancing – 'Dancing is in itself a very trifling, silly thing', says Chesterfield in a letter of 19 November 1745, though acknowledging it as 'one of those established follies to which people of sense are sometimes obliged to conform'; Darcy dances well when it suits him, but points out to Sir William Lucas that ' "Every savage can dance" ' and asserts on being pressed that ' "it is a compliment which I never pay to any place if I can avoid it" ' (*PP* 25–6). He also seems to agree with Chesterfield ('in my mind there is nothing so illiberal, and so ill-bred, as audible laughter ... since I have had the full use of my reason, nobody has ever heard me laugh' 9 March 1748) in his estimate of humour.[15] When Elizabeth (clearly the representative of the anti-Chesterfield lobby here) says she ' "dearly love[s] a laugh" ', he replies with typical pomposity: ' "The wisest and best of men, nay, the wisest and best of their actions, may be rendered ridiculous by a person whose first object in life is a joke" ', clearly categorising himself as among the number of the wisest and best, and exposing himself to Elizabeth's sarcasm (*PP* 57–8). However, his interpretation of Chesterfield is not strictly according to the rubric. He has picked up the maxims without the hypocrisy and double-dealing that Chesterfield recommends. In 1747 (16 October) Chesterfield advises his son to 'Take the tone of the company that you are in, and do not pretend to give it; be serious, gay, or even trifling, as you find the present humour of the company: this is an attention due from every individual to the majority.' Nothing could be farther from Darcy's policy – one could regard him as too honest to behave in such a manner. He exposes the contradictions in this supposed manual of 'practical morality' for young gentlemen.

Chesterfield is not always so expansively democratic; on another occasion (12 October 1748), he seriously warns his son against consorting with those beneath him: 'But the company which of all others you should most carefully avoid, is that low company which, in every sense of the word, is low indeed – low in rank, low in parts, low in manners, and low in merit.' This is a pretty accurate description of the company in which Darcy finds himself at the Meryton assembly, Jane and Elizabeth excepted. Perhaps for the first time, he is being made to realise that the system on which he has been educated (and which he later acknowledges to have been faulty) will not cover every contingency and requires a kind of play-acting for which he is temperamentally ill adapted, and he takes refuge in what can only be described as surliness.

He clings to Chesterfield's stratifications in spite of increasing uncertainty, and such is his acceptance of them as norms that when he finally proposes he can only see himself as generously stooping to Elizabeth's level and fondly imagines her grateful for his condescension. She, of course, sees it quite differently, for her sense of self-worth at first prevents her from understanding his conflicts, or sympathising with them if she did. She actually accuses him of conduct unbecoming a gentleman – the ultimate insult to one of Darcy's stamp until quite recently, and just what he is trying to avoid.

The reader has yet another perception: Darcy is unable to control a powerful attraction to Elizabeth and has allowed himself to act in a totally inconsistent way. Having successfully detached Bingley from Jane, he is now somehow intending to incorporate Elizabeth into his own scheme of things. How can he possibly justify this? Are his passions, like Lydia's, 'stronger than his virtue'? – virtue, in his case, meaning adherence to the standards of his caste and loyalty to his friend. We cannot escape from the certainty that the strongest element in his attraction to Elizabeth is physical:

But no sooner had he made it clear to himself and his friends that she had hardly a good feature in her face, than he began to find it was rendered uncommonly intelligent by the beautiful expression of her dark eyes. To this discovery succeeded some others equally mortifying. Though he had detected with a critical eye more than one failure of perfect symmetry in her form, he was forced to acknowledge her figure to be light and pleasing; and in spite of his asserting that her manners were not those of the fashionable world, he was caught by their easy playfulness. (*PP* 23)

These are Darcy's thoughts, but the faint authorial voice in the background here acknowledges that men do not find women 'uncommonly intelligent' or approve of their 'playful' manners until they have made other 'discoveries', about which Austen does not mince her words.

Darcy is well and truly 'caught' and his is the overriding moral muddle of this novel. It is customary for critics to find Darcy inconsistent as a fictional creation; if we look carefully at the given details of his personality and courses of action, the inconsistency becomes clearly deliberate on the part of the author, not accidental. His situation is complicated beyond any possibility of authorial inadvertence, clumsy revision from an earlier draft, or any of the usual critical escape clauses.[16]

Elizabeth has different problems in her relation to Darcy. There are three elements in her dislike – the mortification of her pride at the Meryton assembly; her conviction that Darcy has victimised a vulnerable dependant – Wickham; and her virtual certainty that he has interfered with Bingley in his relationship with Jane. But she does not despise him simply because he is rich; she is still prepared to judge people on what she thinks are their merits. Her experience is unfortunate – by the middle of the second volume she has met Darcy, his aunt, and two of his cousins. She has no use for the first three, and with reason, but she enjoys the company of Colonel Fitzwilliam, who has 'the readiness and ease of a well-bred man', and Charlotte's speculations (*PP* 181) are by no means presented as fantastic, for:

Elizabeth was reminded by her own satisfaction in being with him, as well as by his evident admiration of her, of her former favourite, George Wickham; and though, in comparing them, she saw there was less captivating softness in Colonel Fitzwilliam's manners, she believed he might have the best informed mind. (*PP* 180)

For the first readers of the novel, still in the dark as to Wickham's iniquities, a marriage to the younger son of an earl (with income from somewhere or other) would have been quite on the cards. However, the hate-relationship with Darcy quickly proves much more potent than Fitzwilliam's tentative interest, and we hear little more of him. Darcy proposes, is summarily rejected, and shortly afterwards one of Elizabeth's causes for dislike vanishes and the others begin to disintegrate.

Her self-castigation after receiving Darcy's letter of explanation is part of a chaotic reaction in which the only clear thread is that she has been misled by appearances in the case of Wickham; her reaction to Darcy's reiteration of the undesirable aspects of her family and his interference with the Jane–Bingley situation is more equivocal and very complex. Her internal discourse (*PP* 212–13) shows her almost imperceptibly going over to his side; she is flattered; her fury gradually turns against herself rather than him, and she is hopeless about 'the unhappy defects of her family', which no one knows better than she. Gradually she begins to forgive him. By the end of her musings, Jane's disappointment has become not the fault of Darcy, but of her family, compounded with Jane's adherence to the principle that a girl should not 'betray a preference' prematurely. Moreover, she feels sorry for him – an entirely new feeling, and not one that is totally justified by events. Such an analysis of the impact of new information on a resisting mind could only have been accomplished in so short a space and so convincingly by the use of free indirect style.

Darcy has so far undergone no change; his outlook is still too simple, and takes too little note of realities. He still believes, against a lot of evidence, that rank, or failing that, enough money to give access to the habits of rank, must ensure all the desirable social niceties of taste and manners. He is blinding himself to the fact that at least one of his relations is as vulgar in her way as Mrs Bennet; he has had cause enough to blush for his aunt's brash impertinence during his stay at Rosings. His cousin, Anne de Bourgh, is moreover no ornament to her station in life – she contributes nothing to any company she is in; and his sister has not been prevented by the instincts of rank and an expensive education from being duped by the pretty son of her father's steward. Nor, we find out later, has her education made her socially confident. What is it that Darcy is so anxious to preserve? Like so much of moral and social wisdom of the time it is an imaginary ideal of past purity that is at the centre of his unease, and Elizabeth is at this point in danger of joining him in accepting its reality.

It is a long time before we meet Darcy again, and he has had time to think about the implications of what he has said to Elizabeth in his letter, and of what she has said to him. As the narrative inexorably moves us on towards the next meeting between the two we have no idea what will happen, because we have no access to Darcy's thought processes. The whole situation is open in a way new to fiction. The internal monologue of Elizabeth prompts us to wonder if a parallel discourse is going on in the mind of Darcy. When the two come 'within twenty yards of each other' we know that something dramatic has happened to Darcy. There is a pause in the narrative as we contemplate the elements in the drama – the backdrop of Pemberley, with all its implications of status and grandeur, and the dramatis personae: Darcy himself, Elizabeth, and the deplorable relations in the background. Elizabeth expects him to flee, but he does not. His whole demeanour demonstrates that he has decided that inclusion is better than exclusion. Vulgarity and its opposite – intelligence, taste, good manners – can exist independently of landed proprietorship and rank; he has found this out at Rosings. Soon, recognising in Mr Gardiner qualities he can respect, in spite of the dust of the counting-house, he invites him into his demesne as an equal, to fish in his river – of all moments in the novel possibly the most significant, and typical of Austen's bathetic irony. In Lady Catherine's words, the woods of Pemberley are already being subjected to pollution.

And what of Elizabeth? As we have seen, she has been undergoing her own metamorphosis, but of a different kind from the one usually assigned her. We left her feeling sorry for Darcy, but by no means converted to his point of view on the subject of gentlemanly conduct. She has been convinced of his perfect adjustment to his duties as a landed proprietor and his acceptance of his responsibilities, without improper pride or ostentation, in the sphere to which he has been called. Her conversations with his housekeeper have seen to that. But she still thinks ill of his behaviour during his stay at Netherfield, his officious treatment of her sister's prospects and his friend's happiness, and of his high-handed manner to herself. But Austen is not prepared to present her as nobly disinterested in what Darcy has to offer. Camilla and Cecilia expend a good deal of fruitless energy trying to prove how little they care for wealth and position. Elizabeth does care for it, and is able to admit it to herself. As she and her aunt and uncle drive into the grounds, she is able to say honestly to herself, ' "... to be mistress of Pemberley might be something!" ' Inside the house, she still muses on the wonder of the possibilities which were opened up to her:

'And of this place,' thought she, 'I might have been mistress! With these rooms I might now have been familiarly acquainted! Instead of viewing them as a stranger, I might have rejoiced in them as my own, and welcomed to them as visitors my uncle and aunt. – But no,' – recollecting herself, – 'that could never be: my uncle and aunt would have been lost to me: I should not have been allowed to invite them.'

This was a lucky recollection – it saved her from something like regret. (*PP* 246)

During the course of the next few days, her adverse thoughts are all obviated – he accepts her uncle and aunt, reintroduces Bingley to the dangerous proximity of a Bennet, and has so modified his behaviour to her that she can hardly believe how much she had disliked him before:

He who, she had been persuaded, would avoid her as his greatest enemy, seemed, on this accidental meeting, most eager to preserve the acquaintance, and without any indelicate display of regard, or any peculiarity of manner, where their two selves only were concerned, was soliciting the good opinion of her friends, and bent on making her known to his sister. (*PP* 265–6)

She begins to think, in short, that she could accept him, and we have to acknowledge that part of her satisfaction in his 'continuing regard' must be the way in which such an alliance will benefit both her and her family. It is open to the reader to decide what is going on here – does the power of sexual attraction override all other consideration? Which of the two is making the greater concession, and why? Within the enveloping conventional love-encounter, innumerable questions introduce themselves.

The crisis of Lydia's elopement with Wickham brings the internal debate of both protagonists to a head. For a time we only know about Elizabeth's. Darcy becomes silent and 'gloomy' after his first shocked reception of the news:

Elizabeth soon observed, and instantly understood it. Her power was sinking; every thing *must* sink under such a proof of family weakness, such an assurance of the deepest disgrace. She could neither wonder nor condemn, but the belief of his self-conquest brought nothing consolatory to her bosom, afforded no palliation of her distress. It was, on the contrary, exactly calculated to make her understand her own wishes; and never had she so honestly felt that she could have loved him, as now, when all love must be vain. (*PP* 278)

We later find out that she is wrong, but in the meantime this passage has a curious effect. The thrust of the fiction here indicates that Elizabeth will not be disappointed – this is, after all, no tragedy – but her internal monologue also follows reader-expectation; we are justified in thinking that the author will have trouble getting Darcy out of this one. The disgrace of a family was one of the few things which justified the breaking even of an official engagement at the time – indeed, actually enjoined the offer of honourable release on the disgraced party. No one would have blamed Darcy for having nothing further to do with the Bennets, and many would have said he ought not, for the sake of his family standing, to continue to countenance them. Fictional conventions, then, would demand that *something* must happen to save Lydia if the marriage of Elizabeth and Darcy is to become possible – but to have the hero himself effect the salvation, especially by the laying out of money, would be most unusual – probably unprecedented in fiction, but, as Austen says in another connection, 'if it be as new in common life, the credit of a wild imagination will at least be all my own'.[17]

Money is a significant symbol of power in all fiction, but in eighteenth- and nineteenth-century novels it often had strong sexual overtones in that it could be used by its normal possessors – men – as a displaced form of seduction. A girl in hock to a man might be regarded as having as good as lost her virginity.[18] A common cliché was for a young woman inadvertently to become indebted to a man, and thus be obliged to marry him if that is what he wants. Camilla is an example of a girl thus entangled, and her sisters, to whom she goes for advice, are quite sure that she must marry Sir Sedley Clarendel, since he has, without her permission, lent her erring brother two hundred pounds which she is without the means of returning. She loves another, and is devastated.

If Darcy were behaving according to the conventions of fiction here he would hesitate – if we are to believe him sympathetic – to put Elizabeth under a financial obligation. Austen ignores this expectation and allows her aunt, her father and herself to accept his generosity with little demur. In another novel, Elizabeth would have to refuse him again out of 'delicacy' – one of the 'forced difficulties' which Austen complains about in her comments on her fellow-novelists. Mr Bennet pays ironic lip-service to convention, but is clearly quite willing to accept the obligation of his whole family to his prospective son-in-law: '"It will save me a world of trouble and economy ... I shall offer to pay him tomorrow; he will rant and storm about his love for you, and there will be an end of the matter"' (*PP* 377). Moreover, while Camilla is struck dumb with agonised embarrassment, so adding immeasurably to her difficulties, Elizabeth is allowed to initiate an explanation from Darcy, he is allowed to admit that he has done it only for *her*, and the reader is actually allowed to suppose that Elizabeth has engineered the scene in order to bring on a renewal of Darcy's proposal. This is an example of how Austen deliberately repudiates the opportunity to exploit the situation in the manner of a traditional novel, where the author would prolong the secrecy, doubts, misunderstandings interminably, as, for instance, with Edgar Mandlebert and Camilla. She herself gives some support for this suggestion by her amused and ironic comment on *Camilla* in a letter to Cassandra soon after its publication – 'Give my love to Mary Harrison, & tell her I wish whenever she is attached to a young Man, some *respectable* Dr. Marchmont [Edgar's mentor in his tormented and vacillating judgements of Camilla's behaviour] may keep them apart for five Volumes.'[19] The further echo of Burney, this time of *Cecilia*, in Elizabeth's encounter with Lady Catherine, contrasting as it does with the deference of the former heroine towards Lady Delvile, has often been noted. Novelists usually avoided castigating aristocratic standards of family purity in outright confrontation.[20] Almost every feature of the traditional love-problem is overturned here.

There is other indication in the letters for the position of *Pride and Prejudice* as primarily an experiment in new possibilities in fiction rather than the vehicle for any moral or didactic purpose. The passage in the letter of 4 February 1813 (part of which has been quoted in the Introduction) about the newly published novel is, I think, widely misunderstood as self-critical:

The work is rather too light, and bright, and sparkling; it wants shade; it wants to be stretched out here and there with a long chapter of sense, if it could be had; if not, of solemn, specious nonsense, about something unconnected with the story; an essay on writing, a critique on Walter Scott, or the history of Buonaparté, or anything that would form a contrast, and bring the reader with increased delight to the playfulness and epigrammatism of the general style. I doubt your quite agreeing with me here. I know your starched notions.[21]

This must be seen as a joke between the sisters which need be only partially expressed. Cassandra's 'starched notions' are obviously about fiction; and the ironic caricature of the sort of criticism that the novel might attract (but emphatically not from its author) refers to discussions culminating in conviction between them that the novel should be as tight in its construction as any stage drama, should not wander in an uncontrolled manner into generalisation and irrelevance and should avoid conscious didacticism.

The closure of *Pride and Prejudice*, apparently conventional in its resolution of the love-affairs in marriage, leaves just as much for the reader to do as the rest of the novel. While foregrounding the happiness of the arrangements, Austen never quite allows us to forget the multiple problems which the alliances bring, especially for Darcy. Avoiding contact with Wickham, especially for his sister, while supporting Lydia 'for Elizabeth's sake' would be a major headache; but keeping Lydia and Kitty apart, coping with Mr Bennet's unheralded visits and reducing the meetings of Lady Catherine and Mrs Bennet to the unavoidable minimum must have made the Pemberley guest-list extremely complicated. It is significant that the novel ends with a reference to Darcy's ease and intimacy with the Gardiners. While Evelina thankfully escapes from the Branghtons of Snow Hill into the aristocratic arms of Lord Orville, it appears that both Darcy and Elizabeth may find their only true refuge from the family tensions of Pemberley in the peace and dignity of Gracechurch Street.

CHAPTER 3

Sense and the single girl

When it comes to a discussion of *Sense and Sensibility,* order of publication is not a reliable indicator of order of conception. In its greater seriousness it belongs, with *Mansfield Park,* to a middle period of development. There is enough evidence to suggest that *Pride and Prejudice,* at least in its earlier manifestation as 'First Impressions', predates *Sense and Sensibility;*[1] its 'light, and bright, and sparkling' atmosphere is closer to the juvenilia and *Catharine.* Mr Collins and Lady Catherine de Bourgh have a good deal of the burlesque about them. There is nobody like them in *Sense and Sensibility;* much of the broad-stroke caricature is harsher and more threatening – Fanny Dashwood and her mother, for instance, are treated with irony, but are powerful and dangerous figures who cannot be neutralised as easily as Lady Catherine is by Darcy and Elizabeth. There is much to support the idea that in *Sense and Sensibility* Austen no longer found the simple moral dichotomies of contemporary fiction merely funny. The novel probes deeper into the mores of contemporary society to find, not the obtuse but ultimately impotent snobbery of Lady Catherine, but selfish greed and malice prepense, which are rendered both respectable and potentially destructive by the support of the society within which they operate. In *Pride and Prejudice* no person is assigned responsibility for the entail which deprives the Bennet females of their future livelihood; the decisions which destroy the prospects of Marianne and Elinor are at best based on carelessness and ingratitude on the part of their grandfather, whose will prevents his son from providing for his second family, at worst on the meanness of their half-brother and his wife. Mrs Ferrars's apparently unassailable command of the purse-strings and Lucy's determined upward mobility at anyone's expense increase the narrative tension. Elinor and Marianne are up against a very much more complex set of powerful economic forces than are the Bennet sisters, and the reader has even less certainty about how they are going to break free.

Sense and Sensibility's gravity of tone tends to produce an assumption in critics that Austen had some particular ideological point to make. Though the simple oppositional framework, sense/sensibility, has long since been abandoned as a critical starting point, others, less simple but even more unsatisfactory, have taken its place. They fall broadly into two groups. Some critics have seen the action, and especially the conclusion, as the defeat of spontaneity and individualism and the triumph of the more sober Christian virtues without the saving grace of Elizabeth Bennet's sparkle; others have sought to prove a less wholehearted allegiance to traditional morality by presenting the novel as an attack on the conventions of Austen's society, often specifically on the operation of capital, and therefore of that rather vague and ill-defined concept, the patriarchy.[2] Neither of these approaches covers everything that the novel has to offer. The fact that two such opposing critical positions can exist so persuasively side by side suggests the existence of other possibilities. The purpose of this chapter is to show once more that Austen is not challenging ideologies but fictions, for the novels that she knew seemed, in making a stand against relativism, to present the problems of living as much too easily solved by the application of theory. At the outset, Elinor and Marianne, like contemporary heroines, both think they can cope with the exigencies of life by adopting theoretically ideal standards. Unlike those heroines, they both find that principle is insufficient – they must be pragmatic to survive. In working out their respective predicaments and the solutions to them, Austen refers obliquely to two modes of contemporary fiction, the polemical/moral novel of the nineties and the sentimental novel along the lines of *Julie, ou La Nouvelle Héloïse* to which it was often a reaction. The first mode is the basis for the 'present' of the novel – the story of the love-affairs of Elinor and Marianne. The second underlies Colonel Brandon's story, which has happened in the 'past' of the novel, and it also has to do with Marianne's declared ideals of romantic love and fidelity. In tying these stories together Austen enables herself to examine both modes in terms of what she regarded as 'probability', and so challenge the simplistic solutions of many of her fellow-novelists.

At first, the novel looks like a re-run of a typical moral plot with which Austen was familiar. It took as its subject the courtship experience of young women, contrasting sober attention to traditional propriety with adherence to the doctrine of 'feeling' and other trendy theories associated with revolutionary politics. Sometimes two young female characters embodied the contrast; examples of this are to be found in the work of two novelists known to Austen when her novel was first drafted around 1797 – Maria Edgeworth and Jane West. In Edgeworth's 'The Letters of Julia and Caroline' (part of *Letters for Literary Ladies*), Julia, against the advice of her sensible friend Caroline, puts a mistaken notion of the personal and artistic satisfactions provided by wealth and position before less grandiose intellectual pleasures and the tranquillity of domesticity, marries the wrong man and goes fatally to the bad. West's *A Gossip's Story* concerns the fate of two sisters, one of whom, Marianne, rejects Pelham, a solid, dull and sensible man, in favour of Clermont, handsome and shallow, who soon neglects her; her response is to form clandestine friendships with women which cause her husband to suspect her of adultery. This destroys the marriage and Marianne's reputation. Louisa, her wiser sister, having failed to persuade Marianne into the more prudent choice, ultimately marries Pelham herself. As Oscar Wilde makes his deluded Miss Prism declare, 'The good ended happily and the bad unhappily', but this is emphatically not 'what Fiction means' for Austen.[3] She set out to subvert this simplistic concept very early, and the process continues apace in this novel. She uses the recognisable structure as her template, though not as a model, for the early draft, 'Elinor and Marianne'.[4] We are fairly reliably informed that it followed *Literary Ladies* in being in the form of an exchange of letters, a mode Austen abandoned in the revisions, probably because it afforded too little scope for the complex interaction of the two sisters which she intended; that she had realised its limitations is clearly shown by her hurried summing-up of the unfinished story of *Lady Susan* – Mrs Vernon is said to feel that she will get nowhere unless she confronts the lady personally (*MW* 311–13).[5] In the final form of *Sense and Sensibility* the oppositional framework is modulated almost to invisibility. When the novel came out with its new title in 1811, readers no doubt thought they had got yet another work of fiction trouncing 'feeling', or sensibility, and lauding 'sense' in the familiar mode, and it is quite certain that Austen was aware that this would be so. But she proceeded to shatter this form of novelistic 'cant' by diffracting the impact of received moralistic vocabulary – a process which had engaged her attention very early in her writing life. Both 'sense' and 'sensibility' were extremely slippery concepts throughout the eighteenth and early nineteenth centuries. Since Locke had first tried to define 'sense' apart from the physical perception of objects in 1690,[6] the term had inevitably taken on subjective meanings ranging from humane intelligence and rationality to downright commercial cunning, depending on the speaker's predilections and prejudices. 'A man of sense' meant, more often than not, 'Someone I (an intelligent and sober person, of course) can agree with.' The term 'sensibility' was also used very flexibly; basically it denoted a humane and compassionate attitude to life, but its French provenance had tended to give it a bad name, associating it with all kinds of excess and fashionable affectation.[7] It was quite possible not to know which of its many meanings was being used on any particular occasion. It is this dubiousness of reference which Austen exploits in *Sense and Sensibility*. Different kinds of sense and sensibility are juxtaposed and set against one another in a complex web of relationships, motives and desires in which only the thoroughly unscrupulous can be seen to be able to triumph over intractable circumstance.

To achieve this moral uncertainty Austen writes against the grain of novels which she found unsatisfactory, though she often enjoyed them. Her single remark about Maria Edgeworth is generally taken to be admiring. It is embedded in ironic comment to Anna in a letter of 1814, in which Austen humorously complains about the competition now being offered by Walter Scott:

I do not like him, & do not mean to like Waverley if I can help it – but I fear I must. – I am quite determined however not to be pleased with Mrs. West's Alicia de Lacy, should I ever meet with it, which I hope I may not. – I think I *can* be stout against any thing written by Mrs. West. – I have made up my mind to like no Novels really, but Miss Edgeworth's, Yours & my own.[8]

As Anna's novel was currently receiving very rigorous criticism, this only implies that Austen thought Edgeworth marginally better than most. There is nothing to suggest unrelieved admiration of any novelist in any of her recorded statements. Her celebrated defence of the novel in *Northanger Abbey* is chiefly an ironical snipe at 'common cant', and actually attacks Edgeworth's 'contemptuous censure [of] the very performances, to the number of which they are themselves adding'.[9]

It is very probable that Austen had Edgeworth and West in mind when she set out to put her own gloss on the concept of sensibility, consciously detaching it from the political anxieties it had recently been associated with and reverting to its earlier identification with true civilised behaviour.[10] Edgeworth and West imply at every turn that sensibility or feeling must in the nature of things be chaotic, unsystematic and destructive. During the period in which *Sense and Sensibility* took shape for publication these two authors appear again: Jane West published *A Tale of the Times* (1799), which overtly politicises the lesson (the central male figure is a jacobin who uses the doctrine of sensibility to deceive gullible women and ultimately to further his own political aims), and Maria Edgeworth produced her 'moral tale', *Belinda* (1801), in which the heroine is subjected to the various dangers of contemporary moral and social trends but emerges triumphant, not only making for herself a marriage which is both rational and romantic, but causing many of those she has encountered on her way to abandon their erratic and dangerous courses. Significantly, her sober good sense is contrasted with the unbridled radicalism of Harriet Freke, the supporter of women's rights.[11]

Austen very soon attacks the notion that sensibility is necessarily anarchic by showing that Marianne has not abandoned all rationality in her allegiance to feeling, but believes that in flouting conventions which seem to her to have no purpose she is obeying the true dictates of reason. There is a Godwinian edge to this position which the narrative does not altogether repudiate. Marianne is said to be 'sensible and clever' (*SS* 6); her considered opinion is that if there is any validity in the judgement of human behaviour then we ought in reason to be open about our feelings and not give support to the vulgar and commonplace. As an ideal there is much to be said for this, and Austen presents Marianne's 'eagerness' as attractive – often more attractive than Elinor's 'prudence' – but as a *modus vivendi* it is doomed by the overwhelming dominance of the vulgar and commonplace in everyday life, which will, either by stupidity or malice, not only resist the efforts of a few idealists to counter it, but often seek to destroy them. The presence of people like Sir John and Lady Middleton, Robert Ferrars, Mr and Mrs Palmer, and Anne Steele demonstrates clearly what Marianne is up against, not to mention the infinitely more dangerous Ferrars–Dashwood combination and Lucy Steele. Though Elinor's 'sense' – which is like Marianne's – tells her that there is substance in Marianne's view, she is aware of the size of the problem and prefers to try to neutralise it by means which Marianne cannot approve:

> Marianne abhorred all concealment where no real disgrace could attend unreserve; and to aim at the restraint of sentiments which were not in themselves illaudable, appeared to her not merely as an unnecessary effort, but a disgraceful subjection of reason to common-place and mistaken notions. (*SS* 53)

This is a considered view, not an abdication of reason. Marianne is not presented as corrupted by dangerous political theories. Her opinions are based upon novels of the sixties and seventies in which intuitive reaction is seen as more laudable than obedience to convention because it is more 'natural' – that is, more rational. The most famous of these, much imitated, were Rousseau's *Julie, ou la Nouvelle Héloïse* (translated into English 1761), Goethe's *Werther*, and Henry Mackenzie's *Julia de Roubigné* (1777), itself a version of Rousseau's, but Marianne is not portrayed as slavishly following them. Elinor does not have to urge Marianne to *think*, as Edgeworth's Caroline urges Julia:

> 'In vain, dear Caroline, you urge me to *think*; I profess only to *feel*.
> "*Reflect upon my own feelings*! Analyse my notions of happiness! explain to you my system!" My system! But I have no system: *that* is the very difference between us. My notions of happiness cannot be resolved into simple, fixed principles. Nor dare I even attempt to analyse them; the subtle essence would escape in the process: just punishment to the alchymist in morality!'[12]

Marianne is presented as quite different from Julia and her point of view is not totally rejected by Elinor as misguided and morally dangerous. She, too, dislikes the commonplace. The basis of the disagreement between the two is about behaviour rather than morality, and is as much a matter of convenience as anything more serious. Elinor makes this clear during a conversation between the sisters and Edward at Barton. Marianne teases:

> 'But I thought it was right, Elinor,' said Marianne, 'to be guided wholly by the opinion of other people. I thought our judgments were given us merely to be subservient to those of our neighbours. This has always been your doctrine, I am sure.'
> 'No, Marianne, never. My doctrine has never aimed at the subjection of the understanding. All I have ever attempted to influence has been the behaviour. You must not confound my meaning. I am guilty, I confess, of having often wished you to treat our acquaintance in general with greater attention; but when have I advised you to adopt their sentiments or conform to their judgment in serious matters?' (*SS* 93–4)

As well as convenience, there is the question of taste. Marianne is given to a sort of literary hyperbole; Elinor, with feelings just as deep, prefers to keep them to herself. But it is never suggested that, because Marianne gives vent to her feelings, those feelings must be regarded as superficial and of no account. Both Julia in *Literary Ladies* and Marianne in *A Gossip's Story* are light-minded and obtuse; their errors are self-generated and blameable; they take up fashionable opinions without examining them. But Marianne's feelings are always presented as understandable and considered. Her regret for the loss of their home is as genuine as Elinor's, but is expressed in the passionate and poetic language which she believes is appropriate to such feelings. Her rhapsodies are presented as overblown and affected, but it should be noted that Elinor is sometimes as affectedly banal. Marianne's habits of mind and expression belong to one fashionable trend; Elinor's ideals of discipline and self-control belong to another, perhaps older, tradition. They are each operating a system which satisfies their sense of the fitting, not obeying an ideological precept. In contemporary novels of instruction (so very different from those of the seventies, where sensibility is the only true morality) Elinor's system would clearly have authorial approval, but in Elinor we are shown a girl who, though obviously sensible, has by no means all the answers and is, in a different way, just as likely to fall into error, just as prone to overdo her convictions, as Marianne. Even her prudence can sometimes be called in question. As soon as this is perceived – and it seldom is – the novel becomes something new to fiction, for the conventional centre of moral authority, previously thought essential, disintegrates as the story develops.[13]

Because of her policy of social complaisance, so much like the attitude of Edgeworth's Caroline and West's Louisa, Elinor at first seems to be carrying the moral weight of the story. Her sober advice to her mother, the whole family's reliance on her judgement, reinforce this early impression. But we are quickly shown that not even she is perfectly organised in her response to the forces of the vulgar and commonplace. While her immediate family's prospects are ruined by Fanny Dashwood's version of 'sense' – close attention to maximising one's income – Elinor herself is indirectly rebuked for showing too much interest in Edward, the heir to the Ferrars fortune. Fanny warns Mrs Dashwood against 'draw[ing] him in' (*SS* 23), than which no expression could be more vulgar and commonplace – except perhaps 'setting one's cap at', a phrase which later arouses Marianne's fury (*SS* 45). Mrs Dashwood immediately whisks Elinor out of Edward's orbit to Barton Cottage, more than a hundred and fifty miles from Norland in Sussex, so that it will be quite clear, if (as she hopes) he continues his pursuit, who is the active party. But Elinor's incipient love-affair will pursue her to Barton anyway, for she has been too open, perhaps even indiscreet, to her sister about her feelings for Edward.

As Austen develops the character of Elinor, we are reminded of other well-known fictional heroines who are confused by the equivocal behaviour of a potential lover. But they have no doubt about what they ought to do, though they sometimes have difficulty in doing it. Camilla is solemnly instructed by her father to have 'no positive wish' in regard to Edgar, for fear of her reputation; she strives to obey, agreeing that unreturned desire on the part of a woman compromises her moral worth.[14] Belinda knows that it is morally imperative that she guard against an 'ill-placed attachment' while Clarence is behaving so mysteriously. They both accept that even their inmost feelings must wait in suspension to be evoked by a plain declaration which leaves nothing untold.[15] Austen sweeps all this aside in the case of Elinor; we learn early that her wish is very positive indeed; she believes that Edward loves her, and is willing to accept his uncertain behaviour as the result of financial dependence on an 'unamiable' mother. She has become intimate with him during the Dashwoods' period of mourning at Norland, and is perfectly willing to expatiate on his excellences to Marianne, with an almost proprietary air:

'I have seen a great deal of him, have studied his sentiments and heard his opinion on subjects of literature and taste; and, upon the whole, I venture to pronounce that his mind is well-informed, his enjoyment of books exceedingly great, his imagination lively, his observation just and correct, and his taste delicate and pure. His abilities in every respect improve as much upon acquaintance as his manners and person. At first sight, his address is certainly not striking; and his person can hardly be called handsome, till the expression of his eyes, which are uncommonly good, and the general sweetness of his countenance, is perceived. At present, I know him so well, that I think him really handsome; or, at least, almost so' (*SS* 20)

When Marianne concludes, not unnaturally, from this panegyric, that they are engaged, Elinor tries to backtrack, but is too honest to deny her feelings. A Camilla-like principle takes second place to the real situation; Austen will not show Elinor *succeeding* in supressing a 'positive wish'. She admits that she feels a 'suspicion – [a] hope of his affection':

'But farther than this you must *not* believe. I am by no means assured of his regard for me. There are moments when the extent of it seems doubtful; and till his sentiments are fully known, you cannot wonder at my wishing to avoid any encouragement of my own partiality, by believing or calling it more than it is. In my heart I feel little – scarcely any doubt of his preference.' (*SS* 21)

Elinor is quite unable to be both honest *and* 'delicate' on the Gregory model. All she manages to say is that she is pretty sure of his 'inclination' and believes that it is only his mother's ambition that stands in his way. Her efforts to conventionalise her attitude make no difference at all to Marianne's conviction that they will ultimately marry. Parental opposition, the only thing Elinor puts forward as a real obstacle, was one of the 'commonplace notions' which Marianne's principles would lead her to discount. Justifiably unconvinced by Elinor's equivocation, she confides in their sister Margaret, unfortunately exposing Elinor to 'impertinent remarks' which she later warns Marianne against (*SS* 68). Much as she may want to avoid notice, Elinor is not initially able to preserve the total silence on the subject of her relations with Edward which she strives to achieve later.

The development of those relations before Lucy Steele's revelation of her engagement to Edward takes up most of the first volume and encloses the beginning and end of Marianne's encounter with Willoughby. This gives plenty of opportunity for parallels which look like contrasts and contrasts which look like parallels. The latter couple's first meeting looks as different as possible from that of Edward and Elinor; swiftly and dramatically Willoughby sweeps Marianne literally off her feet straight into a romantic novel. However, if we persist in seeing Elinor as the sober and disapproving witness on the lines of Jane West's Louisa Dudley, serenely invulnerable to 'ill-placed attachments' we will miss certain shades in her character which are not altogether admirable, though understandable. Bearing in mind that she has heard nothing of Edward since their removal to Barton, the reader should perceive a complex reaction to Marianne's wholehearted response to Willoughby, and his to her; her remarks have a disdainful edge:

'Well, Marianne,' said Elinor, as soon as he had left them, 'for *one* morning I think you have done pretty well. You have already ascertained

Mr. Willoughby's opinion in almost every matter of importance. You know what he thinks of Cowper and Scott; you are certain of his estimating their beauties as he ought, and you have received every assurance of his admiring Pope no more than is proper. But how is your acquaintance to be long supported, under such extraordinary dispatch of every subject for discourse? You will soon have exhausted each favourite topic. Another meeting will suffice to explain his sentiments on picturesque beauty, and second marriages, and then you can have nothing farther to ask.' (*SS* 47)[16]

When Marianne responds ' "Is this fair? is this just?" ' we should be inclined to agree, for Elinor's comments may be partly joking, but are nevertheless slightly sour. The urge to deflate is not endearing, and is not here intended to be so. Elinor is seen to be having a struggle with herself; Marianne as well as the reader might remember her sister's own description of her early relations with Edward and note that Elinor is well aware of the satisfactions to be obtained from the exchange of literary and artistic enthusiasms, even though hers with Edward might have been somewhat more leisurely (*SS* 20). She has no real justification for being so scathing. Marianne is often surprisingly tolerant of Elinor.

Elinor realises that neither she nor anyone has reason to disapprove of Willoughby simply because he is handsome and animated. He is known in the neighbourhood, and is not the subject of any suspicion except that of being rather extravagant. His expectations are good; as a parent, Mrs Dashwood can congratulate herself, and Elinor must be pleased for Marianne. Her only real reservation is one she has about her sister too – 'a propensity ... of saying too much what he thought on every occasion, without attention to persons or circumstances' (*SS* 48–9). It is this element in the character of both her sister and Willoughby, not concrete evidence of double-dealing in the latter, which eventually alerts Elinor to danger for Marianne, for she begins to be puzzled that a regard so public and so enthusiastic does not result in an announcement of their engagement. Curiously, the openness with which she was able to discuss her own doubts about Edward seems difficult in Marianne's case, because the couple's behaviour – the proposed gift of a horse, the permitted theft of a lock of hair reported by Margaret, the expedition to Allenham, all of which take place between pages 58 and 69 – by all ordinary standards would be considered improper for an unengaged couple; an enquiry might be interpreted as an impertinence – 'a doubt sometimes entered her mind of their being really engaged, and this doubt was enough to prevent her making enquiry of Marianne' (*SS* 71). She cannot bring herself to believe that Marianne would behave in this way if she and Willoughby had not come to an explicit understanding. She must remember, too, that Marianne would not consider such mundane matters as money or the opposition of a guardian as worth mentioning. Elinor has to believe that their silence is, for them, normal. What she does not know at this time is that Marianne is really just as much in the dark about Willoughby's intentions as she herself is about Edward's; Marianne later confesses that they were 'every day implied, but never professedly declared' (*SS* 186). From the time of Willoughby's departure she becomes uncharacteristically reticent; Elinor cannot enquire, partly because of her own disinclination to interfere and partly because of her mother's opposition. (It is interesting to note that Elinor and her mother both refrain from enquiring for opposite reasons – Elinor because she is *not* sure of their engagement, Mrs Dashwood because she *is* (*SS* 79)). To all intents and purposes, then, the two girls are at this time in much the same position. Willoughby departs, leaving Marianne lamenting with great intensity, but with no sign of enlightening her family. Edward arrives at last, but only to make Elinor even more uncertain and unhappy than before and to confuse the onlookers as much as they are confused by Marianne and Willoughby.

Elinor's behaviour during Edward's visit serves to show how impossible it is to remain imperturbable whatever the stresses imposed. Austen does not direct the reader, but presents the evidence, through conversation and internal monologue, for Elinor's essential unease. Elinor prefers not to betray feeling because it attracts notice; she often deflects it by taking refuge in the banal, which sometimes verges on the unkind. She has already shown this trait during one of Willoughby's last outpourings of regard for the family before his defection, countering his rhapsodical admiration of Barton Cottage with references to its narrow stairs and smoky kitchen (*SS* 72). During Edward's visit she is at pains to show that she does not share Marianne's romantic nostalgia for Norland; she and Edward vie with each other in the expression of anti-romantic sentiments; their agreement in such matters is an inverted image of the different kind of accord between Marianne and Willoughby, and must bring the two just as close in their own consciousness. It is a species of flirtation which is vibrant with emotional strain, and which leaves Marianne, whom they both snub unmercifully, isolated. It may not be 'improper', but is in its way just as churlish as Marianne's behaviour to the Middletons. Read aright, the text does not give all the justification to Elinor:

'And how does dear, dear Norland look?' cried Marianne.
'Dear, dear Norland,' said Elinor, 'probably looks much as it always does at this time of year. The woods and walks thickly covered with dead leaves.' (*SS* 87)

Marianne launches into a panegyric – almost an anticipation of Shelley – ' "How have I delighted, as I walked, to see them driven in showers about me by the wind! What feelings have they, the season, the air altogether inspired!" ' Elinor again damps her sister's enthusiasm: ' "It is not everyone . . . who has your passion for dead leaves" ' – an impatient and perhaps embarrassed response.

When Marianne tries again to interest Edward in the beauty of nature in the environs of Barton, he too responds with mundane banalities:

'It is a beautiful country,' he replied; 'but these bottoms must be dirty in winter.'
'How can you think of dirt, with such objects before you?'
'Because,' replied he, smiling, 'among the rest of the objects before me, I see a very dirty lane.' (*SS* 87)

The complex interaction of personalities here reveals Elinor's struggle with herself and her feelings. Several times her remarks, apparently made to Marianne, are really directed at Edward and designed to reassure him; she makes clear, for instance, her real unconcern about wealth when arguing with Marianne about the importance of money to happiness (*SS* 91); and there is an invitation to him to come clean when they are, on the surface, discussing the contrast between his and Marianne's character. Elinor has described Marianne as 'earnest' and 'eager' but not really 'lively'; Edward reflects:

'I believe you are right,' he replied, 'and yet I have always set her down as a lively girl.'
'I have frequently detected myself in such kind of mistakes,' said Elinor, 'in a total misapprehension of character in some point or other: fancying people so much more gay or grave, or ingenious or stupid than they really are, and I can hardly tell why, or in what the deception originated.' (*SS* 93)

When these stratagems do not result in any clarification of

Edward's behaviour, Elinor begins deliberately to distance herself
from him. 'Vexed and half angry', she tries to avoid 'every appearance of resentment or displeasure' (*SS* 89), but the next time the
question of the beauties of nature comes up Elinor aligns herself
with Marianne. Edward reiterates his rejection of modern standards
of taste – ' "I know nothing of the picturesque" ':

> 'I am afraid it is but too true,' said Marianne; 'but why should you boast
> of it?'
> 'I suspect,' said Elinor, 'that to avoid one kind of affectation, Edward
> here falls into another. Because he believes many people pretend to more
> admiration of the beauties of nature than they really feel, and is disgusted
> with such pretensions, he affects greater indifference and less discrimina-
> tion in viewing them himself than he possesses. He is fastidious and will
> have an affectation of his own.' (*SS* 97)

Elinor has pulled herself together – her anxiety to be at one with
Edward is now repressed into apparent detachment. But the struggle
is present in the text – Elinor's attitude to Edward fluctuates in a
much more detailed way than, say, Belinda's to Clarence Hervey, or
Camilla's to Edgar. That Austen had *Belinda* specifically in mind
here is evident from the discovery of the lock of hair in Edward's
ring. While Belinda, on Clarence's accidental revelation of Virginia's
hair, is able to congratulate herself: ' "Fortunately ... I have
discovered that he is attached to another, whilst it is yet in my power
to command my affections" ', Elinor, like Catherine in *Northanger
Abbey* when she perceives Henry with his sister, jumps to no such
conclusion (though, ironically, it turns out to be the right one) and
makes no such resolution. Belinda is sure that the hair is not her own
(though it is apparently very similar); Elinor is convinced that the
lock in Edward's ring *is* (*SS* 98, 102). Belinda's reaction is the fictional
stereotype; Catherine and Elinor reach the likeliest conclusions in
the absence of other evidence – Catherine doesn't suppose that
Henry is after all married, and 'lost to her for ever'; Elinor
immediately concludes that the hair is her own.[17] Instead of
promptly abandoning the suitor to a rival, Elinor sees the ring as
comforting proof of Edward's affection through all his equivocations.
While Belinda concludes that Clarence is rather blameably un-
steady,[18] Elinor maintains her approval of Edward, feeling sure that
parental opposition is his problem:

She would be have been glad to know when these difficulties were to cease,
this opposition was to yield, – when Mrs. Ferrars would be reformed, and

her son be at liberty to be happy. But from such vain wishes, she was forced to turn for comfort to the renewal of her confidence in Edward's affection, to the remembrance of every mark of regard in look or word which fell from him while at Barton, and above all to that flattering proof of it which he constantly wore round his finger. (*SS* 102)

Ironically, the truth turns out to be as bad as Belinda anticipates for herself, but Elinor, more realistically, needs better evidence. She may hide her feelings from others, but she does not deny them to herself, even when the truth bursts in upon her, and does not refer, even internally, to any standard of female delicacy which would prevent her from hoping that her 'positive wish' will be realised. In short, she makes no attempt to 'command her affections', only to conceal them. Her inner discourse is quite unlike Belinda's:

Had Edward been intentionally deceiving her? Had he feigned a regard for her which he did not feel? Was his engagement to Lucy, an engagement of the heart? No; whatever it might once have been, she could not believe it such at present. His affection was all her own. She could not be deceived in that. Her mother, sisters, Fanny, all had been conscious of his regard for her at Norland; it was not an illusion of her own vanity. He certainly loved her. (*SS* 139–40)

Both Marianne and Elinor can be seen to be acting in a way which is comfortable for themselves, while persuading themselves that they act according to principle. When Edward leaves, before she is enlightened by Lucy Steele, Elinor is careful to behave normally, persuading herself that she is thereby protecting her mother and sister from 'solicitude' about her. But as they clearly *like* solicitude she must be protecting chiefly herself. She is as much obsessed by Edward as Marianne is by Willoughby – 'her thoughts could not be chained elsewhere' (*SS* 104–5). The difference is, as she admits to herself, 'she was stronger alone' (*SS* 141) while Marianne prefers to share her feelings with others.

This ostensible quiet acceptance tempered with a modicum of human frailty and inner turmoil is Austen's way of transforming the somewhat priggish censoriousness of Edgeworth's and West's Caroline and Louisa, and the conduct-book correctness of Belinda, into a modified stoicism which is attractive as well as believable. As Elinor's crisis develops, Austen clearly shows the element of self-protection in her stoicism, but makes it understandable in terms of Elinor's cast of mind. She is overwhelmingly concerned to conceal her interest in Edward from Lucy and all the world, and in doing so cuts herself off

from her family – 'From their counsel, or their conversation she
knew she could receive no assistance, their tenderness and sorrow
must add to her distress, while her self-command would neither
receive encouragement from their example nor from their praise' (*SS*
141). This resolution particularly isolates her from Marianne, who
continues to believe in the low intensity of her sister's feelings and
the impossibility of controlling her own. Elinor believes in the
healing power of stoicism, but she cannot convince Marianne unless
she demonstrates its efficacy. This she persuades herself she cannot
do because of her promise to Lucy. The absolute bindingness of this
promise must be called in question; Elinor is seen here to invoke
abstract principle when there is a greater good calling for its
abandonment. Austen does not make all her 'good' characters
regard promises as inviolate at all costs – Mrs Gardiner has no
compunction in blowing the gaffe on Darcy, for instance, when she
sees that Elizabeth must learn the whole of the story once Lydia has
let slip part of it. But Elinor makes a conscious decision not to
entrust Marianne with even a part of the tale. By protecting Lucy's
interests (and her own – she would perhaps be seen as pushing her
own claims if she allowed the story currency) Elinor creates a rift
between herself and Marianne which is only healed when the
engagement is published by Nancy Steele. In informing Marianne,
Elinor first tries to pass the matter off as understandable and
acceptable in her usual way (*SS* 263); when Marianne responds
typically, but also more honestly, ' "... if the loss of what is most
valued is so easily to be made up by something else, your resolution,
your self-command, are, perhaps, a little less to be wondered at" ',
Elinor's real feelings at last burst forth in uncharacteristic self-
revelation and pleading for recognition – ' "If you can think me
capable of ever feeling – surely you may suppose that I have suffered
now" ' (*SS* 264). But her agonised outburst really comes too late;
though it brings the girls closer, it does not do much to help
Marianne, as Elinor realises when the awareness of her unhappiness
over four months adds guilt to Marianne's distress: 'It brought only
the torture of penitence, without the hope of amendment. Her mind
was so much weakened that she still fancied present exertion
impossible, and therefore it only dispirited her more' (*SS* 270). Thus
Austen complicates the interaction of human beings in their quest
for right action.

Marianne herself is also a satisfying mix of idealism and self-occupation – perhaps a more common one. She first fails to see how complete honesty in suffering or anything else can create problems for others (Elinor continually covers for Marianne in situations where she rejects compromise). Then, when the going gets rough, she even begins to compromise with openness. When she says to Elinor in the days before the final showdown with Willoughby, ' "our situations are ... alike. We have neither of us anything to tell; you, because you communicate, and I, because I conceal nothing" ' (*SS* 170), she is deceiving herself, because Elinor is ignorant of the very fact which Willoughby can use to repudiate her – he has never asked her to marry him. Marianne does not want this to surface while she clings desperately to romantic ideals of true love unhampered by mundane formal covenants. However, as with Elinor, her impact on the reader is not all of a piece. There are many moments when her directness and sincerity have their appeal, as we can't but appreciate when she speaks out of a full heart to Mrs Ferrars in Fanny Dashwood's drawing-room: ' "What is Miss Morton to us? – who knows, or cares, for her? It is Elinor of whom *we* think and speak" ' (*SS* 235); and when she exclaims at Mrs Ferrars's measures to prevent Edward acquiring even the basic necessities of life, ' "Gracious God! can this be possible!" ', she is more lovable than Elinor, for all the latter's careful attention to propriety (*SS* 267). No reader can avoid agreeing that Mrs Ferrars and her like deserve the censure that only Marianne feels free enough to hand out. When does propriety become weakly ingratiating?

Thus the old simplistic opposition has disappeared. Marianne has really done no more to deserve the calamity which has befallen her than Elinor; indeed, her case is the more pitiable, in that Elinor has the comfort of knowing that Edward still loves her in spite of everything (though he has never 'declared himself'), while Marianne has for a long time to live with the conviction that her whole relation to Willoughby has been based on a sham. She is wrong, and it is appropriate that Elinor should eventually be given the means of consoling her on this very point. Elinor herself has to learn that nothing is simple, and that principle and convention will not always serve in the vexed interactions of life as it is lived. Kenneth Moler is right to point out how a phlegmatic and optimistic attitude to illness can be unjustified, for instance.[19]

In the end, Elinor has something to blame herself for. She is the repository of Austen's message – no one can ever be wholly right or

wholly wrong. After Willoughby's visit and defence of his real
feelings for Marianne, she pities him, and forgives him for becoming
the product of a venal and uncaring society. But even here, perhaps
especially here, she has to compromise, for she never tells Marianne
of the change in her estimate of Willoughby; in fact, towards the end
of the novel, when they are all back at Barton, and Marianne is
willing to give everything she has got to her own rehabilitation,
Elinor deliberately, and in a way untruthfully, puts Willoughby in the
worst possible light, omitting all excuse and apology:

'The whole of his behaviour ... from the beginning to the end of the
affair, has been grounded on selfishness. It was selfishness which first made
him sport with your affections; which afterwards, when his own were
engaged, made him delay the confession of it, and which finally carried
him from Barton. His own enjoyment, or his own ease, was, in every
particular, his ruling principle.' (*SS* 351)

It is a very different Elinor who 'could not quite agree with' her
mother when she asserts that Marianne could never have been
happy with Willoughby (*SS* 338); who 'feel[s] a pang for Willoughby'
even as she wishes Colonel Brandon success (*SS* 339), and earlier had
'for a moment wished Willoughby a widower' (*SS* 335). She consciously decides eventually to 'declare only the simple truth, and lay
open such facts as were really due to his character, without any
embellishment of tenderness to lead the fancy astray' (*SS* 349). It
should not be supposed that this decision necessarily has authorial
support; Elinor's thoughts are presented as her own, with all normal
inconsistency and self-justification. What the reader sees is that
'truth' has had to be treated by Elinor as a very relative matter.

So much for Austen's way with the oppositional courtship novel,
the conventions of which have been sufficiently disturbed. Two
contrasting pairs of lovers are not enough in this new version.
Edward and Willoughby by no means follow the traditional opposition reliable/unreliable, because both from the first behave mysteriously and give rise to justifiable anxiety. But the introduction of
Colonel Brandon upsets the traditional equation altogether and
immeasurably increases the potential of the story to challenge
fictional stereotypes. We (and Elinor) are as duped at first as
Marianne by the image that Colonel Brandon presents – his age,
dull common sense, his unobtrusive demeanour and his flannel
waistcoat. He has no debts and 'two new coats every year', as
Willoughby dismissively remarks (*SS* 51). But the reality is different

and is revealed with typical ironic reference to its source. Austen makes fun later in her spoof *Plan of a Novel* of a narrative device that she thought ridiculous and strained – the long account of a past history, so evident in the novels of Henry Mackenzie and his imitators.[20] Colonel Brandon's story looks at first like one of these. But not only is it much shorter than usual (the tale of Virginia, for instance, takes up two long chapters of *Belinda*), and more dramatic, being told to Elinor with comments and interjection from her instead of as uninterrupted third- or first-person narrative, but is also in itself a critique and subversion of the typical triangular senti-mental plot which had so much influenced Marianne's thinking.

It has not gone unnoticed that Colonel Brandon's story of his lost Eliza is a version of the central text of sensibility, *La Nouvelle Héloïse*, in which patrilinear inheritance is threatened by love. Eliza is forced into marriage with Brandon's elder brother and he returns much later from voluntary exile to find Eliza disgraced, divorced for adultery and dying. This places Brandon in the position of the forbidden lover, like Rousseau's Saint-Preux and Mackenzie's Sa-villon in *Julia de Roubigné*. But he has already, confusingly, been presented as another common fictional stereotype. His age and demeanour in the present of the novel fit him for the position of mentor/guardian – a parallel perhaps to the good Doctor in *The Female Quixote*, whose experience and 'sense' will help to solve every-one's difficulties. In the surface third-person narrative he early damages this expectation not only by falling in love with one of the heroines, but by openly preferring Marianne's romance to Elinor's prudence – ' " there is something so amiable in the prejudices of a young mind, that one is sorry to see them give way to more general opinions" '. Elinor ' "cannot agree with [him] there" ' and as a consequence sounds much the more middle-aged of the two (*SS* 56). When he hints at his past sorrows, she partially recognises this doubling, but hardly appreciates its significance; Marianne does not see it at all. But Elinor reflects with affectionate amusement that if Marianne's romantic enthusiasm had not at this time been satisfied with Willoughby, she might have taken a different view:

Elinor attempted no more. But Marianne, in her place, would not have done so little. The whole story would have been speedily formed under her active imagination; and every thing established in the most melancholy order of disastrous love. (*SS* 57)

But this sentimental text does not need to be 'formed' – it is real. In a sense, both girls are hung up on fictional stereotypes and have not considered the possibility of such things really happening.

The second element in the underlying narrative is Willoughby's seduction of the second Eliza. Much ink has been spilt over the question of why Austen chose to include so complicated a revelation of the iniquities of Willoughby. The most common conclusion is that the plot-structuring, in what is usually seen as an early effort, is flawed: Willoughby has to be seen to be morally unworthy of Marianne, not simply impeded by his financial position, and Brandon is a handy messenger.[21] But such an analysis not only makes awkward Willoughby's partial rehabilitation at the end, but would go to prove *Sense and Sensibility* to be scarred by ad hoc authorial decisions. A deeper exploration of the function of Brandon's story will demonstrate its necessity to the coherence of the work. Both girls have *believed what they have seen* and must be apprised of what they have not; but there is a way in which they are more seriously unenlightened. For Elinor the standard sentimental plot is little more than trivially amusing; for Marianne it is emotionally and imaginatively satisfying in its exaltation of the feelings over convention, the grand and noble over the commonplace. Neither has any notion of its actual potential in life as they know it. For both, it is absolutely necessary that Colonel Brandon's tale should be told in its entirety, but not as something which can be relegated to the realm of fiction. They need to become acquainted with a harsh outer world of 'sense' where romantic love has no legitimacy, where feminine 'softness' and vulnerability are exploited, where bastards do not conveniently die, where deathbeds are sordid and ugly, where idle young men take their sanctioned pleasures without responsibility, and where, above all, virtuous and compassionate men like Brandon may make the wrong decisions in their efforts at damage limitation and fail to prevent disasters. The sentimental plot is converted to a grubby saga of greed and selfishness. Brandon himself, by his own admission, has also been guilty, if only of a certain amount of incompetent dithering. Nevertheless, there is never any doubt of his basic virtue and courage – he is the nearest we are going to get to a romantic hero – not very near. He has to change places with Willoughby in Marianne's consciousness, and on more realistic and informed grounds. The interpolation of the sentimental plot serves to demonstrate the largeness of Brandon's heart and the fatal narrowness of Willoughby's, and to remind all concerned how mixed is the human spirit, and how little appearances are to be trusted. Brandon, apparently the embodiment of 'sense', with a reserved manner and currently staid way of life, is revealed as a man who has in the past been ruled by sensibility and to a great extent, still is; while Willoughby, clearly at first presenting the ideal face of sensibility to Marianne, has reverted to the kind of 'sense' demonstrated so clearly by Brandon's dead father and brother, and by John and Fanny Dashwood – attention beyond all other considerations to the securing of a good income.

This is Brandon's second function – to disperse the connotations of 'sense' and to show up some of its debased interpretations. It is perhaps best shown in his decision to give the living at Delaford to Edward Ferrars, a young man to whom he is not related and whom he does not even know very well, purely on the grounds that he is the victim of 'the impolitic cruelty of dividing, or attempting to divide, two young people long attached to each other'(*SS* 282). The sheer romantic nonsense of this gesture as it would be seen by society at large is reflected in the astonished reaction of John Dashwood, who thinks of nothing except in terms of money. Pointing out that he could have got fourteen hundred pounds for the living if he had had an eye to the main chance and got in before the death of the incumbent, he expresses his criticism in moral terms: ' "*Now* indeed it would be too late to sell it, but a man of Colonel Brandon's sense! – I wonder he should be so improvident in a point of such common, such natural, concern!" ' He then suggests that, as such stupidity is really out of the question for 'a man of sense', Edward ' "is only to hold the living till the person to whom the Colonel has really sold the presentation, is old enough to take it. – Aye, aye, that is the fact, depend upon it." ' Disabused by Elinor of this solution to the knotty problem, John Dashwood is left in wonderment and disbelief (*SS* 295). Colonel Brandon's operation in Austen's fictional world is far more romantic than anything in the world of the sentimental novel.

Sense and Sensibility is very frequently criticised for its denouement, which is held to be a facile, even perfunctory resolution, designed to fulfil the contemporary requirement for a heroine of excessive sensibility to be either punished or reformed. Received opinion has been that Marianne is reformed: brought to her senses by the revelations of Willoughby's viciousness, remorse for her 'ill-placed attachment' and the influence of her sister's sense, she is persuaded to marry a dull but reliable husband who will keep her on the straight and narrow path.[22] If this were so, then we might indeed accuse Austen of poor workmanship and pusillanimous subjection to current orthodoxies. But Austen's closures always have double and treble resonances, and this novel's conclusion is no exception. Its similarity to many other 'sensible' novel-endings is deeply ironic, for we know that Brandon, for whom Marianne's intensity and spontaneity are her chief charms, is the nearest approach to a romantic figure among the men. He is only prudent within certain well-defined limits (he has cleared his estate of his brother's debts). When Elinor and Edward, having been seriously and unsentimentally occupied in the settling for themselves of a decent income, find eventually and typically that they 'have nothing left to wish for, but the marriage of Colonel Brandon and Marianne, and rather better pasturage for their cows' (*SS* 375) they seem to be oblivious to the fact that they are planning for her a thoroughly romantic alliance,[23] not a prosaic practical solution which will pay off arrears of obligation (as readers, we have the opportunity to be much wiser than Elinor). If Marianne abandons some of her more extreme opinions (particularly the one about 'second attachments'), she does so 'voluntarily' and not as a result of persuasion, certainly not 'coercion', as Tony Tanner suggests. She does not need to change in any essential way to be happy with Brandon, for they are alike. If she has been converted it is to an understanding of the reality of the vision in Brandon which she has misread in Willoughby, not to an acceptance of second-best. From the moment she accepts that Willoughby is *selfish* – ' "*My* happiness never was his object" ' (*SS* 351) – she has to see that in Colonel Brandon she has the genuine instead of the spurious article. She has already begun to depend upon him for literary discussion, as she once had on Willoughby (she points out to Elinor, in her plan of intellectual improvement, that she will be able to borrow works 'of more modern production' from Brandon (*SS* 343)). They also have in common an intuitive and impulsive generosity – and they will need it all.

For the conclusion's bantering tone also conceals a more serious aspect of the Brandons' joint lives; they will still take responsibility for Eliza and for Willoughby's child. That personification of the commonest of common sense, Mrs Jennings, had once said of Eliza, whom she then believed to be Brandon's illegitimate daughter, that she could be ' " 'prenticed out at small cost" ' to be out of the way should the Colonel marry (*SS* 196). His behaviour up to this makes such a measure to the last degree unlikely. The marriage is by no means without its complexities. The past will not be banished absolutely. No past ever is, and in this novel there is no escape from the legacy of previous encounters and relationships. Unpleasant people are not banished into the *Ewigkeit* – even Elinor's cool tolerance will be taxed by having Lucy and Nancy Steele as close connections; and Marianne's 'new character of candour' will be pressed to the utmost limit.

However, one result of her experience which contemporary fiction often found *de rigueur* is almost totally missing – no one ever impugns Marianne's reputation, a fate against which Mr Tyrold warns Camilla so seriously. When Elinor protests to Mrs Jennings: ' "I must do this justice to Mr. Willoughby – he has broken no positive engagement with my sister" ' her friend laughs her to scorn – ' "Law, my dear, don't pretend to defend him. No positive engagement indeed" ' (*SS* 196). Her reaction, muted in various ways, is more or less that of everybody who knows Marianne. Her too-obvious response to Willoughby does her no harm of that kind. John Dashwood is concerned when she starts to lose her looks and thus her market price (he rates her at ' "only five or six hundred a-year, at the utmost" ' (*SS* 227)), but that is all. In fact, she knocks down for two thousand – Austen loses no opportunity for ironical twists to the narrative, for this is exactly the sum Marianne has earlier mentioned as her idea of a 'competence', when she knows, in her heart of hearts, that Willoughby is not about to put love before his more material pleasures (*SS* 91).

If Marianne escapes the traditional censure of the imprudent woman, but is rather rewarded, the more blatant misdeeds of others also go unpunished. Lucy, married to the heir to the Ferrars fortune, shows 'what an earnest, an unceasing attention to self-interest, however its progress may be apparently obstructed, will do in securing every advantage of fortune, with no other sacrifice than that of time and conscience' (*SS* 376); Willoughby 'lived to exert, and frequently to enjoy himself' (*SS* 379). The most venal of the cast of characters are the most single-minded, and demonstrate the fact that principle is not always synonymous with virtue. A vision of the essentially anarchic nature of human relationships and the pitfalls in the honest quest for right action becomes, from this novel onwards, Jane Austen's chief fictional concern.

CHAPTER 4

The Frailties of Fanny

With the publication of *Sense and Sensibility* Jane Austen has by no means finished with the stereotypes of the oppositional polemical novel of the nineties, but her next work after the publication of *Pride and Prejudice* brings a somewhat different feature of contemporary fiction more centrally into play – the exemplary girl who battles with worldliness and vice, emerging ultimately victorious after innumerable tribulations, misunderstandings and accusations. She is often, though not always, orphaned, or for some other reason dependent on the protection of powerful relations.

Emmeline, Cecilia, Camilla and Belinda are examples of this kind of heroine, and though, as we have seen, Austen was not unreservedly admiring of either Fanny Burney or Maria Edgeworth, and had already parodied Emmeline in *Northanger Abbey*, they display enough signs of human frailty to be more to her taste than other pattern females who appear in novels which she specifically scorns in her letters to Cassandra and Anna. Sarah Burney's *Clarentine* (1798) concerns a girl who, despite temptations, never deviates, even in thought, from the accepted path of right conduct. Austen is unreservedly scathing about this one in a letter to Cassandra. Two other novelists are mentioned by her in disparaging terms – Hannah More, whose *Cœlebs in Search of a Wife* came out in 1808, and Mary Brunton, who published *Self-control* in 1810. All three novels clearly set out to instruct whilst at the same time entertaining a public hungry for fiction as well as for moral guidance.

For Austen they appear to have represented a trend in fiction of which she could not approve. Of *Clarentine* she remarks in 1807, 'It is full of unnatural conduct & forced difficulties, without striking merit of any kind';[1] in 1809 Cassandra's account of *Cœlebs* does not attract her – 'My disinclination for it before was affected, but now it is real. I do not like the Evangelicals.' She later accuses More of pedantry in her choice of title.[2] She twice jokes about the improbabilities in *Self-control*; she read the novel sometime between 1811 and 1813, when she commented acidly on Laura's fantastic escape down a river in a canoe; and, while collecting opinions of *Mansfield Park* after its publication in 1814 (some adverse), she suggested wryly that she should write a 'close imitation of "Self-control"', and that her heroine should be 'wafted' across the Atlantic in the same way.[3] Contempt for the combined artificiality and didacticism of these novels could hardly be clearer.

Her proclaimed dislike of the Evangelicals needs some discussion. The movement was one of the strongest and most obvious features of the reaction to political radicalism in the nineties and continued to be highly influential long after the initial period of war-hysteria. It was dedicated to the revival of 'serious' and 'active' Christianity, partly as a defensive reaction to Methodism, which, with its outdoor meetings, public conversions and extempore prayer, was regarded as politically subversive, especially after the outbreak of war in 1793, and partly to galvanise a decadent clergy into carrying out its proper duties. It was in the main bourgeois-led and aimed at social control through paternalism; it was to that extent a political movement.[4] It developed a very efficient propaganda-machine – chiefly through Hannah More, whose publications aimed at driving all levels of society into the proper conduct of their lives. In all probability Austen's distaste stemmed from the way it set up unreal models of behaviour in both polemic and fiction – what she might have called 'cant'. Its proponents assumed the divine basis of the social status quo, and by extension the virtues of submission and quietism. The really good person's 'active principle' would convert others, by example rather than pressure, to acceptance and conformity. While deprecating fashionable progressive radicalisms, Austen shows signs of being also repelled by this form of reaction to them. She was not, however, entirely consistent in her pronouncements; a few months after the publication of *Mansfield Park*, in a letter of complicated advice to her niece Fanny about a love problem, she seems to contradict her earlier statement: 'As to there being any objection from his *Goodness*, from the danger of his becoming even Evangelical, I cannot admit *that*. I am by no means convinced that we ought not all to be Evangelicals, & am at least persuaded that they who are so, from Reason and Feeling, must be happiest & safest.' The rest of the letter strongly suggests that the aunt was worried about her previous influence on the niece – she deprecates 'Wit' in favour of 'Wisdom' and presses the girl not to be 'frightened by the idea of his acting more strictly up to the precepts of the New Testament than others.'[5] There is a strong suggestion in the letter that, in the interests of a happy marriage for Fanny, she wants partially to unsay some things she has said before. But 'Reason and Feeling' are crucial words, and she would have found little reason in some of the fictional representations of Evangelical piety currently in print – had doubtless laughed over them with the same niece, as she had with Cassandra and Anna. Put together and in context, her remarks by no means add up to support for Evangelicalism, and emphatically not for the use of fiction as moral propaganda.[6] *Mansfield Park* aims to counteract an increasing tendency for fiction to sermonise through ideal object-lessons.

The 'difficulties' faced by Clarentine certainly leave discernible traces on *Mansfield Park*. Clarentine is a dependent orphan in the family of her father, who had made an unsuitable marriage to a Frenchwoman. She is persecuted by her father's cousin, Mrs Harrington (a Mrs Norris-type figure), especially in view of her childhood friendship with the heir, Edgar. Clarentine grows up beautiful, clever and good – too good to fly in the face of family opposition. When Edgar (who turns out selfish and demanding) proposes to her, she refuses him firmly and fluently in terms of their manifest duty. Nevertheless, she is blamed for the situation and banished to Sidmouth, where she is pursued by an attractive rake, Mr Eltham (overtones of Henry Crawford), who threatens to take her by force if she will not marry him. Clarentine is all the while aware that she has a cousin, William Somerset, whom she can trust to protect her interests, but who is at sea for much of the novel (a hint of Fanny's brother William Price). She tries to escape Eltham's attentions by going to William's old tutor, Mr Lenham, in London. Things are not much better there, since Eltham is in league with Mr Lenham's housekeeper. William comes home, but seems mysteriously involved with a beautiful and worldly Mrs Hertford. Clarentine reacts very much like Fanny Price in wishing that his choice were more worthy of him. In ultimately bringing William and Clarentine together, Burney introduces numbers of perverse misunderstandings which are cleared up in equally unlikely ways. It is an unwieldy novel, with a questionable moral schema, though Burney manages to produce a lively and credible character in Edgar's younger sister, Sophia, when she temporarily vacates the moral high ground for something a little more everyday. Sophia is refreshingly rude about Mrs Harrington, and may be the origin of Mary Crawford.

Cœlebs is even more consciously didactic, and makes few concessions to realism. Charles, the eligible 'bachelor' of the title, goes in search of the perfect wife. After various encounters with marriageable girls who are deficient in education, manners and morality, he finds Lucilla Stanley at Stanley Grove, where the perfect family has reared the perfect daughter. There Charles waits to see how she will shape up to his Evangelical principles before he permits himself to fall in love; Lucilla behaves with perfect circumspection and is usually decorously silent unless she is asked to defend her principles, when she suddenly becomes very fluent. Hannah More here uses the novel to propound the Anglican Evangelical system; she includes many a complicated theological discussion and comment on manners and social obligations. It is a fictional compendium, as announced on the title-page, of 'Observation on Domestic Habits and Manners, Religion and Morals'. Charles, with his self-knowledge and carefully controlled reactions, is about as improbable a young man of twenty-four as could be, and in stark contrast to Edmund Bertram, significantly exactly the same age.

Austen's most acerbic comment is reserved for *Self-control*, another Evangelical novel, more acceptable in twentieth-century terms, perhaps, than *Cœlebs*, in that it is less tiresomely prescriptive and much more exciting. It concerns a beautiful heroine of unimpeachable manners and morals who feels obliged to accept a man approved by her father, and indeed, loved by herself, although he had attempted to seduce her and is, she finds out, vicious in his habits. She regards her promise as binding but makes the date of their marriage conditional upon his reform; during the period set her father dies and she is reduced to penury. She meets a man she prefers, the scion of a perfectly organised and religious family, but still regards herself as irrevocably engaged. Thrown upon the mercy of an unreliable protectress, she is abducted by her betrothed and carried off to Canada. She considers this act as breaking her obligation to him, but can only escape by a solitary and epic canoe-journey, presumably down the St Lawrence. Her fiancé shoots himself, but not before a change of heart causes him to leave a letter making clear that, despite his evil intentions, she has remained unviolated; thus she can regard it as seemly for her to accept her preferred suitor. Laura maintains her moral certainties by continual self-examination and reference to religion on the Evangelical model.

Austen's comments in her letters might lead to the expectation of parody on the lines of the juvenilia. Her insertion into the manuscript of *Catharine* (*MW* 232) of a reference to *Cœlebs* as part of the useless Mrs Percival's educational plan for her ward shows that she was tempted in this direction. But she had moved on fictionally and in *Mansfield Park* has a more serious project on hand. Using a similar overall structure, she sets out either to reverse or blur the assumptions manifested in these three novels. The result is that the work exerts a perennial fascination, though, after some early appreciation of the author's plan, it has been persistently misunderstood by critics who, missing or ignoring the subleties of the narrative, have seen Fanny Price as in the same class as Clarentine, Lucilla and Laura – an attempt at the model female. Within a few years of publication (1821) Richard Whately could congratulate 'Miss Austin' on producing a less-than-perfect heroine, though even he thought she had thereby simply made more palatable the moral lesson required by the novel.[7] But by mid-century things had begun to change; the assumption begins to be made that Fanny Price is *supposed* to be perfectly good, but that the author has underplayed her excellence. The critic of a women's magazine could say '... we like her very much and would be very sorry if her rival had defeated her, but more because we *know* she is a better girl than Mary Crawford, and deserves to be made happy, than because we feel for her as a sister'.[8] This conviction, that Austen must have been trying to create a perfectly good girl and has failed, has spilled over into this century and has done little for the popularity of Fanny as a heroine. The criticism of 1866 would not have allowed for a condemnation of the novel *because* of its heroine's perceived virtues. This was left for later commentators affected by the reaction against supposed late Victorian stereotypes. In 1917, Reginald Farrer was unable to incorporate *Mansfield Park* into his enthusiastic panegyric on Austen as a novelist.[9] '... alone of her books,' he writes, '*Mansfield Park* is vitiated throughout by a radical dishonesty ... Jane Austen is torn between the theory of what she ought to see, and the fact of what she does see.' He thought Fanny 'the most terrible incarnation we have of the prig–pharisee'. This, with infinite modulations, apologies and explanations, has been essentially the twentieth-century view. Without necessarily going all the way with Farrer (who thought on the whole that Austen must have been coerced into this novel by her clerical relations) later critics have assumed the position of model heroine for Fanny. 'She is never, ever wrong', said Tony Tanner in 1966, and his assertion has been backed up by many authoritative pronouncements since.[10] Isobel Armstrong softens down Farrer's critique but still calls attention to 'the difficult gravitas of the text', the primness of the heroine and her conformity to contemporary standards of behaviour.[11] We can't imagine Fanny making excuses for Willoughby, for instance, even in her own head, or speaking her mind to a Lady Catherine. Because she does not appear to challenge convention in the way that Elinor and Elizabeth do, many critics cannot forgive her. Austen stands accused of poor-spirited acceptance of contemporary shibboleths, attributed to an increase of reactionary feeling in the wake of the French Revolution. *Mansfield Park* is often regarded as an anti-jacobin novel: for some, a shameful abdication from the independence of *Pride and Prejudice* (particularly), for others, only to be expected, and in line with the actual support for status-quo values in the earlier novels: despite the vigour and liveliness of their heroines' response to life.[12] Commentators who have noticed anomalies in Fanny's behaviour, inconsistencies in her representation as the conduct-book ideal have, with a few exceptions, seen them as flaws in the perfect carrying out of the author's plan.[13] The critical debate has contracted, then, into an entirely inadequate opposition – either the novel fails because it is too didactic, or it fails because it is inconsistent in its didacticism. But as it quite plainly does not fail, the problem is still there – simply, critics have not yet come up with a plausible reason for its success. Why do we go on reading *Mansfield Park* generation after generation if it is both didactic and dull, an 'artistic failure', and its central character an impossible prig? If, on the other hand, we see the novel as a working through of the unresolvable conflicts facing a young woman who sets out, on the model of the Evangelical heroines of Burney, More and Brunton, to be wholly and consistently good, the anomalies in Fanny's response to her difficulties can be satisfactorily incorporated in a coherent critical reading. But apparent contradictions in her reactions must be faced and explained, as must the calamitous conclusion.

Although *Clarentine* and *Self-control* have many features which remind the reader of *Mansfield Park*, it is *Cœlebs* that is most clearly a target for Austen, especially in the dominance of place. Mansfield Park is a version of More's Stanley Grove, brought into the real world and mercilessly exposed. More's novel was intended to demonstrate the strength of family values in the ruling class and its conscientious carrying out of its duties to its dependants. *Mansfield Park*, on the other hand, demonstrates the weaknesses which More ignores. Sir Thomas Bertram's regime at Mansfield is typical of the way Christianity operated among the rich and powerful. Attention to the virtues of kindliness, good manners, obedience to authority and religious observance went alongside the more or less unrestricted enjoyment of the good things of life if you happened to have access to them. Sir Thomas has imbibed some Evangelical ideas – he believes in residence for the clergy, for instance, submissive behaviour in young women, and the exclusion of 'noisy pleasures' from the domestic scene, but it is clear from the start that these have had minimal effect on most of his children.[14] Unlike Mr Stanley in *Cœlebs* he has not managed to govern his household so that all the inhabitants are consciously and dutifully adapting their behaviour to a pious ideal. Moreover, it is made clear from the start that Sir Thomas is quite unaware of his failure. Self-denial has very little place in the real education of the young Bertrams, which has concentrated on social manners and the superficial and random acquisition of disconnected facts. Tom, Maria and Julia all consider their education to be irrelevant to real life, which consists in horseracing and debt for the young heir, balls and the marriage-market for the daughters. Austen exposes the shortcomings of the girls' education in great detail, dwelling on the shreds and patches of knowledge thought sufficient for young ladies, which Hannah More also deplores. Edmund, the younger son, destined without real choice for the church, turns out differently; he finds out early that his father's somewhat selective adherence to Evangelical principles has some relevance for him. He decides to be a proper parson, with all that it entails in moral concern for his flock and consciousness of responsibility for the moral health of society as a whole. Fanny, from childhood dependent upon Edmund, also builds her life on the Evangelical ideal of active duty. The sociable joys of Maria and Julia and Tom are replaced in Fanny and Edmund by the satisfactions of conscious virtue. Moreover, both Fanny and Edmund educate themselves beyond the Mansfield standard – they read widely and discuss regularly, engaging in rather sententious moral dialogue in which they invariably agree with one another. Fanny thus approaches the More standard of female excellence. So far Fanny and

Edmund together appear to embody the moral weight of the narrative. But from the start they are given problems, for their ideals necessarily imply criticism of what they observe around them, and yet the very code by which they mean to live excludes the possibility of its expression, especially to their elders. One of their early conversations demonstrates the fissures in the apparently smooth surface of their convictions. Edmund advises Fanny when she thinks she may have to go and live with Aunt Norris – both know very well how mean and selfish she is, but their principles will not allow them to rebel and they make the best of it; Edmund mouths some pious untruths about Mrs Norris's upright nature which, he says, is only cloaked by an unfortunate manner, and Fanny escapes from actually criticising her aunt by blaming herself for 'foolishness and awkwardness' (*MP* 25–6). The text asks a difficult question: is refusal to face facts virtuous or not? – and does not provide an answer.

What follows highlights a number of similar key passages, sometimes of dialogue, sometimes of internal discourse, in which Fanny's consciousness, through which most of the novel is mediated, is divided between what she *ought* to do, and what she *wants* to do. Very occasionally a narrator interjects to remind readers that they do not have to think exactly like Fanny, but for the most part we are left with only the intricacies of Fanny's thoughts expressed in free indirect style, or her conversations with others, as guides to whether or not she is living up to her own expectations. The reader may read Fanny differently from the way she reads herself. This is not altogether new – it is clearly the case with Clarissa, for instance; the difference is that Austen's method invites this sort of reader involvement, whereas Richardson was famously uneasy about multiple readings and tried continually to anticipate and forestall them, offering guidance to a definitive conclusion.

The arrival of the Crawfords, who are completely oblivious to Evangelical principles in religion and have no more serious aim in life than the avoidance of boredom, puts the first real strain on the mutually supportive agreement between Fanny and Edmund. The extreme insouciance of Mary and Henry is highly attractive to all the young people living under a comfortable but rather dull social order. The older members see nothing in them to object to; Sir Thomas is absent, in any case, in Antigua. It is usual to regard the Crawfords as representatives of the outer, more wicked, world which is about to attack the moral stronghold of Mansfield. But it should be remembered that there is in fact nothing much to attack.[15] No one at Mansfield is in possession of an unassailable set of principles. Fanny is not strong in her principles – she only thinks she is because she has learned a set of rules which she supposes will guide her in any crisis. Edmund is much the same. The difference between the Crawfords and the Bertrams lies not so much in their respective moral standards, as in the fact that the Crawfords are accustomed to a much more sophisticated and complex metropolitan version of the sexual game than the young Bertrams have any notion of; their ignorance in this respect adds spice to the Crawfords' usual round of shallow flirtation. Austen proceeds from this point to demonstrate how *all* the inhabitants of Mansfield, in different ways, fall victim to the unfamiliar game-strategy of the Crawfords – except perhaps Tom, who is in any case part of their world and clearly quite skilled himself. Both Maria, already engaged, for materialistic reasons, to the booby Rushworth, and Julia are fascinated by Henry, who deliberately sets out to entrap them. Both Fanny and Edmund are precipitated into a situation for which their 'active Christianity' has given them no guidelines – Edmund begins to fall in love, and Fanny, who is, without quite realising it, in love already, begins to experience jealousy. Significantly, Edmund does just what More's Cœlebs does *not* do; he falls for a girl who is the complete opposite of the conduct-book model; he is attracted to her because she is pretty, exciting and enticing, not for her Evangelical piety or upright principles, which are totally absent in Mary. In fact, the whole episode subverts More in a most interesting way. Cœlebs (or Charles, as he is called in the narrative) is extremely cautious in his assessment of Lucilla, making sure that he does not fall in love until he has satisfied himself that her virtues accord with his ideals and those of his dead mother, and that Lucilla is perfectly 'consistent' in them. He muses:

I am aware that love is apt to throw a radiance around the being it prefers, till it becomes dazzled, less perhaps with the brightness of the object itself, than with the beams with which imagination has invested it. But religion, though it had not subdued my imagination, had chastised it. It had sobered the splendours of fancy, without obscuring them. It had not extinguished the passions, but it had taught me to regulate them. – I now seemed to have found the being for whom I had been in search. My mind felt her excellences, my heart acknowledged its conqueror. I struggled, however, not to abandon myself to its impulses. I endeavoured to keep my own feelings in order, till I had time to appreciate a character, which appeared as artless as it was correct. And I did not allow myself to make this slight sketch of Lucilla, and of the effect she produced on my heart, till more intimate acquaintance had justified my prepossession.

'More intimate acquaintance' finds him convinced three chapters later:

I could not persuade myself that either prudence or duty demanded that I should guard my heart against such a combination of aimiable virtues and gentle graces ... [she presented] a fabric of felicity that my heart, not my fancy had erected, and that my taste, judgement, and my principles equally approved, and delighted to contemplate.[16]

Edmund's heart is by no means guarded, he *is* dazzled by the radiance of the being he prefers, and he falls, in More's terms, into dreadful error, delighting to contemplate what he can only approve by distorting his principles. The exchange between Edmund and Fanny at this juncture is very significant, paralleling and referring ironically to More. In chapter 30, Charles and Lucilla discuss the 'modish extravagances' of a city lady, Miss Bell Flam: 'We continued to converse on the subject of Miss Flam's fondness for the gay world. This introduced a natural expression of my admiration of Miss Stanley's pleasures and pursuits.'[17] The dialogue only results in an affirmation of Evangelical principles by Lucilla, and a firmer preference for her modest piety on the part of Charles. Edmund comes to a very different conclusion, and cuts off the conversation when he has arranged his ideas to suit himself. He and Fanny engage in a sort of Socratic dialogue, in which Miss Crawford's character takes a beating, but Edmund makes specious excuses for her and is satisfied; Fanny does *not* see it all as he does (though Edmund assures her she does), and does not say so. Like Charles, Edmund draws her into a discussion of Mary's character and encourages criticism:

'But was there nothing in her conversation that struck you Fanny, as not quite right?'
'Oh! yes, she ought not to have spoken of her uncle as she did. I was quite astonished. An uncle with whom she has been living so many years, and who, whatever his faults may be, is so very fond of her brother, treating him, they say, quite like a son. I could not have believed it!'
'I thought you would be struck. It was very wrong – very indecorous.'

But Fanny wants to go farther than this, and charges Mary with ingratitude, one of the blacker eighteenth-century vices. Edmund will not have this, and begins to equivocate by claiming that it is *excess* of gratitude to her aunt that gives her a difficult choice; he does not want to go beyond 'impropriety' in his charges. But, says Fanny, perhaps the aunt is not all that she should be, not to have taught Mary better; Edmund leaps on this to hope that she may now be in better hands, and proceeds to admire her affection for her brother; Fanny rather righteously objects to Mary's teasing remarks about the letter-writing habits of brothers. Edmund's reply shows how his growing thraldom is causing him to dwell only on the appearance, not the substance, of female excellence:

> 'And what right had she to suppose, that *you* would not write long letters when you were absent?'
>
> 'The right of a lively mind, Fanny, seizing whatever may contribute to its own amusement or that of others; perfectly allowable, when untinctured by ill humour or roughness; and there is not the shadow of either in the countenance or manner of Miss Crawford, nothing sharp, or loud, or coarse. She is perfectly feminine, except in the instances we have been speaking of. *There* she cannot be justified. I am glad you saw it all as I did.' (*MP* 63–4)

To the reader it is obvious that Fanny disagrees completely and is suddenly beset by a number of painful conflicts: she must approve of Edmund, but can see that he is bending the rules; her code has taught her a great deal about moral judgement, little about tolerance and nothing at all about sexual attraction, and in any case she has invested far too much in her relationship with Edmund to be able to risk any kind of breach. She is disappointed in Edmund and is unable to be charitable towards Mary. A couple of pages later free indirect style explores Fanny's state of mind:

> Fanny could not wonder that Edmund was at the parsonage every morning ... neither could she wonder, that when the evening stroll was over, and the two families parted again, he should think it right to attend Mrs. Grant and her sister to their home, while Mr. Crawford was devoted to the ladies of the park; but she thought it a very bad exchange, and if Edmund were not there to mix the wine and water for her, would rather go without it than not. She was a little surprised that he could spend so many hours with Miss Crawford, and not see more of the sort of fault which he had already observed, and of which *she* was almost always reminded by something of the same nature whenever she was in her company; but so it was ... she scrupled to point out her own remarks to him, lest it should appear like ill-nature. (*MP* 65)

The language of tolerance (she 'could not wonder') refers ironically to a mass of confused emotions which Fanny would not want to acknowledge. The paradigm of the instructional novel, in which the heroine's dilemmas are usually more clear-cut and controllable, is being disturbed here.

From this point both Edmund and Fanny rapidly lose their position as moral reference points. While Julia and Maria are allowing that unacknowledged force, sexual passion, to disturb their lives, Fanny and Edmund are essentially doing the same. But of all of them, Fanny has the most serious problem. She has somehow to hang on to her pious principles of grateful submission, while aware that moral chaos is developing around her. The average conduct-novel would give her the strength to repress her personal reactions and show everybody how they *ought* to behave. But Fanny has no such strength; her own feelings run out of control, and she is consequently unable to regulate her behaviour according to the Evangelical ideal. Almost every spontaneous feeling that she has conflicts with some duty which is part of her code. Disgust with Maria and Julia, dislike of Henry Crawford, disappointment in Edmund, jealousy of Mary all lead her into very reprehensible emotions which she tries hard to disguise, or rather to defuse. A small but significant incident exemplifies this. While waiting rather impatiently for Mary to finish her riding lesson, she pretends to herself that she is sorry for the horse: 'if she were forgotten, the poor mare should be remembered' (*MP* 68).[18] Then, unable to throw off her 'discontent and envy' she lapses into headache and languor on the sofa, does not deny it when asked by Edmund, and stands by mute while her aunts are arguing about whose fault it is (*MP* 74). It is Edmund's fault, and she 'had been feeling neglected ... struggling against discontent and envy'. The struggle is admirable, but ineffective. The More standard allows her to be silent; she does not selflessly rebut the concern that is felt, as one might expect. Lucilla Stanley would not have used her silence thus to cloak resentment, for she never experiences any. In Fanny, the feminine meekness of demeanour described in the conduct-books only serves to conceal from onlookers (but, because of the internal discourse, not from the reader) a mind in very human turmoil. Not for the last time we see Fanny using approved feminine silence to avoid positive generosity.

Edmund's resolution after the riding episode to keep Fanny more in mind does not last. At Sotherton he is still preoccupied with

Mary; and Fanny is not only conscious of his neglect, but also of the contradictions between his theory and his practice; he discourses piously to Mary, in true Evangelical manner, upon the duty of the clergyman to guide the conduct of others (he ' "has the guardianship of religion and morals, and consquently of the manners which result from their influence" ' (*MP* 93)), but shows little sign of disapproval of her frivolous remarks about religion, and, dazzled by the company of a pretty girl, is oblivious to the dangerous game being played out by Henry Crawford, Maria and Julia under his nose. Through Fanny, the reader is apprised of all that Edmund is missing; and as she witnesses the interplay of the others we are made aware of certain similarities between her reactions and those of Julia. While Henry is playing one sister off against the other, Julia is described as suffering under the necessity of hiding her feelings of jealousy; when Henry detaches Maria from the party on the terrace and leaves Julia with Mrs Norris and Mrs Rushworth, she has to struggle to maintain decorous complaisance:

The politeness which she had been brought up to practise as a duty, made it impossible for her to escape; while the want of that higher species of self-command, that just consideration of others, that knowledge of her own heart, that principle of right which had not formed any essential part of her education, made her miserable under it. (*MP* 91)

But she does manage to conceal her perturbation, just as, shortly afterwards, we find Fanny doing the same; although her manner is different, and she feels more guilt, she suffers 'disappointment and depression' for much the same reason, and finds these feelings difficult to control. During her walk with Edmund and Mary she becomes conscious of an emotional tension between them which excludes her and which she finds difficult to bear; she needs to sit down – conflict affects her physically (*MP* 94). Fanny may use approved Evangelical self-examination but it does not work. She still feels the unacceptable resentment. The episode also emphasises, in a symbolic way, the inability of Fanny's moral principles to do anything to help others out of their confusion and moral dilemmas; her habits of submission, respect and obedience, as well as her almost invisible position in the family, make this impossible. She tries, ineffectually, and from a sitting position while everyone else is running wildly about, to prevent Maria from going into the park with Henry and to defuse Julia's jealousy. But she is, for all her 'goodness', quite useless (Julia's reference to her as 'child' [*MP* 100] says it all). Her moral standards are ineffective even to herself, because they are too simple to deal with real-life crisis – just as Edmund's are.[19] Austen now shows Fanny almost replicating Julia's behaviour. While attracting far more sympathy from the reader for her plight, Fanny goes on a parallel pursuit of Edmund and Mary (*MP* 103), which results in unspoken, but real, resentment. Fanny has been wanting to see the avenue all morning; now she finds that Edmund and Mary have reached it together and she has been forgotten; her inner monologue serves to show the gulf between what she would like to feel and what she actually does feel: 'Fanny's best consolation was in being assured that Edmund had wished for her very much ... but this was not quite sufficient to do away the pain of having been left a whole hour' (*MP* 103).

Fanny may exercise more control over the expression of her feelings than Julia does, but self-repression is habitual to her; it would be impossible for her to give vent to an outburst such as Julia's to anyone about anything: ' "Why, child, I have but this moment escaped from his horrible mother. Such a penance as I have been enduring" ' (*MP* 100). She is a kinder person than Julia, is more concerned for the sufferings of others, particularly Mr Rushworth, but the strength of the emotional residue is very much the same for her as it is for her cousin. As readers we feel sorry for her, but have no confidence in her ability to stand up to the forces of what is later called 'selfish passion' – whether she likes it or not, she is involved in it herself. We are aware of her love for Edmund long before she is – and of her attempts to transform that love and jealousy into pure concern for Edmund.

These attempts continue during the episode of the play, which also emphasises Fanny's moral impotence – she can do nothing to prevent what she sees as an iniquitous proceeding. But she does begin to recognise what is happening to her – she acknowledges jealousy. The episode repeats, several times, the Fanny/Julia motif: Fanny feels sorry for her – 'could not think of her as under the agitations of *jealousy*, without great pity' (*MP* 136); Fanny recognises their similar feelings, but judges Julia – 'Julia was a sufferer too, but not quite so blamelessly' (*MP* 160); she is conscious of Julia's unhappiness (*MP* 163), and the breach between her and her sister, but 'there was no outward fellowship between them. Julia made no communication, and Fanny took no liberties. They were two solitary sufferers'. Fanny may be 'blameless' in one sense, but the episode's chief impact on the reader is the way in which the system under which they all live excludes any possibility of Fanny's 'active principle' doing anything to help either herself or Julia. And is Fanny really as blameless as all that? At Sir Thomas's unexpected arrival Julia actually voices what Fanny has been trying for throughout the episode: ' "I need not be afraid of appearing before him" ' (*MP* 175). The clash of their manners only points up the parallel of their situations and blurs the fact that Fanny has fallen short in several ways. She has condoned, as will be seen, what was clearly, by both their standards, a moral lapse in Edmund, and she has somehow sufficiently cleared away her earlier conviction that the play *Lovers' Vows* was 'improper' and the language 'unfit to be expressed by any woman of modesty' (*MP* 137) to learn most of it by heart; she believes herself (*MP* 165) 'to derive as much innocent enjoyment from the play as any of them'; and she is only saved from finally agreeing to take the part (temporarily) of the Cottager's Wife by the arrival of Sir Thomas. Bernard Paris points out that she deceives herself about her involvement in the play when she helps to make Mr Rushworth's cloak: 'It is difficult to understand the difference between acting and sewing.'[20] Her principles have not stayed firm. The narrative centres on her consciousness of what *ought* to happen; but she is no more able to cause it to do so than Edmund, the only other person who recognises that anything is amiss. This does not turn her into Nina Auerbach's 'Romantic monster' – just a helpless and muddled girl whose rules are giving way to pressure – both internal and external. For whatever she may try to tell herself, her strongest motivation is a wish keep herself right with Edmund, and this is why she has not opposed, in any effective way, his decision to act. The atmosphere of this episode is one of moral panic rather than the calm certainties of Clarentine or Lucilla.

In addition, Mary, so far the *bête noire*, the wicked interloper, suddenly shows herself to have spontaneously warm and human feelings which Fanny has had all too little experience of at Mansfield. Mrs Norris tries to shame Fanny into doing what Tom and the others want, by a crude reference to her inferior status – ' "I shall think her a very obstinate, ungrateful girl ... very ungrateful indeed, considering who and what she is" ' (*MP* 147). Mary is 'astonished', and does everything she can to comfort Fanny after this brutal and vulgar attack. The authorial voice intrudes here (such guidance from a narrator occurs very rarely, and usually to suggest that Fanny is in error of some sort) to assert that Miss Crawford is 'almost purely governed' by 'really good feelings'. When the next day Edmund announces to Fanny that he is going to rescue Mary from the necessity of having to act what amounts to a love-scene with a stranger, Fanny cannot bring herself to acknowledge Mary's 'really good feelings'; she tries for 'greater warmth of manner' and cannot complete her 'generous effusion' (*MP* 155–6). Is she governed by her concern for the doubtful morality of the whole proceeding? Or does she really want Edmund to leave Mary to her fate, thus obeying the rules they both believe in and staying on her side? The final sentences of the chapter answer this question. Fanny is not concerned about generalised right and wrong; it is Mary who is the enemy – 'Alas! it was all Miss Crawford's doing.' The final words of her internal monologue are: 'Things should take their course; she cared not how it ended . . . It was all misery *now*' (*MP* 157). Although she is presented as telling herself that his moral consistency is her chief concern, the words convey the fact that it is mainly Edmund's relation to herself that she cares about. What Austen is putting forward here is a critique of Evangelical fiction; her target is the ease with which unacceptable human feelings can be camouflaged in simplistic moral systems – a useful set of imperatives can be used to transform and make laudable such things as jealousy and cold-heartedness. When the system fails, as it appears to do with Fanny, an individual is left with an uncomfortable amalgam of self-right-eousness and despair. Moreover, in this case, Fanny, for all her 'goodness', has no means of helping Edmund to deal honestly with his problems, for her own desires are too much involved. Austen has really contrived to muddy the waters here; readers expecting a Clarentine or Lucilla will find Fanny wanting and Edmund too far lost to be redeemable by the usual fictional devices of sudden illuminations and clarifications.

With the return of Sir Thomas, Mansfield becomes 'an altered place'. Mr Yates disappears into the dissipated worlds of London and Newmarket, whither Tom also shortly repairs; Henry decamps to Bath. Maria marries Rushworth and Julia accompanies them to Brighton for the winter. Both sisters are hurt and bewildered by Henry Crawford's behaviour – there is a strong sense as they leave for scenes of wealth and pleasure that this solution is not going to work for them; Maria has nothing but contempt for her husband,

and marries him only to soothe her pride. At this stage Sir Thomas's distorted priorities are clearly demonstrated; he assiduously banishes all signs of play-acting from the surface of Mansfield, but allows himself to be deceived by Maria's speciously calm manner that his fears are groundless and that this is an ordinary, possible marriage; Julia, too, successfully convinces him that she is capable of helping her sister in her new role. Both act more skilfully than they would ever have done on the stage.

Fanny is a silent but perceptive observer. Unlike Clarentine, who, until the heir wants to marry her, is so valued for her good sense and sympathy that she is used as a confidante by the whole Delmington family, she is treated as an irrelevance by everyone but Edmund, who has little more influence in the family, and in any case has an interest in defending the Crawfords from criticism. Once the family circle is contracted, however, Fanny becomes more important. Lost for a companion, Mary makes a friend of her. Perplexed about her feelings for Edmund, perpetually in two minds about her real desires, Mary is in dire need of a confidante. She shows tentative signs of applying to Fanny for help in analysing her reactions. The episode in which this occurs is highly ironic, setting up an expectation of Caroline/Julia or Belinda/Lady Delacour opposition in which Fanny, with her superior sense and self-knowledge will seek to influence the weaker party. In another novel she would at least show compassion and concern. What actually happens is far more complicated and inauspicious. The two girls simply fail to communicate at all, though the reader is continually conscious of what lies in the gaps between them.

Sitting with Mary in Mrs Grant's shrubbery one mild November day, Fanny launches into a rhapsody on the beauties of nature and memory reminiscent both of Dr Johnson and Hannah More's Lucilla.[21] Mary, 'untouched and inattentive, had nothing to say' (*MP* 209). Even to the reader, Fanny's comments sound a trifle stiff and derivative – perhaps Mary's is the silence of contempt for hackneyed pieties. But when Fanny brings the matter down to personalities, admiring Mrs Grant's garden-plan, it becomes clear where Mary's thoughts have been. She responds 'carelessly', ' "I had not imagined a country parson ever aspired to a shrubbery or any thing of that kind." ' The word 'parson', as Kenneth Moler has pointed out, is significant. Hannah More rebukes young women who talk of 'The Parsons', which she calls a 'contemptuous appellation'. Mary has been musing drearily on her half-sister's life as the wife of a clergyman, and on Edmund's exasperating lack of ambition. As Fanny continues with another uplifting panegyric (this time on evergreens, the substance of which is ignored by her companion), Mary tries to cheer herself up, to nudge herself into a highly fanciful compromise about the life she might lead with Edmund:

'I am conscious of being far better reconciled to a country residence than I had ever expected to be. I can even suppose it pleasant to spend *half* the year in the country, under certain circumstances – very pleasant. An elegant, moderate-sized house in the centre of family connections – continual engagements among them – commanding the first society in the neighbourhood – looked-up to perhaps as leading it even more than those of larger fortune, and turning from the cheerful round of such amusements to nothing worse than a tête-à-tête with the person one feels most agreeable in the world.' (*MP* 210)

This is Fanny's cue for encouragement – modified, perhaps, for she must be well aware how much Mary is fantasising. But now it is her turn to have nothing to say, for her heart had been beating 'very quick, and she felt quite unequal to surmising or soliciting any thing more'; she half realises that what Mary is describing comprises most of what would be a paradise to *her*, though neither of them has mentioned Edmund. Tense with alarm, she has no wish to enter into this discussion, and when Mary asks a direct question: ' "There is nothing frightful in such a picture, is there, Miss Price? One need not envy the new Mrs. Rushworth with such a home as *that*" ', Fanny in effect makes no reply, simply repeating the significant words of Mary's question, ' "Envy Mrs. Rushworth!" ' She does not want to come within a whisper of contemplating a change in Mary which might lead her to cast aside her doubts. In fact she prefers Miss Crawford to remain deep in her materialism, for change might mean loss of Edmund. Though she has not yet admitted it to herself, she is in love with Edmund – a fact to which Mary is oblivious – and the state of Mary's soul is the last of her concerns. Several unlikely fictional images suggest themselves – Fanny should set out to improve Mary for Edmund's sake, she should have 'guarded her heart against an ill-placed attachment' like Belinda, she should piously resolve to give up all thought of him and devote herself to good works. This narrative, however, is more than hinting that she wants Mary to remain bad, and Edmund to find out how bad she is.

Both girls fall silent and Mary's evanescently positive mood dissipates, as it must without strong encouragement. The account of Edmund's perception of the scene as he approaches is almost comically ironic. He feels 'particular pleasure' at 'seeing them together'; but they are not 'together'; he can have no conception of the gulf between them and of all that has been left either unsaid or unnoticed. Mary is still preoccupied with her dissatisfactions and soon manoeuvres the talk in this direction, reproaching him roundly for his contentment with his lot in life: ' "I must look down upon any thing contented with obscurity when it might rise to distinction" ', she says, when Edmund argues for the 'modest competence' which he can expect (*MP* 214). Their talk is sufficiently intimate and allusive to increase Fanny's painful anticipations – she only wants to escape from further confirmation of her fears. The episode refers obliquely to many a high-minded fictional inner discourse of self-control and noble renunciation. Fanny is merely human; although she is presented as meaning to be selfless and good, she is also in too much confusion and conflict to carry the moral authority she has seemed earlier to promise.

But she does try to fulfil her own expectations. At the dinner at Mrs Grant's which happens soon afterwards, Fanny realises that she must not any longer allow what she disapproves of to pass without comment. Hannah More had written as early as 1777 that young ladies should usually be docile, but that those who took refuge in decorum to avoid defending what they knew to be wrong 'were not gentle but wicked';[22] Fanny gathers up her energies to oppose Henry's appeal for her agreement that Sir Thomas's homecoming when *Lovers' Vows* was so nearly ready was very unlucky: ' "As far as *I* am concerned, sir, I would not have delayed his return for a day. My uncle disapproved it all so entirely when he did arrive, that in my opinion, every thing had gone quite far enough." ' For her quite unprecedentedly daring, she thinks this speech will repel him, but no such matter – Henry is so jaded by female complaisance that his interest is naturally stimulated by her opposition (*MP* 225). The rest logically follows, though it is a long time before his interest becomes serious enough for him to want to change himself. At first, he only wants to change *her* – ' "to make a small hole in Fanny Price's heart" '. Fanny's relations to Henry closely follow Lucilla's with an unwelcome suitor, Lord Staunton, whose reactions to her rebukes are not dissimilar to Crawford's.[23] The crucial difference is that Lucilla is supported wholeheartedly by her parents and friends in her resistance to his blandishments; Fanny is quite alone.

Henry Crawford is an interesting variant on the fictional rake, for he is not so very bad. Sarah Burney's Eltham drinks, 'play[s] high, fight[s] desperately' and proclaims his willingness to seduce Clarentine if she will not marry him. Even Willoughby and Wickham have more against them than Henry has. The worst one can accuse him of at the outset is an addiction to making rather silly, conceited girls think he will marry them. Maria and Julia excite little sympathy in the reader. His wish to change when he recognises a different kind of woman in Fanny may be illusory, but it is, within his limits, sincere. However, Fanny refuses to countenance the possibility of *any* reform in Henry; she seems to be rigid in her judgements and to lack compassion. But the reader can see that her behaviour is wholly dominated by her feeling for Edmund. The only course she can conceive of is to sit tight and wait for both Crawfords to go away – she has no interest in their lives whatsoever. Clarentine's compassion and therefore her influence finally turn Eltham from his evil ways, though she does not marry him; Fanny wants to have no truck with Henry at all. And, by direct allusion to a fictional stereotype, Austen is at pains to disabuse the reader of any notion of Fanny's superiority in this regard to the general run; she would have been attracted to Henry 'had not [her] heart been guarded in a way unsuspected by Miss Crawford', 'for' she goes on:

although there doubtless are such unconquerable young ladies of eighteen (or one should not read about them) as are never to be persuaded into love against their judgment by all that talent, manner, attention, and flattery can do, I have no inclination to believe Fanny one of them (*MP* 231)

Fanny's lack of response is noted by Sir Thomas at dinner at the Parsonage, but is totally misunderstood by him. He sees her as a model girl, keeping her distance from an attentive male. Henry is detailing his plan to rent a home of his own near Mansfield. Sir Thomas, in neither the reader's nor Fanny's confidence, sees her reaction as 'so proper and modest, so calm and uninviting' (*MP* 246) (again he is deceived by acting) but her real object, which he knows nothing about, is not to accept the compliment of Crawford's attention except by the bare minimum of response, and to avoid 'strengthening his views in favour of Northamptonshire'. Anger and fear are masked by her calm exterior – she has no use for Mr

Crawford. Nor is his plan her only cause for disquiet. Edmund again has to defend his intended profession before Mary. Sir Thomas gives voice to a solemn 'little harangue' about the duty of residence for clergymen, which Edmund supports: ' "Sir Thomas ... undoubtedly understands the duty of a parish priest. – We must hope that his son may prove that he knows it too." ' (*MP* 248). This comes immediately after reminders of the underlying moral instability of Mansfield in references to the hollowness of the Rushworth marriage, which Sir Thomas, with all his claim of high principle, has failed to prevent, and the day at Sotherton, when to Fanny's way of thinking not even Edmund has behaved with entire rectitude.[24] Mary, further irritated by Edmund's steadfast adherence to views which she has already covertly threatened will prevent their marriage, mischievously reminds the company of Henry's behaviour: ' "Only think what grand things were produced there by our all going with him one hot day in August to drive about the grounds, and see his genius take fire. There we went, and there we came home again; and what was done there is not to be told!" ' (*MP* 244–5). The cross-currents of emotion in this episode are emphasised by Sir Thomas's misreading of the whole scene. For a novel of this date it reveals an unusual and total absence of indisputably noble sentiments.

During the run-up to the ball, we are shown Fanny's grip on her moral code slipping even further; she is dominated by one thing only – her feeling for Edmund – and all tolerance and charity go out of the window. Her reaction to the gift of the necklace is wary and suspicious (*MP* 260), and when she receives the chain from Edmund, in her haste to exclude the Crawfords from her relationship with both William and Edmund, she falls into real insensitivity to other people's feelings. She wishes to return the necklace because it is ' "not wanted" '. She tries to soften this down by suggesting that, since it was originally given to her by her brother, Mary would clearly prefer to keep it. This shows the extent of her moral muddle; Edmund himself is shocked and immediately straightens her out; it almost seems as if he has kept a greater hold on generalised charity and loving-kindness than Fanny for the very reason that his love for Mary has made him less rigid:

'She must not suppose it not wanted, not acceptable at least; and its having been originally her brother's gift makes no difference, for as she was not prevented from offering, nor you from taking it on that account, it ought not to affect your keeping it.' (*MP* 263)

This is a general statement, which would apply in any similar situation. Fanny has lost her grip rather seriously. After this episode, in which Edmund clearly shows the strength of his feeling for Mary, Fanny is described as trying hard to 'regulate' her feelings by recourse to duty and prayer, in the kind of self-examination so central to the Evangelical system. This she signally fails to do, and the episode is described without the pious complacency of a Lucilla Stanley or Laura Montreville:

> She would endeavour to be rational, and to deserve the right of judging of Miss Crawford's character and the privilege of true solicitude for him by a sound intellect and an honest heart.
>
> She had all the heroism of principle, and was determined to do her duty; but having also many of the feelings of youth and nature, let her not be much wondered at if, after making all these good resolutions on the side of self-government, she seized the scrap of paper on which Edmund had begun writing to her, as a treasure beyond all her hopes (*MP* 265)

In fact, Fanny succeeds only temporarily in accepting what seems to be the inevitable, and as the time of the ball approaches, and she knows that Edmund is at the Parsonage talking to Mary, she relapses into depression, and only manages to cheer up when poor Edmund comes dispiritedly back after a tiff with Mary about his approaching ordination which seems to have ended all his hopes. Fanny is positively glad – 'She had felt nothing like it for hours' (*MP* 270). Though understandable in the circumstances, this is hardly the reaction of the exemplary heroine. Tony Tanner says: 'We are used to seeing heroes and heroines confused, fallible, error-prone. But Fanny always thinks, feels, speaks, and behaves exactly as she ought.'[25] This statement is not reconcilable with the text; Fanny, behaving as she does in accordance with 'nature' rather than principle, is very 'error-prone'. She forgets all about sharing Edmund's pain and disappointment, and is caught up in her own joy at the likelihood of Miss Crawford's final banishment – 'Now, every thing was smiling.'[26] Does this look like 'that higher species of self-command, that just consideration of others' which we have been told earlier *Julia* lacks? Fanny has all of the faults denied by Tanner, and frequently falls into ordinary human error. Unlike Belinda, Clarentine, Laura, Lucilla and a host of others, Fanny cannot keep her moral balance sufficiently to become the exemplary woman she would like to be, and the text is asking unequivocally whether this can reasonably be expected.

The ball over, and the three young men temporarily absent, Mary again tries to engage Fanny's sympathetic attention. She is sorry for her behaviour to Edmund about his ordination, 'She wished such words unsaid with all her heart' (*MP* 286); she misses him sorely and is worried about his protracted absence and jealous of the daughters of the family with which he is staying; again we see her softened and ready for a radical change of attitude. Here is a soul to be saved, but Fanny once more fails to overcome her own desires and take the opportunity, confining herself to the shortest possible answers. As Mary tries to prise some reaction, Fanny is forced into an acknowledgement that she does not think him likely to marry one of the 'Miss Owens' – or, she hopes, anybody. She is clearly preoccupied with this new danger. Her response is guarded and unsatisfactory – ' "I know nothing of the Miss Owens", said Fanny calmly', when pressed (*MP* 287–9). She will do nothing to encourage Mary, nor – more importantly – will she help in any way to make her more fit, in her terms, to be Edmund's wife. She would prefer Mary to remain hardened in her materialism and therefore unacceptable to Edmund. The kind of selfless love which would enable her to devote herself to Mary's improvement for Edmund's sake – surely more in line with the ideals of *Cælebs* and other contemporary novels – is quite alien to Fanny. Moreover, she is alarmed enough at Mary's suggestion to question Edmund about the Miss Owens on his return: ' "The Miss Owens – you liked them, did not you?" ' (*MP* 355). Her motives are as mixed as anybody's and will not respond to Evangelical pieties.

Austen continually reminds us that Fanny's love for Edmund is the main motive for her determined rejection of Crawford and her dislike and fear of Mary. She can hardly tell Edmund this, and in her conversation with him about it she 'avoids a direct answer'; she uses Crawford's behaviour at the time of the play to explain her rejection (*MP* 348–9). She does the same with Mary; she will neither love Mary nor tolerate Henry because, she convinces herself, they are irredeemably *corrupt*; this makes it possible for her to believe that her feelings are independent of her strong wish to banish the Crawfords and have Edmund once again all to herself. But they are not, and her internal discourse betrays the straightforwardness – even crudity – of her real state of mind – 'If Mr. Crawford would but go away! … go and take his sister with him …' (*MP* 311). Fanny's situation with regard to her unwelcome suitor is in direct contrast to that of

Lucilla. Lord Staunton is known to be a rake, and his promises of reform under her influence are firmly rejected. ' "No, my lord," ' she says, ' "I will never add to the number of those rash women who have risked their eternal happiness on this vain hope." '[27] There is no charming sister, beloved but deluded cousin or stern uncle to complicate Lucilla's decision, nor is she acting, as Fanny is, against the advice of all those she is accustomed to respect. Fanny is in a position of great weakness. There is an all-important passage in which we have the support of the narrator that she could be wrong both about herself and about the Crawfords.

Edmund has returned, and his hopes have revived; he has been able to rid himself – 'nobody could tell how' – of 'the doubts and hesitations of her ambition'. Fanny believes that Mary will now accept his offer. She muses:

and yet, there were bad feelings still remaining which made the prospect of it most sorrowful to her, independently – she believed independently of self.

The interpolation of 'she believed' here must indicate a doubt, even in her own mind. The next sentences of Fanny's internal discourse accuse Mary of something which is at this juncture also applicable to herself:

In their very last conversation, Miss Crawford, in spite of some amiable sensations, and much personal kindness, had still been Miss Crawford, still shewn a mind led astray and bewildered, and without any suspicion of being so; darkened, yet fancying itself light.

There is a reflective irony in this, and to emphasise its message the narrator's voice here interrupts, addressing 'older sages' who might at this point justly impugn the total enlightenment of Fanny's own mind:

Experience might have hoped more for any young people, so circum-stanced, and impartiality would not have denied to Miss Crawford's nature, that participation of the general nature of women, which would lead her to adopt the opinions of the man she loved and respected, as her own. – But as such were Fanny's persuasions, she suffered very much from them, and could never speak of Miss Crawford without pain. (*MP* 367)

This authorial comment puts a stop to any certainty about the purity of Fanny's state of mind. No moral system could blame her for being inexperienced, but a failure of 'impartiality' is much less excusable. But Fanny is unaware of this kind of failure in herself. Again she is shown as unable either to contemplate the reform of Mary or to take up any definitive attitude to what she regards as Edmund's moral relativism; she can neither make the best of things nor make an overall stand against what she thinks is wrong.

And she is to be tested further. She goes to Portsmouth and is there taught a bitter lesson. While she is accusing Mary in her mind of having 'learnt to think nothing of consequence but money', she herself is having to learn how dependent she really is upon ease, refinement and wealth. She has great difficulty in maintaining the proper respect for her parents under conditions of privation to which she is not accustomed. And one aspect of her visit shows her mind to be as 'astray' as Mary's – her project to save Susan, her sister. In their different ways both Susan and Mary may be regarded as victims of a defective moral and social education, but Fanny sees Mary's mind as 'polluted', and therefore unchangeable, while Susan is simply 'far from amiable' and a proper subject for reform. Again her attitude is a disguise for her real wishes. She has no vested interest in keeping Susan in her present unamiable state. When Susan asks for advice, she gives it without stint (*MP* 397). How different from her response to Mary! She wavers in her attitude to Henry, especially during her time of trial in Portsmouth, where he represents for her all the luxury and ease she misses so much, but when letters from Mary and Edmund bring her cousin to the surface of her mind she becomes very clear about where she stands: 'Her friends leading her astray for years! She is quite as likely to have led *them* astray ... Edmund, you do not know *me*. The families would never be connected, if you do not connect them' (*MP* 424). She has earlier shown how much she is affected by the mere mention of Mary's name. On Crawford's visit to Portsmouth he tries to interest Fanny in his management of his estate in Norfolk, and to begin with she is quite impressed 'she was on the point of giving him an approving look' (*MP* 404); the next time he brings up the subject, actually asking for her advice, he has just been speaking of Mary, and Fanny's reaction is very different. She refuses to comment, with as chill a reply as it is possible to imagine:

'I advise! – you know very well what is right.'

'Yes. When you give me your opinion, I always know what is right. Your judgment is my rule of right.'

'Oh, no! – do not say so. We have all a better guide in ourselves, if we would attend to it, than any other person can be. Good bye; I wish you a pleasant journey tomorrow.' (*MP* 412)

And this from a girl who not long ago has been wandering distractedly about the East Room, 'undecided as to what she *ought to do*' (*MP* 153) – she is no stranger to moral dilemma, and could, in the absence of the fresh reference to her major concern, have been more positive and sympathetic; moreover, she is quite prepared to be a 'rule of right' to Susan. At the end of the novel Henry's failure to go to Everingham is on the one hand presented as the result of weakness and vanity; but we can if we choose remember that Fanny had the chance to encourage him otherwise and did not do so. It should also be remembered that a kind answer need not necessarily be equal to a promise to marry him. Fanny is not altogether innocent; though 'without guile' she is not harmless, representing as she does, not open-minded Christian charity, but an inflexible moral system which has little room for generosity and which gives her every opportunity for self-deception.[28] Even a minor degree of approval for Henry's plans might have given him the final incentive to do the right thing. Instead, he goes to Richmond and meets Maria again. The stage is set for the catastrophe.

'Let other pens dwell on guilt and misery' – the well-known first sentence of the last chapter of *Mansfield Park* is apt to distract our attention from the second: 'I quit such odious subjects as soon as I can, impatient to restore every body, not greatly in fault themselves, to tolerable comfort, and to have done with the rest.' It should be noted that the words are 'not greatly in fault', *not* 'completely innocent', and these people are to be restored not to great happiness but to 'tolerable comfort'. That is all that anybody enjoys in the end, and this comfort is built on the wreck of most of Sir Thomas and Lady Bertram's hopes in their fine family. There is a sense, at one level, in the language of the denouement, of picking up the pieces – nobody has got quite what they wanted. Except Fanny – and even she must always remember that she is Edmund's second choice, and that he would have married Mary, faults and all, if events had fallen out differently. We are reminded of the ideal, alternative ending in the last pages –

Would he [Henry] have deserved more, there can be no doubt that more would have been obtained; especially when that marriage had taken place, which would have given him the assistance of her conscience in subduing her first inclination, and brought them very often together. Would he have persevered, and uprightly, Fanny must have been his reward – and a reward very voluntarily bestowed – within a reasonable period from Edmund's marrying Mary. (*MP* 467)

This is a vision of redemption for everyone, which was not to be fulfilled. Who, then, is to blame? On the face of it, it is Henry, but Fanny bears much of the responsibility – for her rejection of Crawford's last appeal is the pivot upon which the novel finally turns towards its calamitous conclusion. And yet, any expectation that she could single-handedly push events in a different direction is unreal. This is why, in spite of everything, she does not come across as a monster of selfishness. Her principles, though rigid, are not strong; her code of good conduct will not bear the pressure of circumstances; but none of this is her fault; she is a victim, not a villain. The fact that Austen chose not to cast Fanny as redeemer shows that her aim was to give the lie to Evangelical fictional certainties, which would have allowed a conventionally happy ending, involving selfless renunciation on the part of Fanny and varying degrees of reformation in all the others. Such things do not happen; and fiction, Austen thought, though it must invent, should not lie.

Mansfield Park goes further than *Sense and Sensibility* in excluding an authoritative centre to the novel. Elinor is steady enough, but cannot escape moral relativism altogether. In *Mansfield Park*, no one is steady. As Sir Thomas contemplates the wreck of most of his hopes, he takes responsibility for it and creates a mood of optimism as the novel closes; but the reader is conscious of the fact that he has no solution to the question of the moral education of those who are *not* 'born to struggle and endure', but to enjoy unlimited ease and luxury; or indeed to any of the other intractable problems of human motive and desire the novel has identified and from which no one – certainly not Fanny – has been able to escape.

The last paragraph is exceedingly subtle in its ironic allusion to the events of the past which have made Mansfield safe for Fanny. It describes her move with Edmund from Thornton Lacey to Mansfield on the death of Dr Grant:

> On that event they removed to Mansfield, and the parsonage there, which under each of its two former owners, Fanny had never been able to approach but with some painful sensation of restraint or alarm, soon grew as dear to her heart, and as thoroughly perfect in her eyes, as every thing else, within the view and patronage of Mansfield Park, had long been.

One can, if one chooses, note the echoing stillness of this conclusion.

Fanny's happiness and safety (suggested as the rewards for Evangelical principles in Austen's letter to Fanny Knight) are based on absence. What she loves is Mansfield virtually empty; there are few figures left on the landscape within its 'view and patronage', and those are reduced from strength to weakness. But what of its old inhabitants? The banishment of so much youth, beauty, hope and energy, however tainted by the world, must be attended with regret. The positive language of the closure, appropriate to a happy ending, conveys at another level a negative vision of loss and compromise. Such an interplay of vitality and paralysis, aspiration and failure, doubt and certainty could produce no positive victory for anyone. In *Mansfield Park* Austen transforms the late-eighteenth-century conduct novel, making a strong bid for the liberation of fiction from its obligations to provide single, unequivocal moral readings.

CHAPTER 5

Men of sense and silly wives – the confusions of Mr Knightley

The 'Opinions of *Mansfield Park*' which Jane Austen collected and preserved gave her evidence that, though some readers were aware of the dispersal of the focus of reader approval present in the novel – they were doubtful about which characters they ought to 'like', and were honest about saying so – others tended to remodel the content to suit their expectations, and missed the novel's subtleties and built-in uncertainties. Lady Robert Kerr, for instance, commented on 'the pure morality with which it abounds' making it 'a most desirable as well as useful work'; 'Mr. Egerton the Publisher praised it for it's Morality' (*MW* 433). Adverse criticism often centred on the short-comings of a character the commentator clearly thought intended to be virtuous by the author; Fanny Knight objected to Edmund's attraction to Mary Crawford and his failure to face up to Henry Crawford's iniquities (*MW* 431); Mary Cooke, a cousin, thought 'Fanny ought to have been more determined on overcoming her own feelings, when she saw Edmund's attachment to Miss Crawford' (*MW* 432–3), showing herself securely attached to the Fanny Burney/Maria Edgeworth stereotype. Austen could be excused for feeling especially frustrated by the last comment, for a reading unbiassed by expectations of moral 'usefulness' clearly reveals that the plot dynamics absolutely require Fanny to fail in this way. Austen was aware that her theory of what a novel should do ran counter for the most part to public expectation, which still believed it should have an unequivocal moral message or fail in its aim. It may have been misunderstandings about Fanny Price and Edmund that drove Austen in her next novel to invent a heroine whom nobody could mistake for an attempt at a conduct-book model – 'whom nobody but myself will much like'.[1] She had plenty of precedent for the deluded heroine (of whom Emma is a version) by early 1814. Charlotte Lennox's *Female Quixote* was still popular with the family;

in 1800 Elizabeth Hamilton, noted by Austen as a 'respectable' writer, had given the world Brigetina Botherim, a burlesque counterblast to Emma Courtney, who imagines herself the heroine of a sentimental romance and relentlessly pursues the embarrassed object of her affections (*Memoirs of Modern Philosophers*);[2] Maria Edgeworth's *Angelina, or, l'Amie Inconnue* (1801) has as its central character a girl who is deceived into sentimental friendship with a drunken trickster; Eaton Stannard Barrett's *The Heroine, or Adventures of a Fair Romance Reader*, published in 1813, was being read by Austen while her brother Henry perused the completed manuscript of *Mansfield Park*; in 1814, Mary Brunton, mentioned earlier by Austen in no very flattering terms, published *Discipline*, a novel about a rich and spoilt heiress who gets her comeuppance at the hands of an older mentor/lover.[3] Moreover, Austen had included the theme already in *Northanger Abbey*, *Pride and Prejudice* and *Sense and Sensibility*, though not as the major ingredient. In *Emma* she takes the familiar stereotype of deluded girl versus mentor/lover, mixes it, among others, with the theme of the dependent girl (Jane Fairfax and Harriet Smith) and the model female (Jane again) and weaves a fiction of amazing intricacy in which none of the stock characters behaves exactly as might be expected and in which the reader's sympathies are never thrust into a moral conduit.

The combination of wealth and beauty in a heroine is a frequently occurring trope in eighteenth-century fiction; she is thereby rendered vulnerable to material indulgence and personal vanity, as well as to predatory suitors. Austen carefully excludes these evils from the life of Emma. She is 'handsome', but we have it on the best authority that she is not vain (Mr Knightley, *E* 39); she is rich, but not addicted to dangerous entertainments such as masquerades (like, for instance, Ellen Percy in Brunton's *Discipline*), for her few visits to Brunswick Square have not provided opportunities for metropolitan dissipation on these lines; and as an unwelcome suitor, Mr Elton is no more than a ludicrous embarrassment. Unlike Mr Percy, Mr Woodhouse is not intent on selling his daughter to the highest bidder – on the contrary, the very thought of marriage is anathema to him. Put like this, it is hard to see how Emma can have any adventures which would fit into a contemporary novel.

Other characters in the story are also subverted versions of stock figures. Both Mrs Weston and Mrs Elton have the familiar outlines of the more mature companion who can be a protective guardian or a threat of some kind. But Mrs Weston significantly exerts no power over Emma and does not attempt to do so; Mrs Elton fails in her attempt. Emma shows her awareness of the stereotype when she contemptuously brushes off Mrs Elton's offer of an introduction in Bath, imaging for herself 'some vulgar, dashing widow' (*E* 275) such as abounded in popular fiction. Perhaps she even had Edgeworth's Harriet Freke in mind. Jane Fairfax is recognisable as the model fictional girl, but turns out to have a discreditable secret, which no traditionally docile young lady was allowed; and Harriet is herself a discreditable secret, though in no way responsible for her position.

But the most confusing element in *Emma* is the character of Mr Knightley. He at first looks very much like Mr Maitland (Ellen Percy's mentor/lover in *Discipline*) and Robert Stuart, who plays a similar role in *The Heroine*, saving Cherry/Cherubina from her romantic-novel delusions, in which she imagines herself to be a noble foundling. Mr Knightley is as ready as they are to hand out home truths to his 'pupil'; contemporary readers could be excused for assuming him to be another pattern gentleman. Even now, there is a tendency to see him as a development of Grandison. 'Austen's model for wisdom', says one recent critic, echoing a long line of commentators who have seen Knightley as carrying the moral authority of the novel.[4] Though one or two critics have found fault with him, it still seems difficult for most to relinquish the idea that Austen was advocating ideal modes of behaviour of one kind or another.[5] Some feminists perceive irony in the presentation of Mr Knightley; Margaret Kirkham in particular sees a fairly equal distribution of praise and blame between Emma herself and Mr Knightley. My analysis closely follows hers – with the difference that I believe that Austen would have repudiated the label of 'Enlightenment feminist' if she had ever heard it.[6] Her main purpose seems to me to have been literary – to produce a critique of fictional figures who control the action of the story because the narrative assumes them to be endowed with special *vertù*; such figures are as often women as men. I think, for example, of the contrast between Lady Catherine de Bourgh, who signally fails in her attempts to control anyone but Mr and Mrs Collins, and both Lady Montreville in *Self-control* and Lady Delvile in *Cecilia*, who, in spite of their unreasonable and intransigent demands, are treated with deference and respect, by the heroines as well as by a prevailing authorial presence. Jane Austen seems consciously to reject any

assumption of status as value. But so far I must agree with Kirkham
– if Mr Knightley is indeed the author's model for wisdom she must
have departed from her usual practice, for nowhere in the major
works do we find a male character who is beyond reproach. 'Pictures
of perfection' made her 'sick & wicked' – and not only female ones.
An examination of some of the less frequented byways of the text
will reveal that, far from being somehow above it all, Mr Knightley
is involved in the same kind of social/moral confusion as Emma and
all the other characters and that it is with a general fictional chaos,
designed to entertain rather by confusion than by satisfying certainties, that the novel is chiefly concerned.

Austen's comments on her reading during the putative gestation
of *Emma* are enlightening. Burlesque novels come in for much less
criticism than serious ones. One favourite novel of this kind, *The
Female Quixote*, has already been mentioned in connection with
Northanger Abbey; it has little obvious influence on *Emma*, for Emma
by no means shares the naiveté or isolation of Arabella. But a certain
foreshadowing of *Emma* may be detected in Eaton Stannard Barrett's
The Heroine ('It diverted me exceedingly,' says Austen in a letter to
Cassandra, 'a delightful burlesque').[7] Based on a similar premiss to
that of Lennox's novel, that too much reading might make a girl
mad, it brings the debate on young women up to date, as well as
offering some trenchant criticism of well-known novels. Like Arabella, Cherry is helped back to sanity by a clergyman; but her real
saviour is Robert Stuart, who analyses her faults but loves her in
spite of them. ' "Had I not seen your failings" ' he says, ' "I should
never have discovered your perfections." '[8] No reader of *Emma* can
fail to see the parallel with Mr Knightley here. Several other
situations also have echoes in Austen's novel – for instance, Cherry's
incredible career of delusion, in which, among other things, she
blows up a ruined church with gunpowder and disguises herself as a
soldier, begins when she loses her governess, who is dismissed for
kissing the butler. Hilarious and disrespectful comment on popular
fiction would also have appealed to Austen; Cherry is presented with
the phantoms of heroes and heroines and finds to her chagrin that,
for instance, in the cloud-cuckoo-land of fiction, Evelina and Lord
Orville lead a cat-and-dog domestic life, and that Pamela has left
Mr B. and run off with Rasselas. However, it is quite certain that
Austen would have had some fault to find in the authoritative
pronouncements of Robert at the end of the novel about fiction in

general. He draws the inevitable distinction between instructive and useful 'fictitious biography... such as The Vicar of Wakefield ... and Cœlebs, which draw man as he is, instead of man as he cannot be, superhuman' (an odd conclusion when we remember the manly resistance to error of all kinds of More's hero, Charles) and 'Romances [which] ... teach [the mind] erroneous notions of the world, by relating adventures too improbable to happen, and depicting characters too perfect to exist'. To Austen's mind this was a false distinction – 'pictures of perfection' constituted the major flaw in all fiction. *Emma* very clearly grows out of this central disagreement with Barrett. Other reading may also have had its effect; in 1805 Austen read Thomas Gisborne's popular work on female education; she finds it more sensible, perhaps, than earlier works by Dr Gregory and Dr Fordyce, but there is enough subversion of his ideal young woman in the person of Jane Fairfax to suggest that her approval was strictly limited.[9]

The location of the novel is carefully designed to maximise the confusions and mislead readers on the watch for reliable moral lessons. Austen is at some pains to show that the world of Highbury is extremely fluid. Upwardly mobile *nouveaux riches*, such as the Coles and Mr Weston, rub shoulders with the impoverished gentry like the Bateses and the main local landowner, Mr Knightley. They attract no accusations of venality and vulgarity – nearly everybody likes them and values their contribution to the social life of the place. Frank Churchill is being brought up in a rather mysterious, wealthier milieu than his father's; Jane Fairfax has gained entry into good society despite her poverty, through her patronage by a moderately wealthy ex-Army officer. Generally, the niceties of rank seem to be ignored. One of Emma's delusions is that she can preserve distinctions of rank when nearly everyone around her is determined to dismiss them. Circumstances continually sideline her and erode her importance; she needs to feel important – hence her eager patronage of Harriet Smith. But at every turn Austen presents Emma's errors as mild and understandable given the confusing environment in which she has to find an identity. Her little snobberies are essentially harmless, for they have no effect.

It is also the shifting nature of Highbury society which makes it such a hotbed of gossip – chiefly gossip about marriage. The ideal of the companionate marriage was well established by the time the novel was written; arranged and dynastic marriages were rare, especially among the 'middling sort'; people were expected to make 'sensible' marriages, but there was plenty of room for manoeuvre, and also for social mobility in both directions. No wonder that in Highbury, whatever else may be going on, it is marriage, actual, projected or speculated about that is on everybody's mind. This includes Mr Knightley, who shows by his interest in Robert Martin as well as by his jealousy of Frank Churchill's apparent attraction for Emma that he is not exempt from this all-pervading preoccupation. Others are more obsessively involved; Mrs Cole, appropriately very interested in the social cross-currents of the place in which she has such an ambiguous position, is the originator of most of the speculations – she is the leader of a kind of Greek chorus of gossipy, sociable women, which includes Miss Bates, Mrs Perry and all the teachers at Mrs Goddard's school, not to mention Mrs Goddard herself, who comment, question and presumably manoeuvre, in this fascinating game of 'pairs'. It is not often observed that Mrs Goddard is an important motivating force in *Emma*.[10] Like that other silent but major character, Robert Martin, she never speaks, but it is she, not primarily Emma, who introduces Harriet Smith at Hart-field, and so sets the plot in motion. We are never told why she does this – why she picks on Harriet; there are other 'parlour boarders' at her school whom she could presumably have brought along to one of Mr Woodhouse's card-parties. But she chooses Harriet, and it is this which gives Emma the signal that Harriet is somehow special, fit in some way to be singled out from other pupils. She already knows that Harriet is 'the natural daughter of somebody' (*E* 22), but she – as well as the attentive reader – suspects that Mrs Goddard knows more, especially as she seems to think Hartfield a suitable background for her. Emma therefore has good grounds for thinking it probable that Harriet may be of gentle, though illegitimate, birth. Recognition that this, though romantic, is not an altogether fanciful speculation exonerates Emma from some of the frivolousness as-cribed to her by Mr Knightley (and ultimately by Emma herself) and those readers who see him as the fount of all wisdom in the novel. It also gives Harriet a special position in the marriage stakes in Highbury, for while most people's origins and situations are known, and their possibilities therefore apparently to some extent circumscribed, Harriet's are a mystery. Emma has some reason for thinking that in her case anything might happen. Of course she has other motives (chiefly her need to feel definitely superior to someone) which are made the subject of ironic authorial comment, and she turns out to be wrong, but the basis of her patronage of Harriet is not the foolish and irresponsible whim described by Knightley and often accepted by critics. It grows out of a pervading game of chance being played by the inhabitants of Highbury – it is almost as if Harriet is a sort of wild card held by Mrs Goddard. Harriet is the extreme example of the doubt about everybody's true social position, the collapsing nature of old ideas about rank, which leads the central characters to fall back, almost unawares, either on unlikely romantic literary stereotypes, or on the reactionary certainties of the conduct books. And it is not only Emma who does so.

By the time of Harriet's entry into the novel, the reader's initial relationship with Mr Knightley has been established. He is introduced in the first chapter as a 'sensible man' (*E* 9); his brisk tone in dealing with Mr Woodhouse's neurotic anxieties and Emma's self-congratulation about having 'made the match' (*E* 11) between Miss Taylor and Mr Weston evinces a sane and rational prudence; his whole persona breathes confidence and common sense. From the start, we feel *safe* with Mr Knightley. Unless we are very vigilant indeed in our reading, we agree with him that Emma is rather a silly girl, interfering in what does not concern her. We feel sure that Mr Knightley will not be engaging in any romantic games of chance. He is apparently a typical hero/guardian on the Grandison model. But Austen enjoys exploiting the reflexes of her readers, and means to disillusion us.

His conversation with Mrs Weston in chapter 5 should begin this process, for here Knightley is shown to be in some confusion about his relationship with Emma. His ambiguous position as Emma's elder brother and substitute father has been variously noted by critics; Glenda Hudson emphasises the fraternal element: 'his concern is brotherly, but there are also clues along the way of his passionate feelings for her'.[11] Juliet McMaster has also noted the heightening of emotional tension in the pupil–teacher relation in Austen's novels.[12] Hudson, I believe, misjudges these 'clues'; 'his desire for her', she says, 'is in no way repressed'. The language of chapter 5 seems to me to be telling us something different, for he does seem to be trying to convince himself that it is her *education* that he is anxious about. The trajectory of Knightley's detached judiciousness, launched in chapter 1, may carry us over the top of this dialogue without proper attention to the actual words. Knightley is clearly at this time influenced by a contemporary theoretical model of the ideal young woman. This model had changed considerably since the middle of the previous century. A girl was not by this time expected to be ignorant; Hannah More, for instance, is insistent that a young woman should be well informed and should not, as Gregory had advised in *A Father's Legacy to His Daughters* in 1774, conceal any knowledge she might have in the interests of flattering a man.[13] Part of the reason for Austen's qualified approval of Thomas Gisborne's *Enquiry* may have been his rejection of imbecility as the best property in the marriage market.[14] But – and here Austen may have perceived a contradiction which militated against 'Nature and Probability' – a girl was not encouraged, even by Gisborne and More, to push herself, to use her knowledge to attempt to exercise power. She must be able to join in conversation when required, but to leave leadership to the men. Emma has offended against this ideal in several ways, and Knightley is deeply dissatisfied with her. As her brother/father/ teacher he feels she ought to be a greater credit to him, and his disappointment, combined as it is with latent sexual attraction, expresses itself in anger – a polite and civilised anger, which strives for balance and liberality, but anger nevertheless. To begin with he asserts that she is too intelligent for her own good – ' "At ten years old, she had the misfortune of being able to answer questions which puzzled her sister at seventeen." ' Instead of using this intelligence to become bookish and contemplative and fulfil the Hannah More ideal – ' "I have done with expecting any course of steady reading from Emma" ' (*E* 37) – she has used her talents to control her social environment and for bossing everybody about; she has committed the cardinal sin of making up her own mind instead of listening to those who might be supposed to know better. He is appalled at the influence she is trying to exert on Harriet because he believes her ideas to be superficial, ill-conceived and snobbish – ' "I am much mistaken if Emma's doctrines give any strength of mind, or tend at all to make a girl adapt herself rationally to the varieties of her situation in life. – They only give a little polish" ' (*E* 39). Mrs Weston tries several times to divert his mind into other channels, and for a moment he appears unprejudiced in his appreciation of Emma's looks and her lack of personal vanity, but soon he is back on the attack, although it is disguised as concern – ' "I wonder what will become of her" ' (*E* 40). The conversation ends with both Mr Knightley and Mrs Weston speculating about a marriage for

Emma: Mrs Weston is concealing 'wishes at Randall's respecting Emma's destiny' (*E* 41) as the wife of Frank Churchill and says nothing; Mr Knightley actually announces his belief that marriage is the only thing that will *subdue* her – ' "I should like to see Emma in love, and in some doubt of a return; it would do her good" ' (*E* 41). This does not seem like the wish of a kindly benevolent mentor – it can be interpreted at one level as rather savage. It is open to the reader to doubt whether he here really knows his own mind. He protests that he has had ' "no ... charm thrown over [his] senses" ' (*E* 37), but his very protestation suggests that he has, and that it has set up an uncomfortable conflict in his mind. He ends the conversation abruptly by talking of the weather – a sure sign of disquiet.

It is their peculiar configuration of relationships that makes it impossible, for much of the novel, for Emma and Mr Knightley to be anything to each other than sparring-partners. They agree about very little, but obviously find their conflicts rather stimulating than otherwise. This is indicated by Emma's revision of her estimate of Frank Churchill when talking to Mrs Weston (*E* 122) and afterwards to Mr Knightley. ' "He ought to come ... I shall not be satisfied, unless he comes" ', she says to the former, brushing aside all talk of extenuating circumstances; for Mr Knightley she produces exactly those circumstances, purely, it would seem, for the sake of disagreeing with him (*E* 145). At times, almost inadvertently, they achieve a kind of instinctual harmony of purpose which hints at latent kindredship of spirit – as for instance during the incipient quarrel between John Knightley and Mr Woodhouse during the family visit to Hartfield, when they both make strenuous and concerted efforts to change the subject of conversation to something other than food and medical men (*E* 103–6), and at the snowy Christmas Eve party at Randalls when both combine to extricate Mr Woodhouse from a situation which John Knightley and Mr Weston are insensitively prolonging (*E* 128); but generally they find it most natural to fall out and refuse to compromise.

The major conflict in volume 1 concerns Robert Martin's proposal to Harriet Smith. Harriet, the unattached young girl whose family background is quite unknown, has been detailed by Emma to provide the romantic adventure her prudent and dutiful side tells her is impossible for herself. Harriet is to be the hidden heiress – possibly of noble blood, although ordinary gentility will do – whose origins will be revealed when she makes a suitable marriage. Emma has to make do with rather ordinary materials here (Mr Elton would be an odd choice as a hero of romance, but so much the better adapted to Austen's purpose), but this only makes her feel that her ambitions for Harriet are not too wide of the mark – unlike Cherry/ Cherubina she indulges in no very extreme imaginings. Unfortunately – or fortunately for the novel's agreeable complexity – we, the readers, have to concur with Knightley that Emma's use of Harriet for what amounts to social engineering is at best unwise. Harriet's position may be open to speculation, but she should not be manipulated. The language of the dialogue constantly directs us to the vast gulf between Harriet's thinking and Emma's and the indoctrination which takes place. Almost every idea that Harriet has by the end of chapter 4, when Emma first learns about Robert Martin, has been placed there by Emma – and we cannot approve of *that*. Consequently, when in chapter 8 Mr Knightley confronts Emma with Martin's expected proposal – which we know has already been refused – we cannot but feel in double harness with him, for we too feel wiser than Emma and are, moreover, in the secret of her delusions about Mr Elton. We are inclined to agree with him that Emma is being ' "no friend to Harriet Smith" ' (*E* 63).

The dialogue which now ensues is a brilliant example of Austen's delight and skill in sporting with the reader's allegiances. Though we know, at one level, that Emma is all wrong, the scene exposes not her irrationality, but Knightley's. Emma is cool, Knightley emotional; Emma consistent, while Knightley shifts his ground several times. Because of this, their opposition is anything but straightforward; both parties to the argument are less concerned with Harriet Smith and Robert Martin than with their attachment to certain contemporary ideas about marriage and status; moreover, they obviously relish the argument for its own sake.

From the outset, Mr Knightley makes a very sweeping assumption:

'I have reason to think ... that Harriet Smith will soon have an offer of marriage ... Robert Martin is the man. ... He is desperately in love and means to marry her.' (*E* 59)

Emma immediately scents an old-fashioned, arranged-marriage stereotype in which the girl meekly accepts the advice of her elders. The fact that she at least suspects that Harriet would be quite happy to concur makes no difference to her response: ' "He is very obliging ... but is he sure that Harriet means to marry him?" ' (*E* 59) –

theoretically and rationally a perfectly justifiable one. But Knightley makes it clear that he regards this as merely a fashionable, feminine ritual gesture – something which an up-to-date female has to *say*, but can't really mean seriously. ' "Well, well" ', he concedes indulgently, ' "means to make her an offer then. Will that do?" ' – Without waiting for a reply, he embarks on a complacent panegyric of Martin:

'I never hear better sense from any one than Robert Martin. He always speaks to the purpose; open, straight forward, and very well judging. . . . He is an excellent young man, both as son and brother. I had no hesitation in advising him to marry. He proved to me that he could afford it; and that being the case, I was convinced he could not do better. I praised the fair lady too, and altogether sent him away very happy. If he had never esteemed my opinion before, he would have thought highly of me then; and, I dare say, left the house thinking me the best friend and counsellor man ever had.' (*E* 59–60)

This is so much occupied with the excellences of Robert Martin and his own good offices that it looks, at one level, like a male conspiracy to trap Harriet before she has time to protest. But the fact that we know that she would probably like to be so trapped obscures the smug certainties of Mr Knightley's discourse and his complete failure to take her wishes into account; his one reference to her – ' "the fair lady" ' – only serves further to diminish her. But smugness can look like judiciousness under certain circumstances, and we cannot get away from the fact that, though he may be wrong in theory, Emma is wrong in fact. They are both so caught up in their own prejudices and preconceived ideas that neither can think clearly, and the immediate real interests of Harriet Smith are submerged. Their argument is partly based on theory and partly on their ongoing personal conflict. Each seems deliberately to produce arguments designed to incense the other.

Emma is by far the more sure of herself. She stands by her theory that Harriet is of gentle birth, and therefore superior to the yeoman, Martin. Knightley's reaction shows him to be a mass of ill-thought-out notions which he is quite prepared to reverse in the interests of getting his own way. He greets the news of Harriet's refusal with stronger and less polite anger than in conversation with Mrs Weston; he becomes 'red with surprize and displeasure . . . in tall indignation' (*E* 60) and straight away presents a total reconstruction of his previous account of the meeting with Martin:

'What are Harriet Smith's claims, either of birth, nature or education, to any connection higher than Robert Martin? ... She is pretty, and she is good tempered, and that is all. My only scruple in advising the match was on his account, as being beneath his deserts, and a bad connexion for him. I felt, that as to fortune, in all probability he might do much better; and that as to a rational companion or useful helpmate, he could not do worse. But I could not reason so to a man in love' (*E* 61)

In his previous account, Martin has been ' "very well judging" ', now his love has overcome his reason; before, ' "he could not do better" ', now ' "he could not do worse" '; and the ' "fair lady" ' is little better than a base-born idiot. Is this the sober and rational thinker we have at one level been led to expect?

Emma, on the other hand, has some very rational arguments. ' "A man always imagines a woman to be ready for anybody who asks her" ' (*E* 60). Mr Knightley brushes this aside, apparently unconscious of the fact that he has done exactly that: ' "Nonsense! a man does not imagine any such thing." ' Of her illegitimacy she maintains that ' "She is not to pay for the offence of others" ' (*E* 62) – a just and compassionate view; and she quite cogently points out that no girl of seventeen should automatically be expected to accept a first offer. But the argument which most incenses Mr Knightley and drives him into further incoherence is her stated view of the general tastes of men in their choice of wives:

'... supposing her to be, as you describe her, only pretty and good-natured, let me tell you, that in the degree she possesses them, they are not trivial recommendations to the world in general, for she is, in fact, a beautiful girl ... and till it appears that men are much more philosophic on the subject of beauty than they are generally supposed; till they do fall in love with well-informed minds instead of handsome faces, a girl, with such loveliness as Harriet, has a certainty of being admired and sought after ... Her good-nature, too, is not so very slight a claim, comprehending, as it does, real, thorough sweetness of temper and manner, a very humble opinion of herself, and a great readiness to be pleased with other people. I am very much mistaken if your sex in general would not think such beauty, and such temper, the highest claims a woman could possess." (*E* 63–4)

Here Emma is voicing the dictates of some of the conduct books about the qualities which are likely to attract a husband. Mr Knightley can hardly deny that she has some authority for her assertion. However, he again brushes aside her argument, accusing her of abusing reason, and goes on to abuse it himself, becoming further enmeshed in confusions and contradictions:

'Nothing so easy as for a young lady to raise her expectations too high ...
Men of sense, whatever you may chuse to say, do not want silly wives. Men
of family would not be very fond of connecting themselves with a girl of
such obscurity – and most prudent men would be afraid of the
inconvenience and disgrace they might be involved in, when the mystery of
her parentage came to be revealed.' (*E* 64)

This is rather hard on Robert Martin, whose prudence has not so far
been questioned, and who has actually been described as a man of
sense. Can he be so in fact if he wants a wife as silly as Harriet? And
if, as Knightley says next, ' "his mind has more true gentility than
Harriet Smith could understand" ' (*E* 65) would not he, too, be
troubled by this supposed ' "inconvenience and disgrace" ' of her
birth and parentage? Has Knightley thought this through? It seems
more likely that we are to suppose that he strongly needs to feel that
the plan which has had his enthusiastic support will succeed, and
consequently strikes out rather wildly to counter arguments against
it. It is really too trivial an incident for such expense of energy and
emotion in the Squire of Highbury. He can't be that concerned with
the affairs of such as Harriet Smith and Robert Martin – except as
they touch his relations with Emma.

For the reader of this novel, though, who is conscious of its
elaborate layering, there is another factor which must have influenced Emma, and cannot but have been observed by George
Knightley, though he is clearly ignoring it in his dialogue with
Emma – and that is his brother John's choice of a wife. J. F. Burrows
dismisses the character of Isabella as having 'little part to play', and
in fact very little critical notice has been taken of her. But Austen
never introduces redundant characters. Throughout the novel we
are reminded of Isabella's 'striking inferiorities' (*E* 433), her narrow
interests and limited perceptions. The silly wife is a significant trope
in Austen's fiction (from Mrs Allen to Lady Bertram there is a long
string of them) and excessive mother-love sometimes a significant
component of it – in this Lady Middleton and Isabella Knightley are
sisters, and equally ridiculous. The difference is that Isabella is
treated with less broad irony than Lady Middleton, and there is no
underlying contempt for her maternal solicitude emanating from
any of the characters, as there is from Elinor in the case of Lady
Middleton. Nevertheless, she is clearly far from bright, and it is open
to the reader to wonder why John Knightley had married her. He is
obviously often irritated by her; for instance, during the Christmas

visit to Hartfield her collusion in hypochondria with her father drives him into open rudeness (*E* 106). Was he attracted by the presumed thirty thousand pounds? Or does he simply prefer a silly wife, though he is, we have to believe, a 'man of sense'? Towards the end of the novel we begin to suspect the latter, for his approval of his brother's engagement to Emma is very qualified. We are never given the exact grounds for his reservations, but the reactions of Mr Knightley and Emma say it all: ' "... he is no complimenter" ', says his brother on showing John's letter, and after reading it Emma is clear that ' "it is very plain that he considers the good fortune of the engagement as all on my side" ' (*E* 464). There can be no other explanation than that he believes that women should be ruled by men and that his brother will have difficulty in governing Emma. If her brother-in-law is in any way typical, then Emma may be exaggerating when she says, ' "Harriet is exactly what every man delights in" ', but the evidence that it is true of some men cannot be denied by Mr Knightley. He must be conscious that Isabella would never have been *his* choice. But instead of confronting the question he evades it and begins to talk about money. His next attack is on what he suspects are Emma's plans for Mr Elton. Elton ' "does not mean to throw himself away" ' (*E* 66). Now a 'rational' primary motive (presumably that to be expected in 'men of sense') in the quest for a wife would be fortune rather than education. Is Harriet too silly or too poor to satisfy a man of sense? Knightley has shown in this quarrel that he doesn't know what he thinks; Emma has shown him that the issues may be more complex than he has assumed, but he is adamant about giving any ground or engaging in a really open debate, and what amounts to bluster has not convinced her. The sort of wise counsel expected of the fictional mentor, which might have deflected Emma from her resolve and at least protected her from Elton's upstart designs, is missing. Knightley goes off in a huff, having been caught playing the Highbury game of chance – and unsuccessfully at that. But there is yet another layer of significance in this episode. Underlying it all is Emma's exposure of a raw nerve in her suggestion that Harriet might actually suit *him* (*E* 64); he studiously ignores this, for he does not want to examine his own wishes in this regard. A ' "charm" ' has been ' "thrown over his senses" ' which he cannot think is rationally based – for Emma does not at this time measure up to the ideal wife for a 'man of sense' any more than Harriet. In high indignation with Emma and himself he turns temporarily, and perhaps more in bravado than reality, to a woman who does. He is already far removed from the certainties of a Grandison, and he is far more muddled than Maitland or Stuart could ever be.

Jane Fairfax is another example of the orphan dependant, this time shifted from the surface narrative into an undetailed and what seems at first a mysterious background. Harriet may be Emma's idea of the perfect wife for a discerning man, but Jane Fairfax comes much closer to Knightley's. Jane superficially corrects much that Knightley thinks is wrong in Emma. She is apparently the perfect conduct-book young woman – well-informed, but discreet; a responder rather than an initiator, scintillatingly accomplished, but at the same time modest and quiet. Emma sees all this, and quite genuinely admires it, but cannot like Jane, because she cannot communicate with her. The reader should note that Emma very readily accepts Mr Knightley's view that she dislikes Jane because 'she saw in her the really accomplished young woman, which she wanted to be thought herself' (*E* 166), but also that it is difficult to like somebody who will not share experience and backs away from intimacy. Mr Knightley's analysis is unfair and ill-informed. Emma is sometimes too willing to accept guilt (her internal discourse should never be taken for the authorial voice). But she cannot escape from her natural reactions, and because she cannot understand Jane's reticence, concludes, and quite correctly, that she is hiding something. Mr Knightley takes a little longer to come to the same conclusion; at first, on her return to Highbury, he gives the gossips good reason to suppose that his interest in Jane constitutes a preliminary to courtship. In volume II there are several instances of concern beyond the call of mere duty on the part of Knightley – he worries publicly about Jane's health, sends her gifts of apples, and so on. It is really small wonder that this is all interpreted by the likes of Mrs Cole as courtship, and that it gives rise to suspicion even in the sensible and unimaginative Mrs Weston (*E* 225). These episodes are usually seen as factors in Emma's misunderstanding of Knightley and to point up her dawning personal and sexual interest in him; it is as if most commentators on the novel feel that Mr Knightley is too solid a character to be suspected of ordinary moves in the courtship game, or of ordinary human muddle-headedness. This is to miss the ironical complexity of the interplay of character at this stage of the novel. Knightley is still recommending Jane as a person whom

Emma ought to befriend, but he is, at the same time, aware of what militates against this, and against his own real involvement with Jane. His clearly embarrassed denial of the charge which Emma finally brings herself to make several weeks later (*E* 287) represents a crisis in the relationship between himself and Emma, for he also tells her why he could never seriously consider Jane as a wife (although we may believe him to be being less than honest about this). Implicitly accepting as justified Emma's own earlier criticism of Jane as too reserved for friendship (*E* 171), he says:

'Jane Fairfax is a very charming young woman – but not even Jane Fairfax is perfect. She has a fault. She has not the open temper which a man would wish for in a wife.' (*E* 288)

And again:

'Jane Fairfax has feeling ... Her sensibilities, I suspect, are strong – and her temper excellent ... but it wants openness. She is reserved, more reserved, I think, than she used to be – And I love an open temper.' (*E* 289)

Here Mr Knightley has done something quite uncharacteristic of the fictional hero/guardian – he has changed his mind. There is a coded message here to Emma that not only has he decided that she has been right in her estimate of Jane – with which he has earlier strongly disagreed – but that he has relinquished his conduct-book womanly ideal and prefers Emma's ' "open temper" '; he is saying, in effect, that a stormy relationship with someone he can trust is better than a calm one with someone whose thoughts may be hidden from him. He is inviting Emma to go on saying exactly what she thinks and at least hinting that he will no longer invoke his own superiority to oppose her. However, she fails to notice this, for she is unable at this stage to regard Mr Knightley in the light of a possible suitor; she is too caught up in her own stereotype of what a suitor should be. Moreover, she is not being entirely 'open'.

Mr Knightley much later confesses that it is jealousy of Frank Churchill that enlightens him about his own feelings for Emma. It is clear that the whole of Highbury considers Frank the obvious husband for her. His character is based upon the Lord Chesterfield idea of the 'gentleman' – one for whom manner and general agreeableness are of first importance. Knightley despises him from the start, but is sufficiently caught up in the stereotype to believe that he will be irresistibly attractive to Emma. Emma's ideas about love are literary rather than the result of observation. She is impressed with Frank's manner; he measures up to all she has heard and read about handsome and eligible young men, and she tries, with little success, to fall in love with him. In spite of her internal monologue about her feelings, the reader is aware that her 'love' is more a matter of determination than tender emotion and means very little. She doesn't even like him very much, and quite soon she has to admit this to herself – ' "I do not look upon him to be quite the sort of man … His feelings are warm, but I can imagine them rather changeable" ' (*E* 265). From the time of Frank Churchill's return, then, we have both protagonists relinquishing their apparently ideal mate; the difference between them is that Knightley had been able, at least indirectly, to say this to Emma, while she has not been able to enlighten *him*. He goes even further at the ball at the Crown, generously bowing to her superior judgement in the matter of Harriet, throwing aside his habitual dislike of dancing to remain in her company, and at last denying that he could ever think of her as his sister (*E* 331). Emma completely fails to recognise these signs, and it never occurs to her to disabuse anyone about her feelings for Frank. As far as anyone knows she and Frank are still destined for each other. And nobody can ask her. Questioning an unengaged girl about the state of her affections was not permitted to any but her parents or guardians. Nor would it have been proper for Emma independently to deny emotional involvement with a man who had not yet made her an offer. The result is that Knightley, along with everyone else in Highbury, remains convinced that the pair will ultimately marry. Both are quite happy to let this continue – Emma because it makes her feel more interesting, Frank from other, even less pardonable motives. So complete is her internal rejection of Frank that in the next chapter but one she hands him over to Harriet (*E* 341) – but only in her imagination. Knightley knows nothing of this.

This misunderstanding renders Knightley both vulnerable and powerless. He is like Fanny Price in that he has to stand silently by while he watches (as he thinks) the girl he now loves give herself up to a shallow and insensitive man, in whom he shortly discovers evidence of even worse qualities. His attempts to warn her of Frank's relationship with Jane fail, for, as the reader knows, they talk at cross-purposes – ' "I will answer for the gentleman's indifference" ' says Emma incautiously, unconsciously confirming Knightley's worst fears (*E* 350–1). It is a mistake to conclude that Knightley here reaches the truth about Jane and Frank. The text makes clear that he is alarmed but mystified. He is quite oblivious to Emma's regrettable fantasy about Jane and Mr Dixon. Still convinced that Frank will marry Emma (after all, she has the money, and Frank must be regarded as a 'sensible' man) he believes that Frank is somehow manipulating both girls, and that Emma's chances of a happy and stable marriage are doomed. He speaks out of a sense of real concern at what he sees as her danger and is saddened to find that Emma remains in her usual relation to him; she flouts his warning as ridiculous, hinting at confidentiality between herself and Frank. Knightley naturally feels defeated: 'She spoke with a confidence which staggered, with a satisfaction which silenced, Mr. Knightley' (*E* 351). Their behaviour to each other, though their relationship is subtly changing, takes its usual form of attack and repulse. But this time the situation, at least for Knightley, is far more serious than their feud about Harriet Smith. His conviction that Emma will become the victim of such hollow flattery as Frank hands out is almost as perverse as Emma's current chimera – that Frank will marry Harriet; but perverse or not, he believes that he can no longer be involved in Emma's destiny and decides to bow out. He is not pleased to see Frank Churchill at the alfresco gathering at Donwell but keeps his distance from Emma, showing that he has at that time no thoughts of renewing the battle. This episode, like the ensuing scene at Box Hill, is a *tour de force* in the manipulation of point of view, for Emma is preoccupied with other things, and is only later to understand the significance of Frank's petulant mood on his late arrival; he has met Jane as she flies from the scene, and knows that she is reaching the end of her tolerance of the situation between them – ' "I met *one* as I came" ' he says (*E* 364).

Mr Knightley joins the outing to Box Hill, and there sees Emma and Frank engaged in febrile badinage which a disinterested observer would be able to recognise as semi-hysterical and enjoyable to neither. Emma hates what is going on – she is finally extremely glad to get away from such 'questionable enjoyments' (*E* 374). But they have led her to do something completely out of character – her internal moral monitor, which has until now prevented her real irritation and impatience with Miss Bates from breaking through to the surface, has failed, and she has wounded her with a silly witticism (*E* 370). Neither Mr Knightley nor anyone else present can know that Emma's behaviour is almost entirely controlled by the Frank–Jane quarrel which, as it reaches its crisis, is poisoning the atmosphere and leaving Emma isolated and almost desperate. The reader perceives most of the action through Emma's consciousness, but is at the same time aware of how it must look to Knightley. He thinks he sees the girl for whom he has admitted to himself feelings which have nothing much to do with current standards of female excellence on the Gisborne model being corrupted by a shallow and decadent man who means to indulge in some such caddish scheme as to marry her for her money while at the same time conducting a relationship with another woman. At this time he puts little past Frank in the way of selfish unconcern and thinks that Emma is allowing herself to be dragged down to his level. He has no reason to think that he has any hope of saving her, but his concern drives him to obey old habits of remonstrance, this time with far greater seriousness than ever before: ' "I must once more speak to you as I have been used to do ... I must, I will, – I will tell you truths while I can, satisfied with proving myself your friend by very faithful counsel, and trusting that you will some time or other do me greater justice than you can do now" ' (*E* 375–6). There is a finality in the ' "once more" '; it is almost a farewell – and indeed, the next day he leaves for London, to avoid (as we find out later) the painful spectacle of the final stages of Frank's courtship of Emma. But not before he discovers that he has at last triumphed. At the time Emma's response is her usual one – combat; she 'tried to laugh it off' and deny that it was ' "so very bad" ' (*E* 374). But in reality she is devastated, and by the next day Mr Knightley is aware of what can only be described as a victory. Her acknowledgement this time of her fault and of his justification results in what must be one of the tenderest of low-key love-scenes in all fiction:

He looked at her with a glow of regard. She was warmly gratified – and in another moment still more so, by a little movement of more than common friendliness on his part. He took her hand; – whether she had not herself made the first motion, she could not say – she might, perhaps, have rather offered it – but he took her hand, pressed it, and certainly was on the point of carrying it to his lips – when, from some fancy or other, he suddenly let it go. – Why he should feel such a scruple, why he should change his mind when it was all but done, she could not perceive. – He would have judged better, she thought, if he had not stopped. – The intention, however, was indubitable; and whether it was that his manners had in general so little gallantry, or however else it happened, but she thought nothing became him more. It was with him, of so simple, yet so dignified a nature. – She could not but recall the attempt with great satisfaction. (*E* 385–6)

Typically, Austen places this at a point where neither party can possibly know that it *is* a love-scene, so caught up are they in their erroneous speculations, and yet Emma's preoccupation with its implications are clear from the complexities of her inner monologue here. The reader is informed of their love for each other before the protagonists have clearly formulated it themselves.

For Emma and Knightley are now farther apart than they have ever been in their picture of the true state of affairs among their friends and between themselves. In fact, though nobody yet knows it, we are in the concluding stages of the Churchill–Fairfax story, while Emma is currently convinced that Harriet and Frank are in love with each other; disabused of this, she falls into the even greater error of supposing Mr Knightley to be in love with Harriet. Emma is still possessed with the delusion that female vacuity is the essential requirement for a 'sensible' husband, and, though finally enlightened as to her own feelings, is quite unable to see herself as a desirable wife.

For one thing she is disgusted with herself. The Box Hill episode has a lasting effect. From that time she begins a long period of penance and self-castigation which has its origin in Knightley's rebuke about Miss Bates. When she becomes aware of the true state of her feelings on hearing Harriet's pretensions, this intensifies. As many critics have indicated, the free indirect style here is deceptively like an authorial voice; but we should not be deceived. Emma's gloom and despondency after hearing the news of Jane and Frank's engagement (*E* 422–3) have no more substance than any of her other speculations, for we know that despite the Dixon fantasy, she has done no lasting damage to Jane, whose miseries are over; and moreover, her suggestion that Jane has had ' "something to conceal" ' (*E* 203), has turned out to be true; her communication of her suspicions to Frank is embarrassing to herself but reflects even less credit on him; the idea of a marriage between Harriet and Mr Knightley is preposterous and need not really trouble Emma if she were not still caught up in her delusions. Even her self-accusation of neglect of the Bateses is, by her own estimate 'more in thought than fact' (*E* 377). She has not perhaps fulfilled the conduct-book ideal, but has done her best in the circumstances. Miss Bates clearly strains everyone's tolerance. But she is giving in to what she supposes is Knightley's plan of reform for her – she has no notion that by this time he regards her as more sinned against than sinning, and has moreover abandoned all thoughts of changing her in any way. He is indeed at this point preparing to come hotfoot to comfort her for her supposed disappointment in Frank Churchill.

So they have both been wrong – both confused and misled, partly by others, but partly by their own prejudices. Those who see Mr Knightley as mentor, pure and simple, tend to overlook the enormous development his character undergoes during the course of the novel. At the beginning he is entirely the self-confident paternal/fraternal guardian and pedagogue, inflexible in his concept of true womanly behaviour, sure that he knows what is best for everybody. Gradually his position is undermined, for in the long run experience teaches him that his attitudes are too rigid, that Emma's intuitions are sometimes better than his 'reasonable' assumptions and that love has little to do with rules of conduct. The revelation of Jane Fairfax as an ordinary mortal tempted into that heinous collection of offences – 'an ill-placed attachment', an unsanctioned engagement and a clandestine correspondence – is a shock to his system from which he does not recover. His victory at Box Hill is nowhere near as important as it might have been earlier, for now he can be in the position of a reader reading *Emma* for a second time – knowing the secret of Jane and Frank gives everything a different gloss. It certainly cheers Emma up, and the reader, entangled so intimately in her feelings, is relieved and refreshed at her clean blast of righteous anger to Mrs Weston – even though we know, as Mrs Weston does not, that it is Frank's impudent use of her Dixon invention that incenses her most. But the novel ends on an ironical note, for once Emma is disabused of her latest fantasy about Harriet she is contrite, and wishes to get full value for her penitence. She is still apt to see herself in the guise of an Ellen Percy or a Cherry Wilkinson – in need of admonition. While Mr Knightley tries to escape from the patriarchal/fraternal role, Emma shows every sign of submitting herself in conventional womanly manner to her husband's dominion whether he likes it or not – 'What had she to wish for? Nothing, but to grow more worthy of him, whose intentions and judgment had been ever so superior to her own' (*E* 475). This is the expression of her mood on hearing of Harriet's engagement to Robert Martin. A moment's clear thought would remind her, and the astute reader, that Harriet's final acceptance of Martin is better based than when Knightley announced, *tout court*, that he ' "means to marry her" ' (*E* 59). At least she has had some experience upon which to base her choice. But now Emma wants to believe that her knight has been right all along. This is the final ironical twist in the plot, and one that somewhat damages its standing as the straightforward feminist tract described by Margaret Kirkham and others, for we see a woman who has apparently every chance of enjoying an equal relationship with her husband rejecting it out of hand. This novel is not about rewards and punishments, though it does deal in changes of heart.

But as we have found, Austen's endings are never conclusive and the language of this one leaves a number of perplexities to the reader not quite prepared to accept the fairy-tale formula. Does she really mean us to accept the victory of the patriarchal stereotype? Will Emma really become as blindly uncritical as Isabella? Or (even more unlikely) will Mr Knightley relinquish old habits of domination and really step down? Since their relationship was born of conflict neither resolution seems probable; their pre-nuptial felicity looks romantic but not permanent; even in their new-found harmony they show a tendency to spar. When Emma is informed of Harriet's engagement to Robert Martin she at first finds it difficult to believe, and suggests that Mr Knightley has made some mistake. His rejoinder, ' "Do you dare say this? ... What do you deserve?" ' is countered by her ' "Oh! I always deserve the best treatment, because I never put up with any other" ' (*E* 474). Light-hearted at the time, it has overtones both of the past and the shape of things to come; it is left open to the reader to reflect that Mr Knightley may again assert his superiority and Emma refuse to accept it, that they may both again obstinately hold on to untenable opinions for the sake of argument. Five other marriages are presented in the novel for consideration alongside Emma's. John and Isabella Knightley have been sufficiently discussed. We have also seen Mrs Weston coping with her husband's unreasonable sociability and optimism and Mr Elton's deterioration as he adapts himself to his mean-minded wife. Frank Churchill seems to regard his future wife as an *objet d'art* upon which to hang jewellery, and we can imagine, though we do not see, Harriet's subordination to the wider Martin family at Abbey-Mill. In contrast with all of these the marriage of Emma and Mr Knightley holds the possibility of becoming a balance of opposing but equal forces, rather than the subjection of one personality to another. Mr Knightley's removal to Hartfield shows how little he feels threatened (as brother John might have been) by the domination of a woman. Perhaps this balance is what we are intended to understand by the novel's closing words: 'the perfect happiness of the union'. Entertained – and perhaps obliquely instructed – as we have been by their conflicts, we have to hope that Emma and Mr Knightley *quarrel* happily ever after – a unique conclusion for a novel of its time.

CHAPTER 6

Rationality and rebellion: 'Persuasion' and the model girl

Of all six completed novels *Persuasion* most resists a late twentieth-century reader's attempts to exonerate Austen from charges of prescriptiveness and didacticism. If Anne Elliot was 'almost too good' for the author, a reading based on an assumption of Austen's attachment to conventional contemporary wisdom will certainly leave her too good for us.[1] Marilyn Butler, among others, avers that 'Anne comes near to being dangerously perfect' and much modern criticism finds her somewhat tediously fault-free.[2] Curiously, though, it is the one work of Austen's which attracted prompt contemporary criticism on moral grounds; in 1818 the following was included in a review in *The British Critic*:

[The novel] contains parts of very great merit; among them, however, we certainly should not number its *moral*, which seems to be, that young people should always marry according to their own inclinations and upon their own judgement; for that if in consequence of listening to grave counsels, they defer their marriage, till they have wherewith to live upon, they will be laying the foundation for years of misery, such as only the heroes and heroines of novels can reasonably hope ever to see the end of.[3]

These two attitudes, nearly two hundred years apart, provide us with a bewildering paradox – is the novel supporting or rejecting contemporary rules of conduct? What was Austen up to in *Persuasion*? Various answers have been put forward; like *Mansfield Park* it continues to provoke explanations, if not apologies, for its moral stance – most often critics find something wrong with it, some failure of coherence or consistency. If we examine the novel within the framework of the present study, we should be able to come close to an answer to the questions surrounding *Persuasion* without implying that Austen somehow did not quite achieve her aim.[4] The five other novels, and the fragments, have all manoeuvred among available stereotypes to find a new way of presenting in fiction the problems of human interaction in life as Austen perceived it, rather than life as it might, according to contemporary conduct-theory, desirably be lived. *Persuasion* is no exception, but it takes a somewhat different direction.

Emma had come in for a good deal of criticism on the grounds that its heroine was no compliment to the female sex. In 'Opinions of *Emma*' (*MW* 438), Miss Isabella Herries 'objected to my exposing the sex in the character of the Heroine', and Fanny Knight's current admirer, James Wildman, was apparently of the same opinion. Austen replies:

> Do not oblige him to read any more. – Have mercy on him, tell him the truth & make him an apology. He & I should not in the least agree of course, in our ideas of Novels and Heroines; – pictures of perfection as you know make me sick & wicked – but there is some good sense in what he says, & I particularly respect him for wishing to think well of all young Ladies; it shews an amiable & delicate Mind. – And he deserves better treatment than to be obliged to read any more of my Works.[5]

There was very little likelihood that Austen would, at this stage, fulfil expectation by writing an exemplary novel or create a 'picture of perfection'. What she did was to invent a character with whom no one could find fault on the grounds of manners or behaviour ('with manners as consciously right as they were invariably gentle' (*P* 153)), who fulfils outwardly all the ideals of the conduct books, and subject her to narrow and mindless interpretations of those ideals. This heroine is thereby forced into a pragmatism which throws her back on *feeling* as 'her spring of felicity' (*P* 252) and the reference-point of her judgement. But this novel is not a new, late celebration of sensibility, a '*Woman of Feeling*'. Anne is deeply convinced that reason and feeling are not oppositional but complementary; what goes against feeling goes against reason also. She is more like Marianne than she is like Elinor. But she is not influenced by fashionable moral and social theory. She has come to her conclusions from experience – she has found out that inflexible adherence to rule and precept does not invariably increase the sum of human happiness and may well do the opposite. Who has gained by her sacrifice? As the result of the failure of traditional 'sensible' solutions to make sense of her life, Anne has to go back to first principles, and in the intolerable tension between what she feels is right and what is forced upon her by contemporary judgements, is nearly drained of energy; she almost fails to give her life back its meaning. The novel presents no single solution to any of her problems and the dénouement is a matter of luck rather than judgement. The best we can say of the ending is that time and chance are kind to Anne Elliot. Deserving as she may be, the reader must be aware that she could have remained disappointed and alone for the rest of her life.

In the *Plan of a Novel* of (circa) 1816, Austen postulates a heroine very like Anne: 'a faultless Character herself – , perfectly good, with much tenderness & sentiment, & not the least Wit – very highly accomplished, understanding modern Languages & (generally speaking) everything that the most accomplished young Women learn, but particularly excelling in Music – her favourite pursuit – & playing equally well on the Piano Forte & Harp – & singing in the first stile' (*MW* 428). Austen adds a modicum of 'Wit' and subtracts the harp and the singing (significantly, in emphasising the waste of Anne's real musical talents – 'having no voice, no knowledge of the harp, and no fond parents to sit by and fancy themselves delighted' (*P* 47)), but otherwise this is both Austen's rather contemptuous concept of the conventional heroine *and* Anne Elliot to the life. However, what happens to her is not according to that convention. The novel is essentially a critique of the common fictional adventures of such a girl, which were often only one degree removed from the ludicrous junketings described in the *Plan*. Fictional 'cant' is still the author's target.

As we have seen, Austen's admiration for the works of Fanny Burney was becoming a little detached and ironical even in 1796, just after the publication of *Camilla*. She remembers sending her love to 'Mary Harrison' hoping that when she is 'attached to a young Man, some *respectable* Dr. Marchmont may keep them apart for five volumes'.[6] Anne and Captain Wentworth are kept apart for *two* – thus fulfilling a fictional expectation, but without the obsessive moralising of Marchmont and Edgar's most unlikely submission to his opinion and easy conviction of Camilla's guilt. But Burney's later publication, *The Wanderer*, which came out during Austen's confident period after the success of *Pride and Prejudice*, is clearly part of the immediate stimulus for *Plan of a Novel* and more seriously for *Persuasion*.[7] Juliet Granville's adventures as she tries to earn a meagre living and later flies from her brutal pursuers through the English countryside are undeniably the source of the caricature heroine in *Plan*:

often reduced to support herself ... by her Talents & work for her Bread; – continually cheated & defrauded of her hire, worn down to a Skeleton, & now & then starved to death –. At last, hunted out of civilized society, denied the poor Shelter of the humblest Cottage ... having at least 20 narrow escapes of falling into the hands of Anti-hero – & at last in the very nick of time ... runs into the arms of the Hero himself ... (*MW* 430)

Not an exact parallel, perhaps, but recognisable enough. Burney had many axes to grind in her novel – it is a complex examination of social attitudes which deserves a good deal of respect – but her serious purpose drives her to present thoroughly unlikely characters and situations and inflates her language, which often bears no resemblance to any recognisable human dialogue. The multiplicity and intensity of Juliet's tribulations, from which she surprisingly emerges sweet, modest and clean, producing alternately 'a torrent of tears' and 'mantling blushes', would come for Austen in the category of 'unnnatural conduct and forced difficulties' which she cites as her grounds for finding Sarah Burney's *Clarentine* 'foolish'.[8] In *Persuasion* conduct is to be natural, the difficulties will derive predictably from common rather than extraordinary situations, and the outcome will be satisfactory, but quite independent of anyone's deserts.

At the opening of the novel, Anne has lost her moral bearings. That is not to say that she does not behave according to Christian principles of tolerance and endurance, but that she has no faith in the value of these things. She adopts approved virtues in a rather mechanical, joyless way because she has little alternative. This is due in great part to the chief difference between her and most of the other Austen heroines – her isolation. Not even Fanny Price is so deprived of a companion to whom she can speak. Unlike Elizabeth Bennet and Elinor Dashwood, Anne is caught between two selfish and uncongenial sisters; the only person who appears to care at all whether she lives or dies is Lady Russell, a good woman of limited intelligence who relies on a set of narrow and cautious precepts and rates reason above – not equal to – feeling. In context we can see her as a responsible woman reacting adversely to what she saw as dangerous new ideas. There is more than a hint in the text that she is familiar with the radical/conservative debate; she 'gets all the new publications' (*P* 146) and Elizabeth is bored by her interest in 'new poems and states of the nation' (*P* 215). When Anne accepts her advice and breaks her engagement to Frederick Wentworth, she has literally no one else to turn to, no one else with whom to discuss her life-choices. During the eight years which elapse before she meets Wentworth again, her isolation becomes total, since she can no longer communicate even with Lady Russell. In her own mind she separates her duty to submit to the 'grave counsels' of her elders from *their* duty to make sure their advice will lead to certain good – a hopeless expectation. She forgives herself for her submission, but at the same time blames the system within which she lives for its chill caution and ungenerous prudence. She feels sure that given the chance she would never act according to its precepts – 'she felt that were any young person, in similar circumstances, to apply to her for counsel, they would never receive any of such certain immediate wretchedness, such uncertain future good' (*P* 29). So far, she has not had the chance, for her family situation deprives her of all influence and her circle of acquaintance is too narrow. She has adopted a negative and passive view of life in which she allows herself to be either ignored or used for other people's convenience. There is a sense in which she is almost punishing Lady Russell by refusing either to recover or to discuss her situation: 'But in this case [that of Charles Musgrove's proposal], Anne had left nothing for advice to do; and though Lady Russell, as satisfied as ever with her own discretion, never wished the past undone, she began now to have the anxiety which borders on hopelessness for Anne's being tempted, by some man of talents and independence' (*P* 29). Having initially accepted advice, Anne sees no reason to comfort her friend for its effects. She simply does not talk to her about it.

It is important for our understanding of the novel to examine the background to Lady Russell's advice and its impact on a contemporary reader. Few in 1818 would have argued against the general inadvisability of an almost penniless, though 'gently' reared, girl engaging herself to marry an actually penniless, if optimistic, young sailor on the off-chance that he might one day succeed in making enough money to keep them both – and their children. In general, Lady Russell would have been held to be right. The undesirability of long engagements was received opinion. Older and supposedly wiser heads would not depend on the first flush of love and commitment to last; suppose a girl or young man met someone they liked better? Better not to trust to the vicissitudes of time and change. After eight years, Anne no more believes this in her own case than she had done at nineteen, when she was persuaded that her love would only be a burden to him:

She was persuaded that under every disadvantage of disapprobation at home, and every anxiety attending his profession, all their probable fears, delays and disappointments, she should yet have been a happier woman in maintaining the engagement, than she had been in the sacrifice of it; and this, she fully believed, had the usual share, had even more than a usual share of all such solicitudes and suspense been theirs (*P* 29)

A little later, the narrator's voice calls this 'romance' (*P* 30), and this description, even in its pejorative sense, would have attracted a good deal of contemporary agreement. But we do not have to identify Anne's beliefs with the narrator's. Anne could have no means of knowing what the outcome would be; her prudence at nineteen may have been 'unnatural', but is it therefore to be rejected as useless? As usual with an Austen novel the narrative leaves questions open at the same time as appearing to answer them. We can imagine, if we choose, how Anne might have fared if the engagement had continued and Wentworth had not succeeded; had, perhaps, ended up like his friend Harville, disabled on half pay. Anne finds the Harvilles' efforts to be happy in inadequate seaside lodgings charming and cosy – a harder head would call this romance also. How might she have coped, in reality? We are told, significantly, that Mrs Harville is 'a degree less polished than her husband' (*P* 97) – hardened perhaps by material deprivations. Anne knows very little about such things, except that the warmth of the Harvilles' domestic life seems to contrast strongly with the coldness of her own family situation. Even a less cautious observer than Lady Russell might easily pronounce her in error. Austen's habit of driving the allegiances of readers against the grain of their convictions is very evident here. And we are not even quite sure that the narrative tilts *against* Anne, for the example of Benwick's engagement to Fanny Harville, undertaken before they had the means to marry, is given as an example of what might have happened in the case of Anne and Wentworth if Sir Walter had been less of a snob and Lady Russell less entrenched in principle. Admiral and Mrs Croft seem to have taken some risk in marrying without much attention to material considerations. No single situation is put forward for reader approval. Anything could have happened.

But Anne's particular situation is aggravated by the unhelpful personality of her lover. We are surely not expected to suppose that Wentworth is justified in demanding that Anne choose between himself and the only other person in the world who cares a fig for her. He compounds her misery by his version of a contemporary expectation of female conduct. Meekness combined with ignorance had long since been rejected by those promulgating the rules; moralists like Hannah More were now constructing even more improbable models like Lucilla Stanley, who were able to impress onlookers with their firmness of opinion in situations which those onlookers approved, while in general keeping a very low profile indeed. Wentworth demonstrates this double expectation – he loves Anne partly for her traditional womanly virtues (her 'gentleness, modesty, taste, and feeling' (P 26)) but expects her to rise up in revolt against those traditions when, and probably only when, it suits him.[9] His confusions on this score are several times made clear; he states as his twin requirements in a wife 'a firm mind, with sweetness of manner' (P 62); he seems little interested in how that sweetness can be maintained while she defies the counsels of her family. He is a long time working out what Tony Tanner has called a combination of 'flexibility and firmness, the concessionary and the adamant' which is necessary in all human dealings, and does not recognise the complexity of his demands.[10] His confusion is made specifically evident; he does not wish his putative wife's firmness of mind to extend to insisting on coming to sea with him; his argument with his sister at Uppercross makes this very clear, and his manner of extricating himself from this exchange is symptomatic of unease and uncertainty:

'Now I have done ... – When once married people begin to attack me with, 'Oh! you will think very differently, when you are married.' I can only say, 'No, I shall not;' and then they say again, 'Yes, you will,' and there is an end of it.'
He got up and moved away. (P 68–70)

Anne is constantly the overhearer of Wentworth's rather desperate attempts to make a consistent structure for his wishes and desires; his conversation about the hazelnut with Louisa contains the same kind of obstinate theorising. His analogy has no validity, for the nut that clings to the tree will rot, while those that fall will germinate (P 88). After eight years, he is still an angry man, emotionally confused and refusing to see reason. Much later he admits this.

The story requires the two to meet again, and Austen makes sure that the re-encounter is believable, though entirely the work of chance. Sudden and unpredictable meetings after years of inexplicable silence are legion in the fiction of the time; this one is different. Ironically, Sir Walter's financial difficulties lead directly to it, when the Crofts come to Kellynch as his tenants. To give ample space for further exploration of the couple's attitudes, Anne is typically rejected as a companion in Bath by her elder sister, Elizabeth, (who substitutes the ambitious gold-digger, Mrs Clay) and demanded as support by her discontented sister Mary Musgrove at Uppercross. The social mores of the time would make an exchange of visits between the Musgroves and Crofts inevitable; the shared profession of Admiral Croft and his brother-in-law and the 'peace [which was] turning all our rich Navy Officers ashore' (*P* 17) would make a visit from Wentworth very likely.

He comes, and the event gives readers the opportunity to observe even more closely than the narrative has so far allowed, the nature of the relationship between him and Anne. Light is soon thrown on what might be supposed to be the root cause of Lady Russell's uneasiness all those years ago, however she might rationalise it into purely economic consideration. We have already been told that Wentworth and Anne 'were gradually acquainted, and when ac-quainted, rapidly and deeply in love' (*P* 26). Lady Russell would see this as a dangerous version of the Romeo–Juliet story – 'too rash, too ill-advised, too sudden'. 'Rational esteem' may be present, but the chief component of this love is something more basic, and Austen does not flinch from demonstrating it. The necessity for novel heroines (such as Burney's Camilla and Juliet) to be cool in their response to awkward suitors or rejected lovers is here ignored. Twice during this early phase of renewal Anne is shaken to the foundation of her being by his touch; once even through the body of the little child clinging to her back; it 'produced such a confusion of varying, but very painful agitation, as she could not recover from' (*P* 80); and again as he assists her into the carriage of his sister and brother-in-law: 'his will and his hands had done it ... it was proof of his own warm and aimiable heart, which she could not contemplate without emotions so compounded of pleasure and pain, that she knew not which prevailed' (*P* 91). All the time Anne is also aware of his continued 'high and unjust resentment', but this makes no differ-ence. Indeed, the strength of her feeling overcomes what is clearly seen both by herself and by the reader as unscrupulousness and arrogant petulance in his flirtation with the Musgrove daughters. By all contemporary fictional standards Anne ought to disapprove enough to resolve to have nothing more to do with him. But it never crosses her mind. What we are seeing here is not the anxious internal debate about what is *right* which so often dominates the proceedings in Burney and Edgeworth, for instance, but the unstructured reactions of strong emotion. Without generalising, the narrative comes down heavily in favour of the 'single and constant attachment' which Elinor Dashwood tries so valiantly to reject when she thinks her hopes of Edward are gone forever; her words could easily be Lady Russell's, but they could never issue from the lips of Anne Elliot: 'And after all ... that is bewitching in the idea ... and all that can be said of one's happiness depending entirely on any particular person, it is not meant – it is not fit – it is not possible that it should be so' (*SS* 263). Though Anne sees that a 'second attachment' is possible for others, even forsees Benwick's and is more tolerant of it than Wentworth is, for herself it is not on the agenda. It is not a moral question; she is not aiming at any *'beau idéal'* of female conduct; her 'high-wrought love and eternal constancy' (*P* 192) are the products of passion, not principle. She simply cannot help herself.[11] But what she does not do for a time is revive within herself the energy to rekindle Wentworth's response. She almost hands him over to Louisa.

By many of Austen's contemporaries her failure to cure herself of this 'ill-placed attachment' might be interpreted as weakness – even obstinacy in thus clinging to the past. We might now rather describe it as a loss of moral energy and recognise it as a destructive form of sublimation; Austen appears in some sort to present it as such. Anne contents herself with defusing the petty disagreements between her sister and her husband and in-laws and indulging the often selfish demands of her more positive companions. She is aware that she is wasted, but tells herself that there is nothing she can do. Her attitude is summed up in her physical response to life – why has she abandoned dancing in order to accompany others? (*P* 72). It cannot be that at twenty-seven her joints are too stiff for the exercise. Some of her dejection seems almost wilful – the creation of a desert called 'duty' in which to protect herself from the necessity for positive action.

A change of heart is necessary for the dynamics of the story – Anne must move from passive to active in order to regain a positive purpose in life. Perhaps the most remarkable feature of this novel is the way in which the author minutely charts the re-establishment of communication between Anne and Wentworth. It begins at Lyme. Still feeling marginalised, her first encounter with Benwick shows Anne indulging in self-pity and other negative feelings. If we read chapter 11 of the first volume with attention to the depth of reference of its free indirect style, we find her ignoring certain clues to Wentworth's state of mind as if she is afraid even to begin to hope. While contemplating the idea of Benwick, whom she is about to meet, and the tragedy of his loss, she thinks of herself as in worse case: ' "he has not, perhaps, a more sorrowing heart than I have. I cannot believe his prospects to be so blighted forever" ' (*P* 97); she has missed the purport of Wentworth's account – his acknowledgement of the strength of such a feeling as he supposes Benwick to have had: 'He considered his disposition as of the sort which must suffer heavily, uniting very strong feelings with quiet, serious, and retiring manners, and a decided taste for reading, and sedentary pursuits' (*P* 96–7). It is open to the reader to wonder whether he has almost inadvertently begun to speak once more to Anne. She begins to be more obviously the focus of his thought from the time when the as yet unrecognised Mr Elliot admires her during the pre-breakfast walk – 'He [Wentworth] gave her a momentary glance, – a glance of brightness, which seemed to say, "That man is struck with you, – and even I, at this moment, see something like Anne Elliot again" ' (*P* 104); this accelerates with the disaster on the Cobb and culminates with his overheard statement at Mrs Harville's: ' "but, if Anne will stay, no one so proper, so capable as Anne!" ' – an indication, if ever there was one, of his abandonment of his view of her as feeble (*P* 114). But Anne is by no means ready to interpret all this as anything but an effort to get the best nursing for Louisa – now, she teaches herself to suppose, the object of his affection. She cannot yet accept the idea of constancy in a man. (For different reasons, Emma has also shown this kind of obtuseness; perhaps Austen regarded it as more believable than the stoical determination to repress desire which is evident in many contemporary novels). Accustomed to pessimism, she protects herself from hope that she thinks is bound to be unjustified. While she swiftly recognises Benwick's melancholy as an indulgence in an *expected*, theoretical and literary, sensibility rather than real suffering, and wryly comments to herself that she could well do with the same advice as she proffers to him, she fails to notice the resurfacing of Wentworth's powerful attraction to her. She is too ready to accept his flirtation with Louisa as actual courtship. She misinterprets everything because with him she cannot be detached.

The reader should see Wentworth at first exasperated by his permanent emotional commitment to Anne, and gradually coming to perceive that he cannot and does not want to escape; this is invisible to Anne, and incidentally to everyone else, for Wentworth tells her later that he is almost 'entangled' in an engagement with Louisa at this point. The reader is, as so often with Austen, at the third point of the triangle, which shifts the attention outward from the main action and shows the protagonists to be deceived or deceiving, without the direct intervention of a narrator. (There is again a parallel here with Emma and Mr Knightley.)[12] Though Anne's 'second spring' has already begun, some cautious fear in her refuses to believe it. Wentworth has clearly shown his appreciation of her judgement and his instinctive intimacy with her when he seeks her opinion about their encounter with Louisa's parents – (' "Do you think this a good plan?" ' (*P* 117)); but after they have all gone away to Lyme, leaving her to await the advent of Lady Russell, she takes refuge in brooding melancholy, injecting her situation with the poetry of tragic loss:

A few months hence, and the room now so deserted, occupied but by her silent, pensive self, might be filled again with all that was happy and gay, all that was glowing and bright in prosperous love, all that was most unlike Anne Elliot!

An hour's complete leisure for such reflections as these, on a dark November day, a small thick rain almost blotting out the very few objects ever to be discerned from the windows, was enough to make the sound of Lady Russell's carriage exceedingly welcome; and yet, though desirous to be gone, she could not quit the mansion-house, or look an adieu to the cottage, with its black, dripping, and comfortless veranda, or even notice through the misty glasses the last humble tenements of the village, without a saddened heart. – Scenes had passed in Uppercross, which made it precious. It stood the record of many sensations of pain, once severe, but now softened; and of some instances of relenting feeling, some breathings of friendship and reconciliation, which could never be looked for again, and which could never cease to be dear. She left it all behind her; all but the recollection that such things had been. (*P* 123)

In their way, these thoughts are as literary as Benwick's, who Anne has been so sure will revive to love again, and on whom she has enjoined a more positive effort to 'fortify the mind' by recourse to works other than poetry. Anne is not without a sense of humour, and is herself 'amused at the idea of her coming to Lyme, to preach patience and resignation to a young man whom she had never seen before; nor could she help fearing ... that, like many other great moralists and preachers, she had been eloquent on a point in which her own conduct would ill bear examination' (*P* 101). But her self-criticism does not prevent her from now indulging in what must be described as a consolatory but also somewhat enjoyable wallow in romantic melancholy much like Benwick's. She too has been reading Byron. We are later informed that she can read Italian (*P* 186) – the quotation from Dante which introduces *The Corsair* – 'nessun maggior dolore, / Che ricordarsi del tempo felice / Nelle miseria' aptly sums up her state of mind.[13] There are clear structural and narratorial reasons why the time-scale of the novel is the period 1806 to 1814 – the absence and wholesale return of naval officers is necessary to the plot – but the fact that it coincides with the publication and frenzied popularity of Byron's Turkish tales is used here by Austen in a similar contrapuntal way to her use of contemporary novels; aware of her immediate readers' inevitable acquaintance with these works, she constantly refers to them in a way that is both ironic and revealing. In the three poems which are mentioned by Anne and Benwick in their conversation at Lyme – *The Giaour, The Bride of Abydos* and *The Corsair,* (*P* 100, 109) – a male lover has lost the woman of his heart in sensational circumstances involving abduction, murder and sudden death; the heroes are as a consequence dedicated to lifelong desolation which occasions their withdrawal from the scenes of action and their total resistance to consolation. That Benwick is *not* inconsolable very soon becomes evident – Anne is aware of 'some dawning of tenderness towards herself' (*P* 167) and his need to replace Fanny Harville rather than mourn her forever is later proved by his engagement to Louisa. But Anne sees far more of a parallel with Byron's heroes in herself, and her thoughts constantly echo his lines – especially certain passages from *The Giaour.* [14] Her internal monologue quoted above has much in common with his lament:

> The keenest pangs the wretched find
> Are raptures to the dreary void,
> The leafless desert of the mind
> The waste of feelings unemploy'd.
> Who would be doom'd to gaze upon
> A sky without a cloud or sun?　　　　(957–62)

Echoes, more perhaps in the vocabulary than the sense, recur; the Friar muses of the Giaour: 'But sadder still it were to trace / What once were feelings in that face' (859–60); Anne notices Wentworth looking at her: '*Once* she felt that he was … observing her altered features, perhaps, trying to trace in them the ruins of the face which had once charmed him' (*P* 72). She is only too willing to interpret Mary's rather spiteful report that Wentworth 'should not have known her again' (*P* 60) in the light of the Giaour's description of himself:

> The wither'd frame, the ruin'd mind,
> The wrack by passion left behind.
> A shrivell'd scroll, a scatter'd leaf,
> Sear'd by the autumn blast of grief!   (1253–6)

Anne is often shown to identify herself with autumnal decay – once even as she notes the evidence that the farmer at Winthrop was 'counteracting the sweets of poetical despondence and meaning to have spring again' (*P* 85), and we can be fairly sure that some of the quotations with which she toys on that walk were from Byron.[15]

But as these intermittent references reinforce Anne's conviction of permanent desolation, her vision of herself as tragic victim, the reader who knew *The Corsair* might have seen something which, for the time being, Anne does not, though she is so intimately aware of Wentworth's presence. Anne observes his demeanour when Mrs Musgrove thanks him for his care of her scapegrace son, now dead: 'There was a momentary expression in Captain Wentworth's face at this speech, a certain glance of his bright eye, and curl of his handsome mouth' (*P* 67); Conrad, the Corsair, can also evince contempt in a similar way: 'And oft perforce his rising lip reveals / The haughtier thought it curbs, but scarce conceals' (Canto I, ix, 205–6); but though he is also, like Wentworth, 'Too firm to yield, and far too proud to stoop' (Canto I, x, 255), Conrad is in fact an icon of male constancy to a single love: 'Yes, it was love – unchangeable – unchanged, / Felt but for one from whom he never ranged / Though fairest captives daily met his eye' (Canto I, xii, 287–9). It should be remembered that Captain Wentworth's opportunities to find a new love must have been legion during his eight-year absence, war notwithstanding. Readers who recognise something Byronic in Wentworth will know that Anne is misreading him.[16] But typically, the whole exalted, overblown scenario of Byron is brought down to

earth – Anne may have been unkindly used, perhaps, but nobody is
threatening to throw her or anyone else into the sea in a sack.
Austen has 'read the Corsair, mended [her] petticoat'[17] and has,
now, something 'else to do'. Anne is shown to be overdoing her part
as romantic heroine; she must snap out of it.

She does, but it is not initially Wentworth who is responsible for
her throwing off her Byronic desolation; as in the brief resurgence of
her confidence at Lyme, it is Mr Elliot, heir to her father's estate, a
rich man, and, in the eyes of such as Lady Russell, in every way
suitable as a rational replacement to the also Byronic Wentworth.
When Anne arrives in Bath in no very buoyant frame of mind, it is
Mr Elliot who brings a glow to her cheek and makes even her
unobservant and indifferent father comment on the improvement in
her looks (*P* 145–6). From the first it is her cousin who brings Anne
into the focus of attention at Camden-place, almost shaming her
father and sister into taking some notice of what she has to tell them:
'When he questioned, Sir Walter and Elizabeth began to question
also' (*P* 144). Anne had been impressed with him in Lyme, and
continues to be so, for he knows exactly how to please her:

> He was quite as good-looking as he had appeared at Lyme, his countenance
> improved by speaking, and his manners were so exactly what they ought to
> be, so polished, so easy, so particularly agreeable, that she could compare
> them in excellence to only one person's manners. They were not the same,
> but they were, perhaps, equally good. (*P* 143)

There is an indication here that Anne is too charmed to be quite
telling herself the truth, for Wentworth has shown himself to be far
less concerned to please than to speak his mind; he has certainly
failed to put himself out, as Mr Elliot does, to conciliate Lady
Russell. Anne is more honest later as her situation reaches a crisis.
For the time being, though:

> There could be no doubt of his being a sensible man. Ten minutes were
> enough to certify that. His tone, his expressions, his choice of subject, his
> knowing where to stop, – it was all the operation of a sensible, discerning
> mind. (*P* 143)

Some contemporary readers may have been ahead of Anne here,
for Mr Elliot has modelled himself on a careful reading of Lord
Chesterfield, whose advice to his son consistently recommends *devious-
ness*. In enjoining him, in a letter dated 18 November, o.s. 1748, to
model his behaviour on the diplomatic community in Turin he says:

Observe their natural and careless, but genteel air; their unembarrassed good-breeding; their unassuming, but yet unprostituted dignity. Mind their decent mirth, their discreet frankness, and that *entregent* [tact], which, as much above the frivolous as below the important and secret, is the proper medium for conversation in mixed companies.[18]

Later (22 May, 1749), he becomes more explicit:

I recommended to you in my last an innocent piece of art – that of flattering people behind their backs, in presence of those who ... will not fail to repeat, and even amplify, the praise to the party concerned. This is, of all flattery, the most pleasing, and consequently the most effectual ...

The principal [sic] of these things is the mastery of one's temper, and that coolness of mind, and serenity of countenance, which hinder us from discovering, by words, actions, or even looks, those passions or sentiments by which we are inwardly moved or agitated ...[19]

The Frenchified cad was a popular figure in fiction; both Frank Churchill and Mr Elliot are subtle and plausible versions of this model. Anne is from the first puzzled by Elliot's transformation, and charitably concludes that he is courting Elizabeth and is therefore keeping an eye on Mrs Clay – a proceeding of which she does not disapprove. For this reason she is half convinced of his views on 'good company' (*P* 150–1) when she comments on the vacuousness of Lady Dalrymple and her daughter – at least they keep her father out of the way of Mrs Clay's scheming.[20] Much more importantly, though, she is thoroughly trapped by his Chesterfieldian ploy of 'flattery behind the back', especially that flattery which Chesterfield famously held highly effective with women – of the understanding.[21] At the evening party at Lady Dalrymple's, to which Anne doughtily refuses to go, he and Lady Russell vie in praise of Anne:

To her [Anne], its greatest interest must be, in having been very much talked of between her friend and Mr. Elliot, in having been wished for, regretted, and at the same time honoured for staying away in such a cause. – Her kind, compassionate visits to this old schoolfellow, sick and reduced, seemed to have quite delighted Mr. Elliot. He thought her a most extraordinary young woman; in her temper, manners, mind, a model of female excellence. He could meet even Lady Russell in a discussion of her merits; and Anne could not be given to understand so much by her friend, could not know herself to be so highly rated by a sensible man, without many of those agreeable sensations which her friend meant to create. (*P* 158–9)

Something in the nature of an epiphany in her view of human worth and excellence occurs when Lady Russell speaks to her of the possibility of a marriage. For a moment Anne's 'imagination and her heart were bewitched' (*P* 160) by the idea of being restored to a beloved home as its mistress – until that same imagination brings Mr Elliot before her. Then she knows him; but of her two varieties of condemnation, the second is more important. She first ranges over his probable past and wonders how thoroughly he has given up his 'bad habits'; as she does so, she realises how 'clever, cautious' he is – he does not openly repudiate anything. The next paragraph is crucial in the reader's appreciation of Anne's thorough rejection of the Chesterfield programme, and an understanding that, notwithstanding her rather pious reflections, a modicum of 'carelessness on ... serious matters' or the odd bit of Sunday-travelling might be forgiven under certain conditions:

> Mr. Elliot was rational, discreet, polished, – but he was not open. There was never any burst of feeling, any warmth of indignation or delight, at the evil or good of others. This, to Anne, was a decided imperfection. Her early impressions were incurable. She prized the frank, the open-hearted, the eager character beyond all others. Warmth and enthusiasm did captivate her still. She felt that she could so much more depend upon the sincerity of those who sometimes looked or said a careless or a hasty thing, than of those whose presence of mind never varied, whose tongue never slipped. (*P* 161)

One might call this almost a contest between Byronic and Chesterfield man in which the former carries the palm.

This moment of recognition begins the final phase of the novel, which follows in structure many contemporary works which filled their last volume with what Austen regarded as 'forced difficulties' before successfully uniting the favoured lovers. Such fictional strategies are satirised in *Plan of a Novel*; while the 'Hero – all perfection of course – [is] prevented from paying his addresses to her, by some excess of refinement', the heroine is pursued 'by the vile arts of some totally unprincipled and heart-less young Man, desperately in love with [her] ... Often carried away by the anti-hero, but rescued either by her Father or the Hero –' (*MW* 429–30). There is so much that ironically parallels this in the last chapters of *Persuasion* that it is impossible to imagine that it was not recognised by those relatives and friends who helped to concoct it. But the whole thing is translated into Austen's fictional 'probability' – Mr Elliot is, as Anne finds out from Mrs Smith, pretty 'vile and unprincipled' but far too cool a customer to do any 'carrying away' or expose himself to accusations of anything but heartless self-interest, at no time an uncommon human trait; and it is not 'Scruples' like those of the 'Hero' of the *Plan*, or of Edgar Mandelbert of *Camilla* and Albert Harleigh of *The Wanderer*, that have so far fettered Wentworth, but his own foolish pseudo-pursuit of Louisa and his unfounded jealousy of Mr Elliot. The meeting of Anne and Wentworth after they both know of his release from Louisa is almost – but not quite – as sudden and startling as the conventional 'forced difficulty' which Austen so much deplored, and Anne is frustratingly unable to extricate herself from Mr Elliot on that occasion (*P* 175–7). Moreover, at the same time we are informed that Bath is abuzz with rumours of their impending engagement – it even reaches into the 'noisy parlour and a dark bed-room behind' of Mrs Smith's obscure dwelling. Small wonder that Captain Wentworth thinks he may be too late, that he has behaved badly, and that Anne might settle for what her family must surely want for her and for themselves. Like Mr Knightley, he thinks of the Frank Churchill/Mr Elliot model as inescapably desirable to women.

Realising all this, Anne has, against all heroinely modesty and reticence, to take matters into her own hands. Her final anxieties have nothing to do with anything but the near impossibility of private communication between two people in the midst of the obsessive socialising of contemporary life. Austen demonstrates very clearly the strength and manipulativeness of public opinion – how very little control people had over their own lives. Somehow, Anne has to demonstrate her indifference to Mr Elliot and she is continually frustrated. He seems to be everywhere – first in Milsom-street, causing Anne to have to refuse the protection of Wentworth's umbrella;[22] outside the White Hart, where the Musgroves and Mary are visited by Wentworth; at the concert, where Elliot commandeers her as a translator of Italian – thus, incidentally, using a little more opportunistic flattery (*P* 186–90). Anne realises that it is for her to give Wentworth encouragement, and she does not scruple to do so; she says whatever she can to demonstrate her real feelings, and her manoeuvrings at the concert amuse her by their likeness to those of Burney's Miss Larolles, that incorrigible husband-hunter in *Cecilia* – and they are as little effective (*P* 189); Wentworth remains touchy, seemingly determined to regard himself as again rejected. No Dr Marchmont is needed here to cause him to keep his distance – the whole situation militates against communication. In a key passage of Anne's internal discourse, she refers directly to the fictional stereotype: 'Surely, if there be constant attachment on each side, our hearts must understand each other ere long. We are not boy and girl, to be captiously irritable, misled by every moment's inadvertence [recognisable as a reference to Edgar Mandelbert's maddening perversity and Camilla's naive ineptness], and wantonly playing with our own happiness' (*P* 221). But she does not manage to hang on to this rational analysis of the situation. The very next moment, she falls into the mistake of giving Wentworth the impression that she is intimate enough with Mr Elliot to know the minutiae of his plans, and has some difficulty in devising a way which proves that she cares little about whether he goes or stays (*P* 222–3). Fanny Burney uses grand and glittering public scenes like Vauxhall and the Pantheon to confuse and threaten her heroines with misrepresentation and actual danger; Austen places hers in a thoroughly ordinary, mundane inn. But the constantly mobile, changing social atmosphere at the White Hart has much the same effect, given the difference of scale. Anne is reduced to a state of exhausting emotional agitation which is beginning to interfere with her necessary social poise. Desperate measures are required of her – she must speak unequivocally if indirectly through the unremitting interaction of others in a way which Wentworth cannot fail to understand.

The episode (*P* 231–8) which finally convinces him has, I think, been much misunderstood. It can be read, not as a great statement of the condition of women and a plea for understanding, put forward by the author and intended to summarise the message of the novel, but as Anne's final desperate effort to enlighten Wentworth. The greater substance of Anne's impassioned speech to Captain Harville about the constancy of women as contrasted to that of men is not only inconclusive, but is directed at the already convinced. Anne knows what Wentworth thinks of Benwick, for he has told her, unequivocally, before the concert, and his statement had no whisper of ambiguity: ' "A man does not recover from such a devotion of the heart to such a woman! – He ought not – he does not" ' (*P* 183). Both Harville and Anne believe that Fanny ' "would not have forgotten him [Benwick] so soon" ' (*P* 232), *but* both men who are present and involved in the conversation profess at different times high standards of constancy and fidelity. Harville refers to his wife and family as ' "these treasures of his existence" ', for whose sakes he would do anything (*P* 235). Anne's speech is something of a puzzle unless it is seen in the context of what is going on in her mind and those of the others present. The whole novel has shown the heroine to be a person of strongly variable moods – she is easily thrown into despondency; this is one of the flaws in her character which make her real rather than ideal. Her own exertions to convey the truth to Captain Wentworth and conversations with him begun and interrupted leave her typically pessimistic; after the episode in which Mr Elliot is espied from the window, and Anne has intrepidly suggested that she would like to abandon the whole tedious card-party at home and go to the play, Captain Wentworth first seems to be about to refer to the past – ' "It is a period, indeed! Eight years and a half is a period!" ' (*P* 225). Typically this promising beginning is interrupted by the hurly-burly of the social scene they are in and the chill incursion of Sir Walter and Elizabeth. Wentworth's reception of Elizabeth's invitation to that same card-party – 'Anne caught his eye, saw his cheeks glow, and his mouth [that Byronic mouth again] form itself into a momentary expression of contempt, and turned away, that she might neither see nor hear more to vex her' (*P* 227). Immediately she is thrown into gloom and retreats to Camden-place to brood. The next day at the inn she is again a prey to fluctuating agitations as Mrs Croft, a woman of no mean intelligence and Wentworth's sister to boot, inveighs against 'uncertain engagements' in his hearing and provokes an ambiguous reaction – 'one quick, conscious look at her'. Naturally, 'her mind was in confusion' (*P* 231).

We are not to suppose, then, that when she is drawn into conversation with Captain Harville everything she says is the result of measured, logical thought, or that any of it represents the author's position on 'female difficulties'. Anne's response to Harville is at first formulaic – her description of a woman's life as inescapably 'quiet, confined' (*P* 232) is conventional but by no means universally applicable – there is actually present in the room one woman who has refused to put up with such a life – Mrs Croft, that determined seafarer; in fact nothing in the novel supports this fiction about women's lives, which seem to be more often scenes of unrelenting activity of one kind or another; and Harville quickly points out that Benwick has recently been as quiet and confined as any woman could be, and has yet forgotten Fanny within the year. Anne is in difficulties and falls back on a difference in the nature of men which not only can Harville immediately rebut, but which she already knows Wentworth does not believe. By this time, she has also become aware that Wentworth may be listening and in effect grasps the opportunity to issue a challenge which she knows he will have somehow to answer. Both Harville and Anne become more animated as the conversation develops, and as Anne responds 'eagerly' to his protestations of devotion to his family, she states clearly, though in a code which Harville will not quite grasp, that if Wentworth had gone down in the leaky *Asp*, his first command, there would have been no chance of any recovery for her – whereas he, similarly bereaved, she suggests, would, like Benwick, have been easily consolable. ' "All the privilege I claim for my own sex ... is that of loving longest, when existence or when hope is gone" ' (*P* 235). Which, being interpreted, is 'I still love you and always will; perhaps, because you are, like Captain Benwick, a man, it is not the same with you.' It is then that Wentworth is goaded into writing his letter ' "Dare not say that man forgets sooner than woman, that his love has an earlier death. I have loved none but you" ' (*P* 237).

The scene is dramatic in its structure, not discursive; it opens up a number of questions but seems deliberately to leave them unanswered. Its chief purpose is to bring Anne and Wentworth together in a way that is both natural and exciting. It is well known that Austen originally arranged, in the cancelled chapter, for the couple to be accidentally alone when they finally reach an understanding.[23] Perhaps one reason for the change was that such a lucky development was extremely unlikely in the unrelentingly public nature of social life at the time. It *might* happen, but would not ring true in fiction. The real reason is probably that the scene in its final form generates far more tension between the protagonists. It is a typical Austen scene in its focal depth and richness of allusion to the wider matrix of the main action. That Anne is clear about her real motives in this speech is demonstrated by its effects on her: 'She could not immediately have uttered another sentence; her heart was too full, her breath too much oppressed.' She has been unequivocally given the final cast. In the cancelled chapter, Austen rather coyly begs forgiveness for her heroine for her forwardness: 'If she *had* no horror of a few minutes tête-à-tête with Captain Wentworth, may she not be pardoned?'[24] But in the final version Anne has courageously to seize a much more unpromising opportunity, in the full glare of a public place, and the author makes no apology.[25]

Anne and Wentworth come then to an understanding and the novel ends happily for all the favoured characters and not particularly unhappily for the rest. Captain Wentworth admits that he will be happier than he deserves – but then so will Mr Elliot, and Sir Walter and Elizabeth will still have their great relations to 'resort to for comfort'. So what *was* Austen up to in *Persuasion*? In my view she makes no generalised statement in the novel about society – the irresponsible landowner Elliots are *not* replaced by solid and steady Crofts and Wentworths at Kellynch; things go on much as they did before; nor does Lady Russell's disillusionment represent any 'turning away' on the author's part from 'old values', as Tony Tanner has suggested.[26] It certainly doesn't preach that the gentle, modest, unassuming girl will always get her man if she simply sits back and waits. But for chance, and a certain compromise with the most extreme rules of female reticence (which may have existed only in fiction), Anne would have remained unmarried for the rest of her life. Nor does it in any way suggest that a girl might benefit from reliance on any mentor, male or female. Lady Russell 'had been unfairly influenced by appearances' and had to 'admit that she had been pretty completely wrong' (*P* 249); however, Captain Wentworth is no Grandison, but a mass of human frailty which Anne is prepared to put up with without much in the way of rational motive. One might say that she, too, is going on taste as much as on thoughtful analysis of character; and a reading against the typical optimism of the conclusion might suggest that she will often have to mitigate the effects of Wentworth's intolerance of fools (especially those in her own family), shield people from that 'curl of his handsome mouth', and act as umpire between him and Lady Russell. She, too, has been subject to the ordinary weaknesses of the human condition; when Captain Wentworth proclaims her as 'maintaining the loveliest medium of fortitude and gentleness' and as demonstrating 'the resolution of a collected mind' he is speaking as a lover, and a penitent one, and may pardonably be exaggerating (*P* 242). The reader has been aware of Anne's mind as anything but collected, and her fortitude has faltered many times. Her defence of her past conduct as she tries to reconcile Wentworth to the continued presence of Lady Russell in their lives is an acknowledgement that there can be no certainties in moral judgements. ' "It was" ', she says, ' "one of those cases in which advice is good or bad only as the event decides" ' (*P* 246). The startling contrast – if we will only notice it – between the relativity of this statement and her apparent submission, at the same time, to the fixed necessity of filial obedience, especially for women, demonstrates that Anne cannot close the debate but has to compromise – she has *not* found a solution to the struggle to distinguish right from wrong. ' "I was right," ' she says, ' "perfectly right in being guided by the friend whom you will love better than you do now. To me, she was in the place of a parent." ' Here 'right' has no absolute moral reference; it was right for her, she goes on to say, because it prevented her from feeling guilty. That is all she can say. Confusion of character discourse with the authorial voice and a predetermined moral programme for the novel often cause this speech to be interpreted as a definitive conclusion, but there are elements in the last two chapters which will directly contradict this impression. It is no bit of extraneous novelistic atmosphere that the first instalment of the lovers' final *éclaircissement* takes place among the 'sauntering politicians, bustling house-keepers, flirting girls … nursery-maids and children' (*P* 241). As the focus moves away, in an almost cinematic manoeuvre of the point of view, we see the principals, absorbed in their own story, as part of a bevy of individuals who will act according to an infinite variety of unpredictable motives, causing thereby much provocation and be-wilderment to the Lady Russells of this world, who may mean well, but whose certainties are unjustified. 'This may be bad morality to conclude with,' says the author at the opening of the final chapter, speaking in general and directly to the reader about what she saw as the chaotic nature of much human conduct, 'but I believe it to be the truth.'

CHAPTER 7

'Sanditon' – conclusion

Incomplete as it is, we can perceive in the twelve chapters of *Sanditon* that have come down to us the twin targets of Austen's irony – 'cant' and contemporary attitudes to literature. Most of the characters are gathered, and the attack is about to begin. It is futile to try to guess how the story would have developed, for though we can interpret Austen's unique qualities as a writer in the completed work, we cannot reproduce them, and would be foolish to try. But some speculations must be discussed, for, as with the finished novels, questionable assumptions can be made in connection with *Sanditon* about Austen's views on the purpose of fiction.

Comment on the fragment encapsulates a dissatisfaction with Jane Austen from which most critics have so far been unable to escape. Attitudes have changed over the years, but the reservations have remained. George Henry Lewes is typical of nineteenth-century condescension – Austen deserves, to his way of thinking, but a remote niche among the immortals, because her work, though exquisite, lacks grandeur – 'miniatures' he says, 'are not frescoes'.[1] Twentieth-century critics, especially recent ones, have tried to correct this attitude by identifying an engagement with 'important' large-scale social and economic issues – the missing quality is supplied from present-day concerns. Difficulty in establishing these elements in the novels has usually resulted in the perverse conclusion that she could not have been doing the job very well – that the novels are 'flawed'. The unfinished state of *Sanditon* is a godsend to critics anxious to close the argument and prove Austen once and for all the serious social commentator that they would like her to be. Since two-thirds of the novel is not there, the task of finding the evidence, against the message of the text, is that much easier than with the completed novels. The strategy is usually to assert that what we have of *Sanditon* represents a new departure in subject, style and method and then to show that these differences indicate some change of heart, or a hardening of attitude. Its location at an embryo seaside resort assists these speculations because, contemplating our own decaying piers and promenades, as well as the devastation of the Spanish coast, we now regard such places, at least in theory, as purely commercial enterprises which enrich the greedy, pander to the vulgar enjoyments of the masses and ruin the landscape. Feeling ran considerably less high in the late eighteenth and early nineteenth century. The setting of *Sanditon* is not perhaps as significant as has been thought.

Some critics assume that Austen was attacking the whole concept of the resort when she made a central figure, Mr Parker, a naive amateur entrepreneur, bent on making his home-village as famous as Brighton and Weymouth and thereby losing much of the solid comfort of his previous life. Marilyn Butler says: 'Jane Austen is the most concerned of the three [novelists, the others being Scott and Edgeworth] to compare her contemporary resort with a notional older way, an inherited organic community reminiscent of the imaginative construct made by Burke.' Echoing her, Tony Tanner asserts: 'They [the old values of the settled Heywoods] are inscribed in the book to serve as a measure of the loss and transformation, or deformation, which prevail in the new social world of the novel.'[2] This assumption of social criticism is often supported by a notion that Austen herself did not like resorts; it is true that she did not initially want to live at Bath instead of Steventon, but she seems to have enjoyed herself there. The idea that she objected to Weymouth is based on one letter to Cassandra, and on Mr Knightley's condem- nation of Weymouth as one of 'the idlest haunts in the kingdom' (*E* 146). We should not confuse Mr Knightley's opinions with those of his creator, and the remarks in the letter, typically mocking and ironic, do not add up to a settled opinion of her own:

Your account of Weymouth contains nothing which strikes me so forcibly as there being no ice in the town. For every other vexation I was in some measure prepared ... but for there being no ice what could prepare me? Weymouth is altogether a shocking place, I perceive, without recommenda- tion of any kind, & worthy only of being frequented by the inhabitants of Gloucester. I am really glad that we did not go there, & that Henry and Eliza saw nothing in it to make them feel differently.[3]

In any case, Austen certainly liked Lyme (as does Anne Elliot) – as much a commercial watering-place as any other, where she enjoyed bathing so much that she 'staid in rather too long'.[4] Some novelists were at the time commenting on the dissipation and irresponsibility of the patrons of such places and condemning them as perversions of real, traditional communities – Marilyn Butler mentions particularly Scott's *St Ronan's Well* – but this sort of thing can only be perceived in *Sanditon* if we are already convinced that Austen's other novels are, if only indirectly, defending tradition against change.[5] If it is accepted, as I have maintained, that Jane Austen was all along consciously avoiding taking sides in contemporary debates, there is nothing to suggest *moral* disapproval of Mr Parker's activities – it is his self-deception that is highlighted. Her choice of such a budding resort seems rather to have rested on her need for a location which would be limited in extent, have the required '3 or 4 families' fixed in the place and interacting with one another in ways which involved inheritance and other money dealings, as well as the possibility of a naturally occurring influx of people from outside. Sanditon really differs very little from the 'country village' recommended to niece Anna as an ideal scenario; as Raymond Williams has pointed out, Austen's communities are not feudal and ossified, but scenes of constant social flux: 'it must be clear that it [the 'world of the novels'] is no single, settled society, it is an active, complicated, sharply speculative process'. Sanditon, then, according to this persuasive view, differs little from Highbury or Meryton.[6] Mr and Mrs Parker and Lady Denham are the fixed characters, apparently collaborating in the project; the latter's impecunious dependants, Sir Edward Denham, his sister and Clara Brereton, are semi-permanently part of the Denham ménage; Charlotte Heywood, untravelled and socially inexperienced, is introduced by the Parkers, whose hypochondriac relations provide comedy, at least for the time being; and we hear of, and briefly see, Sidney Parker, a young man about town, who apparently has little use for the resort project. Add to these characters some young women from the visiting school, the mulatto heiress, Miss Lambe, and the two shallowly fashionable, husband-hunting Miss Beauforts, and you have a typical cast of characters, with plenty to do in the way of walking about and meeting each other – not this time in Ford's of Highbury, but in Mrs Whitby's circulating library.

Linked to and supporting the notion that *Sanditon* was at last to reveal some kind of ideological commitment on the part of the author is another common assertion – that the fragment is more

concerned with topography than Austen's other novels. Brian
Southam has commented on what he sees as the novelty in Austen of
'a distinctive *genius loci*, created through its topography';[7] Marvin
Mudrick makes topography, with the Romantic poets and 'sex as
comedy' one of the 'new ingredients' in *Sanditon*.[8] Leaving aside the
poets and the sex for the moment, these assertions about topography
must be challenged; they are only tenable if we accept the common
nineteenth-century assessment of the completed novels as stuffily
confined to drawing-rooms and enclosed gardens. Topography plays
a crucial part in all the novels, not for ideological comment but as an
essential ingredient in psychological analysis. Practically all the
determining events occur out of doors in very vividly identifiable
locations;[9] Catherine Morland looks down on the whole city of Bath
while she listens to the Tilneys' disquisition on the picturesque and
inadvertently tells them a great deal about herself; the grounds of
Rosings and Pemberley are the essential settings for Elizabeth's
meetings with Darcy; and who can fail to notice the background of
Barton Cottage with its great hill down which Marianne careers,
straight into the arms of Willoughby? Or Mansfield Parsonage
garden, where Fanny does *not* communicate with Mary Crawford;
Sotherton and the 'wilderness' where Fanny's helplessness is so
clearly demonstrated? Nothing could be more topographical than
Emma's thoughts about the environs of Donwell Abbey; and what
about Uppercross and Lyme and Bath in *Persuasion*? One could
extend the list almost indefinitely. The importance of place and its
effects on behaviour become startlingly evident as experienced
readers of Austen watch visual adaptations of the novels on film and
television – the locations never quite satisfy the viewer's perception
of where things happen. Austen always used topography as a
powerful matrix for her characters' states of mind. Even the
rhapsody about the environs of Lyme, though it is diffused through
the narrator's voice, is linked to Anne Elliot's mood just before she
meets Captain Benwick for the first time; both are finding, not
distraction, but food for the indulgence of melancholy in the beauties
of nature – something we have also seen Anne do on the walk to
Winthrop. Austen's special use of the environment to clarify event
and mood may be clearly seen if we compare her spare and closely
relevant natural description with the very formal, forced enthusiasm
of Juliet in *The Wanderer*, when, at the height of her 'difficulties', she
contemplates the beauties of the New Forest:

Chiefly she was struck with the noble aspect of the richly variegated woods, whose aged oaks appeared to be spreading their venerable branches to offer shelter from the storms of life, as well as of the elements, charming her imagination by their lofty grandeur; while the zephyrs, which agitated their verdant foliage, seemed but their animation. [10]

and the South Devon coast above Teignmouth:

She clambered up various rocks, nearly to their summit, to enjoy, in one grand perspective, the stupendous expansion of the ocean, glittering with the brilliant rays of a bright and cloudless sky: dazzled, she descended to their base, to repose her gaze on the soft, yet lively tint of the green turf, and the rich, yet mild hue of the downy moss. Almost sinking, now, from the scorching beams of a nearly vertical sun, she looked round for some umbrageous retreat; but refreshed the next moment, by salubrious sea-breezes, by the coolness of the rocks, or by the shade of the trees, she remained stationary, and charmed; a devoutly adoring spectatress of the lovely, yet magnificent scenery encircling her.[11]

This is set-piece interpolation – it seems to belong to another era altogether – and it is beyond the bounds of probability that Juliet can be thus distracted from her still friendless, desperate state, whereas Anne's engagement with nature is closely linked to her personal concerns. On the way to Winthrop she observes 'the last smiles of the year' and thinks of the 'declining year' as reflecting 'declining happiness, and the images of youth and hope, and spring, all gone together' (P 84–5). In a typical Austen use of the narrator's voice to suggest what a character may be only subliminally aware of, hope is injected into the sense of loss: 'and after another half mile of gradual ascent through large enclosures, where the ploughs at work, and the fresh-made paths spoke the farmer, counteracting the sweets of poetical despondence, and meaning to have spring again' (P 85). Using less than half the number of words, Austen, as very often, evokes here a scene and a mood in a brilliantly skilful use of an environment for fictional purposes. Sanditon has no scene which is radically different; Charlotte's view from her 'ample Venetian window' reflects her relish for her new experience in all its variety: 'the miscellaneous foreground of unfinished Buildings, waving Linen, & tops of Houses, to the Sea, dancing & sparkling in Sunshine and Freshness' (MW 384); and just as Anne's preoccupations are replicated on the walk to Winthrop, so are Charlotte's as she walks to Sanditon House:

These Entrance Gates were so much in a corner of the Grounds or

Paddock, so near one of its Boundaries, that an outside fence was at first almost pressing on the road – till an angle *here*, & a curve *there* threw them to a better distance. The Fence was a proper Park paling in excellent condition; with clusters of fine Elms, or rows of old Thorns following its line almost every where. – *Almost* must be stipulated – for there were vacant spaces – & through one of these, Charlotte as soon as they entered the Enclosure, caught a glimpse over the pales of something White and Womanish (*MW* 426)

The whole of this scene is shrouded in mist – 'it was a close, misty morn^g' – which increases our consciousness of Charlotte's partial and misleading perception of what is going on around her. It is a sharply illuminating device (in spite of the mist) but not new to Austen. Topography is an important element in *Sanditon*, but it will not do as a new departure.

In fact, the fragment shows every sign of not departing from, but probing deeper into, the exploration of human motive and desire, with a special emphasis on self-deception, which has been the business of the other novels. Scenes where multiple points of view complicate the fictional message abound, even in this short space (I think especially of chapter 7, in the Parkers' drawing-room, and the arrival of the Parker siblings in chapter 9).

Another major claim for this novel above the rest is that it expresses concern about a transition from Enlightenment to Romanticism. This is not tenable, chiefly on the grounds that it cannot be deduced from the texts of this or the other novels that Austen had any notion of a break in the history of literature at this stage. She was not versed in nineteenth- and twentieth-century literary categories. What Austen is identifying in this fragment is not evidence of decadence on the literary scene, but the spouting of unexamined opinion – 'cant'. Sir Edward's disquisition on poetry is not very different from Robert Ferrars's equally vapid monologue about cottages – both are predominantly satirical characterisations (*SS* 251–2). Charlotte, though socially a *tabula rasa*, is an experienced reader; she is well up in contemporary poetry (like Anne Elliot) and is at first delighted with Sir Edward's equal interest. During the course of the conversation, however, she recognises 'cant', though she does not use the word. Sir Edward discourses on Scott, Burns, Montgomery, Campbell and Wordsworth in half a page of incoherent praise:

But while we are on the subject of Poetry, what think you Miss H. of Burns lines to his Mary? – Oh! there is Pathos to madden one! – If ever there was a Man who *felt*, it was Burns. – Montgomery has all the Fire of Poetry, Wordsworth has the true soul of it – Campbell in his pleasures of Hope has touched the extreme of our Sensations – "Like Angel's visits, few & far between." Can you conceive any thing more subduing, more melting, more fraught with the deep Sublime than that Line? – But Burns – I confess my sence of his Pre-eminence Miss H. – If Scott *has* a fault, it is the want of Passion. – Tender, Elegant, Descriptive – but *Tame*. – The Man who cannot do justice to the attributes of Woman is my contempt. – Sometimes indeed a flash of feeling seems to irradiate him – as in the Lines we were speaking of – "Oh! Woman in our hours of Ease" –. (*MW* 397)

It quickly becomes evident that Sir Edward has a very narrow and superficial acquaintance with the work of the poets he mentions with such enthusiasm, and is speaking only for effect. Charlotte is astute enough to recognise this, and finds his glib and derivative remarks on the sea ('the deep fathoms of it's Abysses, it's quick vicissitudes, it's direful Deceptions'):

rather commonplace perhaps – but doing very well from the Lips of a handsome Sir Edward, – and she cd. not but think him a Man of Feeling – till he began to stagger her by the number of his Quotations, & the bewilderment of some of his sentences ... – He seemed very sentimental, very full of some Feelings or other, & very much addicted to all the newest-fashioned hard words – had not a very clear Brain she presumed, & talked a good deal by rote. (*MW* 396–8)

She is clearly not about to put up with this kind of false claptrap and would prefer a more rational dialogue on one of her favourite topics. However, she herself is not exempt from a prevailing tendency to use literature as a basis for snap judgement. She thinks of herself, and the reader is co-opted into this assessment, as a 'sober-minded young lady', but even she catches herself out in categorising Clara Brereton according to the prevailing novelistic notion of the heroine:

And as for Miss Brereton, her appearance so completely justified Mr. P.'s praise that Charlotte thought she had never beheld a more lovely, or more Interesting young Woman. – Elegantly tall, regularly handsome, with great delicacy of complexion & soft Blue eyes, a sweetly modest & yet naturally graceful Address, Charlotte could see in her only the most perfect representation of whatever Heroine might be the most beautiful & bewitching, in all the numerous vol:s they had left behind them on Mrs. Whitby's shelves.- Perhaps it might be partly oweing to her having just issued from a Circulating Library – but she cd. not separate the idea of a complete Heroine from Clara Brereton. Her situation with Lady Denham so very much in favour of it! – She seemed placed with her on purpose to be ill-used. Such Poverty & Dependance joined to such Beauty & Merit, seemed to leave no choice in the business. (*MW* 391)

However, the apparent mutual affection of the pair convinces Charlotte that even she, the 'sober-minded' can be too influenced by novel-reading ... but are we being doubly duped? Is Charlotte so determined not to be deceived that she deceives herself? Perhaps Clara *is* being ill-used; or perhaps – a nice turn-up for the book – is ill-using Lady Denham. This seems quite likely, because Lady Denham's decision to take Clara under her protection goes clean against her previous rooted objection, and is given no clear motivation. It also goes against her projected self-image as self-aggrandising and mean. It is perfectly possible that Clara has some mysterious hold over her. Charlotte may not be so clear-sighted as she thinks she is – she sees Lady Denham as 'mean' but is herself puzzled by her relationship with Clara.

Her judgement of Sir Edward, however, is supported by the shift in point of view – we know from his own thoughts that he is silly and vain, and that he not only 'talks by rote' about fashionable literary trends, but indulges in a Richardsonian fantasy in which he 'carries off' an unwilling Clara as soon as he can arrange – and afford – a harbourage in 'Tombuctoo' (*MW* 405–6). In this connection it is surely impossible not to remember Charlotte Lennox's Arabella in *The Female Quixote*, whose preoccupation with being 'carried off' by the most inoffensive and unlikely men provides much of the humour. Sir Edward seems to be going to develop into a male version of Arabella, a latter-day Don Quixote who plans to carry off virtuous females instead of tilting at windmills, with equally comic results. Clara 'sees through' him, and has 'no intention of being seduced' – perhaps Sir Edward is as much her victim as he plans to make her his.[12] As Charlotte peeps between the trees she is aware of some relationship between them; Sir Edward and Clara are sitting 'near each other & appeared ... closely engaged in gentle conversation'; Charlotte immediately concludes that they must be lovers: 'It could not but strike her rather unfavourably with regard to Clara; – but hers was a situation which must not be judged with severity' (*MW* 426). Charlotte is clearly not succeeding in extricating herself from, perhaps, the ethos of Fanny Burney's *The Wanderer*, where elegant manners and blue eyes are presented as sufficient indicators of virtue to the truly perceptive. Margaret Kirkham sees Sir Edward's self-identification with Lovelace as a more definite challenge to Richardson than has previously been evident – a feminist dislike of the dashing masculine villain, perversely attractive in his villainy.[13] But the touch is lighter than this; what is being held up to ridicule is his shallow stupidity rather than his plan of abduction itself, which has no chance of succeeding.

With the mystery of Sir Edward and Clara, Lady Denham's apparent determination to keep her hands firmly on the purse-strings and the presence of the handsome Sidney in the offing, there is plenty of scope in the situation as it is laid before us for any number of false assumptions and unexpected revelations, all arising out of very ordinary situations, and out of a construct of reality based on the characters' reading. The conclusion of *Sanditon* would probably have produced no more absolutes in virtuous conduct than had hitherto been provided, nor any clear condemnation of contemporary social and political trends. We may not be able to guess how *Sanditon* continued and concluded, but we can confidently assume that the the dispersal of attention which is characteristic of the other novels would have left the significance of the action open to the reader's ingenuity, with the narrator standing at the margins, rarely, if ever, giving any direction.

This repudiation of the obligation to give a moral lead, this decision to present human interaction in an untendentious way which invites a number of reader-reactions, gave fiction a new dimension – it was brought much closer to the condition of drama. But it was drama with a difference, for the addition of internal monologue, or '*style indirecte libre*', creates a potential for the novel which drama will always lack. Many episodes in Austen's novels, in their narrowness of range, their confinement to a relatively small space, their careful grouping of characters, resemble scenes in a play, but the depth of imaginative focus is immeasurably increased by the fact that we have access to the thoughts of one or more of the persons involved, as well as a subtext of suggested life which lies outside the main action, supporting and complicating it. There are many such episodes, but powerful examples would be the scene at Pemberley when Darcy first meets Mr and Mrs Gardiner, the painful collisions at Box Hill, and Anne Elliot's *cri de cœur* across the sitting-room of the White Hart. Nothing quite like this had been done before.[14]

The chief result of this enhanced dramatic quality in prose fiction is that the characters more than ever before take on a life of their own. Because we are given so little direction by the narrator, we are drawn into speculation about them; we have a strong sense that they live and breathe outside the confines of the text. Thus the novels acquire a range of reference which quite belies their apparent restriction in time and space. Nineteenth-century critics praising Austen for her truth to life were unable to analyse what struck them as so original – G. H. Lewes's prolix encomium of 1859 (see p. 5 above) is typical in its mixture of enthusiasm and marginalisation.

Nor could anyone assert that her special qualities were widely imitated. The novel of the nineteenth century built for the most part on the picaresque and on the Radcliffean Gothic – these influences are clear and demonstrable. Austen's spare and economical method was widely admired – but not used as exact precedent. Her influence, though, may have been less direct. There is no doubt that during this phase of its development the novel gradually acquired an immensely increased psychological range; both 'good' and 'bad' characters are portrayed with more subtleties and contradictions; what Johnson had objected to in the 'mixed' character became the norm. It was this analytical approach which above all set the nineteenth-century novel apart from many of its eighteenth-century forebears, and Jane Austen stands at the point of change. 'Pictures of perfection' did not altogether disappear from fiction (Dickens, for instance, has a number of almost caricature 'good' women), but Becky Sharp rapidly became a more satisfying fictional construct than, say, Caroline Percy in Edgeworth's *Patronage*.[15] We have come to regard doubt rather than certainty as the normal condition of fiction. In excluding what appeared to her 'absurd', Austen believed she was merely improving upon her inheritance and clearing away the dross which had collected around it. But what she perhaps thought of as necessary adjustment grew into fundamental innovation, only partially recognised at first, but ultimately ensuring for her fiction an extraordinary durability.[16] So complex does the relationship between reader, character and author become as she reshapes the novel to her own design, that it must surely be universally acknowledged that no critic will ever succeed in having the last word.

Notes

INTRODUCTION

1 A personal version of two lines from Scott's *Marmion*, vi. 38, when he omits to describe a love-scene: 'I do not rhyme to that dull elf / Who cannot image for himself'.

2 R. W. Chapman (ed.), *Jane Austen's Letters* (Oxford University Press, 2nd edn 1952, reprinted 1964), May or June 1814, pp. 387–8.

3 *Letters*, 11 October 1813, p. 344; Mary Brunton, *Self-control* (London, 1810; reprinted London: Pandora Press, 1986).

4 *Letters*, 8 October 1807, p. 180; Sarah Burney, *Clarentine* (London, 1798).

5 For a comprehensive but succinct examination of serious academic discussions (mainly in Scotland) of the status of the novel (as distinct from periodical criticism) see Paul G. Bator, 'Rhetoric and the Novel in the Eighteenth-Century British University Curriculum', *Eighteenth-Century Studies* 30, number 2 (Winter 1996–7), 173–91. For more extended work on the subject, especially on the concept of probability, see Douglas Lane Patey, *Probability and Literary Form* (Cambridge University Press, 1984) and Robert Newsom, *A Likely Story: Probability and Play in Fiction* (New Brunswick and London: Rutgers University Press, 1988).

6 See Claudia L. Johnson, *Jane Austen: Women, Politics and the Novel* (University of Chicago Press, 1988), chapter 1, esp. p. 27.

7 Mary Hays, *The Memoirs of Emma Courtney*, ed. Eleanor Ty (Oxford University Press, 1996); Maria Edgeworth, *Letters for Literary Ladies*, ed. Claire Conolly (London: J. M. Dent, Everyman, 1993); Jane West, *A Tale of the Times* (London, 1799).

8 Jane West, *Letters addressed to a Young Man* (London, 1801) and *Letters to a Young Lady* (London, 1806).

9 *Letters*, 30 August 1805, p. 169.

10 *British Critic* 39 (May 1812), 527, reprinted in B. C. Southam, *The Critical Heritage* (London: Routledge and Kegan Paul, 1968, revised and reprinted 1986), p. 40.

11 Sir Walter Scott, *Quarterly Review* 14 (March 1816), 188–201.

12 Letter to Sir William Elford 20 December 1814 in A. G. L'Estrange

(ed.), *Life of Mary Russell Mitford* vol. 1, p. 300, reprinted in Southam, *Critical Heritage*, p. 54.

13 Richard Whately, '*Northanger Abbey* and *Persuasion*', *Quarterly Review* 24 (January 1821), 352–76, reprinted in Southam, *Critical Heritage*, p. 95.

14 *Letters*, 16 December 1816, p. 469.

15 George Henry Lewes, 'The Novels of Jane Austen', *Blackwood's Edinburgh Magazine* 86 (July 1859), 99–113, reprinted in Southam, *Critical Heritage*, pp. 148–56, esp. pp. 148 and 166.

16 J. E. Austen-Leigh, *A Memoir of Jane Austen* (London, 1870, 71, reprinted R. W. Chapman (ed.), Oxford University Press, 1926).

17 Richard Simpson, *North British Review* 52 (April 1870), 129–52, reprinted in Southam, *Critical Heritage*, pp. 241–65.

18 Reginald Farrer, 'Jane Austen', *Quarterly Review* 228 (July 1917), 20–33. Disagreement with 'Aunt Janeism' manifested itself also in less positive ways: see for instance, H. W. Garrod, 'Jane Austen: a Depreciation' in *Essays by Divers Hands* (London: The Royal Society of Literature, 1928).

19 I. A. Richards, *The Principles of Literary Criticism* (London, 1924). New Criticism in its earlier days concerned itself mainly with the language of poetry, as the titles of the work of its prominent exponents often demonstrate: F. W. Bateson, *English Poetry and the English Language* (Oxford University Press, 1934); Cleanth Brooks, *The Well-wrought Urn* (New York: Reynal and Hitchcock, 1947) and W. K. Wimsatt, *The Verbal Icon: Studies in the Meaning of Poetry*, (1954, reprinted London: Methuen, 1970). See also David Lodge, *The Language of Fiction: Essays in Criticism and Verbal Analysis of the English Novel* (London: Routledge and Kegan Paul, 1966) for an analysis of ways in which New Critical techniques were incorporated into the study of prose fiction.

20 F. R. Leavis, leader of a distinctive group of critics associated with Downing College, Cambridge from 1936. With D. W. Harding, Denys Thompson and L. C. Knights he edited the influential periodical *Scrutiny* from 1932 to 1953.

21 D. W. Harding, 'Regulated Hatred: an Aspect of the Work of Jane Austen', *Scrutiny* 8 (March 1940), 346–62, esp. p. 351.

22 Q. D. Leavis, *Fiction and the Reading Public* (London: Chatto and Windus, 1932) and a series of articles entitled 'A Critical Theory of Jane Austen's Writings' from 1941–2: *Scrutiny* 10 (June 1941), 61–87; (October 1941), 114–42; (January 1942), 272–94; and *Scrutiny* 12 (Spring 1944), 104–19; Lionel Trilling, *The Opposing Self* (New York: Viking Press, 1955), especially the chapter on *MP*.

23 Mary Lascelles, *Jane Austen and her Art* (Oxford University Press, 1939, reprinted 1968).

24 Notably Sheila Kaye-Smith and G. B. Sterne, *Talking of Jane Austen* (London: Cassell, 1943). A less adulatory view of Austen can also be found earlier – Charlotte Bronte protested to Lewes and W. S. Williams in 1848 and 1850 that she found nothing to admire in the author (see

Southam, *Critical Heritage*, pp. 126–28); R. W. Emerson thought her 'vulgar' and 'sterile'; see *Journals* vol. IX, (Boston, 1913), p. 336.

25 See Peter Garside and Elizabeth MacDonald, 'Evangelicalism and *Mansfield Park*', *Trivium* 10 (1975), 34–50. The essay offers a very detailed and useful survey of the cross-currents of this aspect of Austen criticism since 1944, with an excellent bibliography. Its conclusions will, however, be challenged later in this study.

26 Arnold Kettle, *An Introduction to the English Novel* vol. 1 (London: Hutchinson, 1951), pp. 90–104, esp. p. 93.

27 Marvin Mudrick, *Jane Austen: Irony as Defense and Discovery* (Berkeley and Los Angeles: University of California Press, 1952); Mudrick adds a detailed critique of Q. D. Leavis's essays in *Scrutiny* as an appendix.

28 A. Walton Litz, *Jane Austen: A Study of her Artistic Development* (London: Chatto and Windus, 1965).

29 Alistair M. Duckworth, *The Improvement of the Estate* (Baltimore and London: Johns Hopkins University Press, 1971); Marilyn Butler, *Jane Austen and the War of Ideas* (Oxford: Clarendon Press, 1975, reprinted 1987).

30 Nancy Armstrong, *Desire and Domestic Fiction: A Political History of the Novel* (Oxford University Press, 1987); Mary Poovey, *The Proper Lady and the Woman Writer: Ideology as Style in the Works of Mary Wollstonecraft, Mary Shelley, and Jane Austen* (University of Chicago Press, 1984).

31 Margaret Kirkham, *Jane Austen: Feminism and Fiction* (Hassocks, Sussex: Harvester Press, 1983; reprinted London: Athlone Press, 1997); Claudia L. Johnson, *Jane Austen: Women, Politics and the Novel* (University of Chicago Press, 1988).

32 Kirkham, *Jane Austen*, p. 152.

33 Raymond Williams, *The Country and the City* (London: Chatto and Windus, 1973).

34 See Edward Said, *Culture and Materialism* (London: Chatto and Windus, 1993, reprinted Vintage, 1994), pp. 100–16. Brian Southam develops this theme in 'The Silence of the Bertrams: Slavery and the Chronology of *Mansfield Park*', *Times Literary Supplement* (17 February 1995), 13–14.

35 *Memoir* p. 89: 'every circumstance narrated in *Sir Charles Grandison*, all that was ever said or done in the cedar parlour was familiar to her; the wedding days of Lady L. and Lady G. were so well remembered as if they had been among living friends'.

36 *Letters*, 4 February 1813, pp. 299–300.

37 '*Northanger Abbey, Sense and Sensibility* and *Pride and Prejudice*' in Edward Copeland and Juliet McMaster (eds.), *The Cambridge Companion to Jane Austen* (Cambridge University Press, 1997), p. 35. Several of the essays in this collection indicate new directions in Austen criticism which are very welcome. There is still present, however, some need to identify a specific moral stance for Austen. Brownstein later (p. 55) speaks of the 'moral point' of Austen's fiction: 'on the one hand we are not so very different from our neighbours, and that on the other we must tirelessly

discriminate among our common traits in order to understand the extreme importance – and moral implications – of the differences'. In another chapter, '*Mansfield Park, Emma, Persuasion*', which provides many unusual analyses of point of view in the three later novels, John Wiltshire, p. 62, speaks of 'ethical anxiety in the reader that is not entirely resolved'. With earlier critics he finds flaws in Austen's practice: for instance, on p. 63, having identified a balancing tension of internal discourse between Mary and Fanny in *MP*, he finds that Austen can't quite sustain what she has undertaken. Isobel Grundy's chapter, 'Jane Austen and Literary Traditions', refers in fine detail to Austen's reading, highlighting many novelists who attracted the family's derision for one reason or another. However, the essay as a whole is inclined to play down the real seriousness of Austen's *general* impatience with the condition of contemporary fiction and to insist on an underlying respect, particularly for Richardson and Burney; Grundy states, for instance, on p. 203, that Austen 'tends to stand a little outside the beaten paths of discipleship' – perhaps an understatement. Analysis of Austen's reading is also to be found in Jan Fergus, *Jane Austen and the Didactic Novel* (London: Macmillan, 1983). Fergus relates Austen's work to a limited range of contemporary novels, but nevertheless sees her as belonging to a didactic tradition, though educating the emotions rather than the judgement.

I THE JUVENILIA, THE EARLY UNFINISHED NOVELS AND NORTHANGER ABBEY

1 Edgeworth, *Literary Ladies*; Jane West, *A Tale of the Times* (London, 1799).
2 John Gregory et al., *The Young Lady's Pocket Library, or Parental Monitor* (1790; reprinted with an introduction by Vivien Jones, Bristol: Thoemmes Press, 1995).
3 'A woman especially, if she have the misfortune of knowing any thing, should conceal it as well as she can' (*NA* 111). This refers ironically to Gregory, *A Father's Legacy*, p. 13: 'But if you happen to have any learning, keep it a profound secret, especially from the men, who generally look with a jealous and malignant eye on a woman of great parts, and a cultivated understanding.'
4 Gregory, *A Father's Legacy*, pp. 11–12.
5 Mary Wollstonecraft, *A Vindication of the Rights of Woman* (1792; reprinted, with an introduction by Miriam Brody Kramnick, London: Penguin Classics, 1985), chapter 5, 'Writers Who have Rendered Women Objects of Pity', section III, pp. 196–201.
6 Hannah More, *Cœlebs in Search of a Wife* (1808; reprinted with an introduction by Mary Waldron, Bristol: Thoemmes Press, 1995).
7 Thomas Secker 1693–1768, Archbishop of Canterbury, *Lectures on the Church Catechism* (1769). The footnote in *MW* spells the name 'Seccar'.

8 B. C. Southam, *Jane Austen's Literary Manuscripts: A Study of the Novelist's Development Through the Surviving Papers* (Oxford University Press, 1964), pp. 39–40.

9 Charlotte Smith, *Emmeline, or the Orphan of the Castle* (1788; reprinted London: Pandora Press, 1988); *Ethelinde* (London, 1789).

10 Southam, *Literary Manuscripts*, p. 58.

11 *Letters*, 23 March 1814, p. 486.

12 W. and R. A. Austen-Leigh, *Jane Austen: Her Life and Letters* (London, 1913), p. 230.

13 J. E. Austen-Leigh, *A Memoir of Jane Austen*, 2nd edn (London, 1871), p. 130.

14 *Letters*, 13 March 1817, p. 484; 'Miss Catherine is put upon the Shelve for the present '.

15 Charlotte Smith, *Emmeline*, pp. 6, 47, 124.

16 Ibid., p. 159.

17 Charlotte Lennox, *The Female Quixote* (1752; reprinted World's Classics, Oxford University Press, 1989); Richard Brinsley Sheridan, *The Rivals*, 1775.

18 Madeleine de Scudéry, 1607–1701, author of *Artamène, ou le Grand Cyrus*, and *Clélie*, Arabella's favourite works.

19 *Letters*, 7 January 1807, p. 173: 'the "Female Quixotte" ... now makes our evening amusement; to me a very high one, as I find the work quite equal to what I remembered it'. The family had abandoned Madame de Genlis's *Alphonsine* in favour of Lennox's novel.

20 Charlotte Smith, *Emmeline*, p. 23.

21 *The Female Quixote*, book VII, chapter 4.

22 Ann Radcliffe, *The Mysteries of Udolpho* (1794; reprinted, with introduction by Bonamy Dobrée and explanatory notes by Frederick Garber, World's Classics, Oxford University Press, 1980), p. 324.

23 Eliza Parsons, *The Castle of Wolfenbach*, 1793 and *The Mysterious Warning* (misnamed *Mysterious Warnings* by Isabella Thorpe), 1796; Peter Teutold, from the German of Lawrence Flammenburg, *The Necromancer; or the Tale of the Black Forest*, 1794; Regina Maria Roche, *Clermont*, 1798; Francis Lathom, *The Midnight Bell*, 1798; Eleanor Sleath, *The Orphan of the Rhine*, 1798; and P. Will, *Horrid Mysteries*, 1796. These seven novels were reprinted under the editorship of Devendra P. Varma by the Folio Press in 1968. His preface to *The Castle of Wolfenbach* contains a detailed account of the search for these novels, some of which were long thought to be Austen's inventions, together with some discussion of the reasons for her choice. See also Michael Sadleir, *The Northanger Novels: A Footnote to Jane Austen*, (English Association Pamphlet 68, 1927).

24 Eaton Stannard Barrett, *The Heroine, or Adventures of a Fair Romance Reader* (1813).

25 Radcliffe, *The Mysteries of Udolpho*, p. 672.

26 Austen's closures have attracted a variety of comment and explanation;

see, for instance, Lloyd W. Brown, *Bits of Ivory: Narrative Technique in Jane Austen's Fiction* (Baton Rouge: Louisiana State University Press, 1973) and sections on Austen in D. A. Miller, *Narrative and its Discontents: Problems of Closure in the Traditional Novel* (Princeton University Press, 1981).

2 THE NON-HEIRESSES: *THE WATSONS* AND *PRIDE AND PREJUDICE*

1 Fanny Burney, *Cecilia* (1782, reprinted, World's Classics, Oxford University Press, 1996) and *Camilla, or a Picture of Youth* (London: Strahan, 1796; reprinted E. and L. Bloom (eds.), World's Classics, Oxford University Press, 1983).

2 The connection with *Cecilia* has been made many times; see, for example, R. Brimley Johnson, *The Women Novelists* (London, 1918), pp. 117–30; R. W. Chapman (ed.), *PP*, Appendix, p. 408–9; Q. D. Leavis, 'A Critical Theory of Jane Austen's Writings', pt 1, *Scrutiny* 10 (1941–2), 61–87; Frank W. Bradbrook, *Jane Austen and her Predecessors* (Cambridge University Press 1966), pp. 97–100. Kenneth Moler, in *Jane Austen's Art of Allusion* (Lincoln: University of Nebraska Press, 1977), has carefully investigated Austen's whole debt to contemporary novelists, but generally in terms of influence rather than challenge.

3 Butler, *War of Ideas*, pp. 217, 216.

4 See Southam, *Literary Manuscripts*, chapter 4, for facts and speculation concerning the abandonment of this novel.

5 See ibid., chapter 3, pp. 52–4, for a discussion of Cassandra's note, which is reproduced in *MW*, facing p. 242.

6 Austen-Leigh, *Life and Letters*, pp. 96–8.

7 *Letters*, 29 January 1813, p. 298.

8 *Letters*, 23 March 1817, to Fanny Knight about *Persuasion*, p. 487: 'You may *perhaps* like the Heroine, as she is almost too good for me.'

9 Mary Wollstonecraft, *Maria, or the Wrongs of Woman* (London: Joseph Johnson, 1798, reprinted, Janet Todd (ed.), London: Chatto and Pickering, 1991).

10 Both Duckworth, *Improvement of the Estate* (pp. 128–31) and Butler, *War of Ideas* (pp. 215–16), for instance, see Darcy as the representative of the social stability and conservatism that they regard as the moral aim of the work.

11 Philip Drew, 'A Significant Incident in *Pride and Prejudice*', *Nineteenth-Century Fiction* 13 (1958), 356–68, sees Darcy's whole demeanour in his early social manner as affected by his chagrin at the Wickham–Georgiana episode.

12 Butler, *War of Ideas*, p. 216.

13 See *Letters*, 22 May 1817, p. 495: 'Ly P– writing to you even from Paris for advice! It is the Influence of Strength over Weakness indeed. Galigai de Concini for ever and ever.' Both Chapman (*Letters*, Notes, Letter 145)

and Bradbrook (*Jane Austen and her Predecessors*, p. 28) see this as a reference to Chesterfield's letter of 30 April 1752, in which he denounces the execution of Eleonore Galigai as a sorceress in 1617. She gave as her defence, to quote Chesterfield, that 'strong minds undoubtedly have an ascendant over weak ones'. Bradbrook generally supports the idea that internal evidence in the novels proves Austen's acquaintance with the work (pp. 28–34), but has little to say about *Pride and Prejudice* in comparison with the other novels.

14 Philip Dormer Stanhope, 4th Earl of Chesterfield, *Letters to his Son and Others*, ed. Robert K. Root (London: Everyman's Library no. 823, 1951), p. 37.

15 See Bradbrook, *Jane Austen and her Predecessors*, pp. 31–2.

16 These criticisms are made explicitly in Lascelles, *Jane Austen and her Art*, pp. 22 and 162, Mudrick, *Jane Austen: Irony as Defense and Discovery*, pp. 117–19, and Moler, *Jane Austen's Art of Allusion*, pp. 93–4, but are implied also in Marilyn Butler's assertion of the novel's moral inconsistency.

17 *NA* 243, on the subject of Henry's unromantic reasons for marrying Catherine.

18 Clarissa, for example, considers very carefully what material assistance she can accept from Lovelace; in Mary Brunton's *Discipline* (London, 1815, reprinted London: Pandora Press, 1986), Ellen Percy's inability to resist her lover's plans for an elopement stem partly from the fact that she has borrowed money from him. The sentimental novel tends to ignore materialistic notions of this sort, as has been noted above. In *SS* (pp. 58–9) Austen refers to a fashionable disregard for convention in the contrast between Marianne's wish to accept the gift of a horse from Willoughby, with no thought of impropriety, and Elinor's more conventional concern for her reputation.

19 *Letters*, 5 September 1796, p. 13.

20 Charlotte Smith's Emmeline is very concerned not to offend her suitor's aristocratic family; as is Laetitia Hawkins's Rosanne, in a novel of the same name which Austen found contained 'a thousand improbabilities' (*Letters*, circa December 1814, p. 422). Rather than 'pollute' the Brentleigh family with Rosanne's 'tainted' blood, Hawkins kills off the hero near the end of the novel.

21 *Letters*, 4 February 1813, pp. 299–300.

3 SENSE AND THE SINGLE GIRL

1 See Chapman (ed.), *Novels of Jane Austen*, 'Introductory Note to *Sense and Sensibility*', vol. 1, p. xii. Cassandra's note states that 'First Impressions' was completed in August 1797 and that *SS* was begun in November of that year.

2 Marilyn Butler's original exposition of Austen as conservative in *War of*

Ideas has resulted in a large number of critical works both for and against in which discussions of *SS* have been prominent. Claudia L. Johnson's statement of the feminist case in *Jane Austen: Women, Politics and the Novel* is of particular relevance to this novel (see chapter 3); Nicola J. Watson, in *Revolution and the Form of the British Novel 1790–1825: Intercepted Letters, Interrupted Seductions* (Oxford: Clarendon Press, 1994) supports Butler's case in a complex analysis of the demise of the epistolary novel – see pp. 87–90.

3 Jane West, *A Gossip's Story*, London, 1796. The quotation from Wilde is from *The Importance of Being Earnest*, Act II.

4 J. M. S. Tompkins first identified the possible influence of *A Gossip's Story* in ' "Elinor and Marianne": a Note on Jane Austen', *The Review of English Studies* 16 (1940), 33–43.

5 There is a family tradition that the original of *SS* was written as an exchange of letters – see Austen-Leigh, *Life and Letters*, p. 96. Nicola Watson, *Revolution and the Form of the British Novel*, acknowledges these reasons for Austen's rejection of the epistolary form (pp. 83–4), but sees its abandonment as part of a more general rejection of individualism as ideologically unacceptable.

6 *Essay on Human Understanding*, ed. Raymond Wilburn (London: Everyman's Library, Dent and Sons, 1948), II, I. iv.

7 Hannah More's poem *Sensibility* (1782), reprinted in Hannah More, *Poems*, with an introduction by Caroline Franklin, *The Romantics: Women Poets 1770–1830* 12 vols. (London: Routledge/Thoemmes Press, 1996), pp. 167–87, praises sensibility, but warns against hollow affectation and excess:

> *She* does not feel thy pow'r who boasts thy flame,
> And rounds her every period with thy name;
> Nor she who vents her disproportion'd sighs
> With pining *Lesbia* when her sparrow dies:
> Nor she who melts when hapless *Shore* expires,
> While real mis'ry unreliev'd retires!

She and Henry Mackenzie apparently exchanged letters of mutual admiration in 1778 – she for his novels, he for the sensibility of his hero and heroine in her play *Percy*. Only his reply has been preserved (William Roberts, *Memoirs of the Life and Correspondence of Mrs Hannah More* (London: Seeley and Burnside, 1834), vol. I, pp. 134–5). 'We are perfectly agreed', he writes, 'about the *pleasure* of the *pains* of sensibility.' She clearly had some doubts by 1782 about the more enthusiastic followers of Mackenzie.

8 *Letters*, 28 September 1814, p. 404.

9 *NA*, p. 37, probably referring to Edgeworth's 'Advertisement' to *Belinda* in 1801, in which she insists that the work is not a novel, but a 'moral tale'.

10 Adam Smith thought that displays of emotion were indicative of a higher level of civilisation than impassive endurance, which he saw as a concomitant of the primitive way of life. See *Theory of Moral Sentiments*

4th edn (London, 1774, first pub. 1759), part II, Section 2, pp. 317–18. See also Gerard A. Barker, *Henry Mackenzie* (Boston: Twayne, 1975), esp. pp. 65–6, for a discussion of Smith's influence on the doctrine of sensibility.

11 Jane West, *A Tale of the Times* (London, 1799); Maria Edgeworth, *Belinda* (London: Joseph Johnson, 1801; reprinted Kathryn J. Kirkpatrick (ed.), World's Classics, Oxford University Press, 1994). These two novelists may now seem to keep uneasy company in this discussion, since West cannot be said to have survived at all compared with Edgeworth. I defend the juxtaposition on the grounds that the two novelists had similar preoccupations, which Austen aimed to dislodge from fiction, and that she could not know at the time how fleeting West's high reputation would prove to be.

12 *Literary Ladies*, p. 39.

13 Kenneth Moler, *Jane Austen's Art of Allusion* chapter 2, esp. p. 73, notes the faults in Elinor and her difference from the stock 'sensible' sister, but concentrates his attention on only two aspects, her misjudgement of Willoughby, and her failure to take Marianne's illness seriously.

14 Fanny Burney, *Camilla*, p. 358.

15 Maria Edgeworth, *Belinda*, pp. 138–40.

16 Contemporary readers would probably be reminded here of Mackenzie's Emily Atkins in *The Man of Feeling*, whose seducer uses her interest in literature as a means of evoking her trust in him. It is notewothy that such a comparison bears no part in Elinor's estimate of Willoughby; indeed, it could not have, because she and Edward also have a mutual interest in reading.

17 *Belinda*, p. 139; *NA*, p. 53: 'Catherine immediately guessed [her] to be his sister; thus unthinkingly throwing away a fair opportunity of considering him lost to her for ever, by being married already.'

18 *Belinda*, p. 144.

19 Moler, *Jane Austen's Art of Allusion*, p. 73.

20 'The Father to be induced, at his Daughter's earnest request, to relate to her the past events of his Life. This Narrative will reach through the greatest part of the 1st vol.' *MW*, pp. 428–9.

21 See, for instance, Mary Lascelles, *Jane Austen and her Art*, p. 73.

22 See especially Tony Tanner, *Jane Austen* (London: Macmillan, 1986), p. 100.

23 Brownstein, '*Northanger Abbey*', p. 48, on the contrary, refers to 'the thoroughly unromantic resolution, coupling Marianne with the colonel in the flannel waistcoat'.

4 THE FRAILTIES OF *FANNY*

1 *Letters*, 8 February 1807, p. 180.

2 Ibid., 24 and 30 January 1809, pp. 256, 259.

3 Ibid., 11 October 1813, November or December 1814, pp. 344, 423.

4 Ford K. Brown, in *Fathers of the Victorians* (Cambridge University Press, 1962), gives the fullest account of the history and impact of the movement. See also Leonore Davidoff and Catherine Hall, *Family Fortunes* (London: Hutchinson, 1987), pp. 81–95, and Oliver MacDonagh, *Jane Austen: Real and Imagined Worlds* (New Haven and London: Yale University Press, 1991), chapter 1, for accounts of the movement. Marilyn Butler, in 'History, Politics, and Religion' in J. David Grey (ed.), *The Jane Austen Handbook with a Dictionary of Jane Austen's Life and Works* (London: Athlone Press, 1986), p. 104, sees the movement as partly supported by the aristocracy, but most of its leaders, though rich, were rather short on ancestry and much involved in respectable trade. Hannah More, for instance, was very much a self-made woman; see Mary Waldron, 'Ann Yearsley and the Clifton Records', *Age of Johnson* 3 (1990), 311, and *Lactilla, Milkwoman of Clifton: The Life and Writings of Ann Yearsley, 1753–1806* (Athens, Ga.: University of Georgia Press, 1996), pp. 25–6.

5 *Letters*, 18 November 1814, p. 410.

6 For the controversy surrounding Austen's possible support for Evangelicalism in *MP*, see Peter Garside and Elizabeth McDonald, 'Evangelicalism and *Mansfield Park*', *Trivium* 10 (1975), 34–50. This summarises the seminal text of Evangelicalism, William Wilberforce's *Practical View of the Religious System of Professed Christians in the Higher and Middle Classes in this Country Contrasted with Real Christianity* (London: Cadell and Davies, 1797) and quotes a number of opinions on its influence on *MP*, including those of Kaye-Smith and Sterne in their 1943 study *Talking of Jane Austen* and Q. D. Leavis (ed.), *Mansfield Park* (London: Macdonald, 1957), p. xii. See also David Monaghan, '*Mansfield Park* and Evangelicalism: a Reassessment', *Nineteenth-Century Fiction* 3 (1978), 215–30. Monaghan's essay surveys the critical work on *MP* from 1943 to 1978, noting the disagreements and fine distinctions among treatments of Austen's attitude to Evangelicalism.

7 *Quarterly Review* 24 (January 1821), 352–76. See Southam, *Critical Heritage*, p. 101.

8 *Englishwoman's Domestic Magazine* (August 1866). See Southam, *Critical Heritage*, p. 213.

9 'Jane Austen', *Quarterly Review* 228 (July 1917), 20–33.

10 Tony Tanner (ed.), *Mansfield Park* (London: Penguin Books, 1966), introduction, p. 8.

11 Isobel Armstrong, *Jane Austen: 'Mansfield Park'*, Penguin Critical Studies (London: Penguin Books, 1988), p. 99.

12 Critics who represent the dismissive and the more apologetic aspects of this judgement of the novel are Kingsley Amis, 'What Became of Jane Austen?', *Spectator* (4 October 1957), 33–40; Nina Auerbach, 'Jane Austen's Dangerous Charm – Feeling as One Ought about Fanny Price'

in Janet Todd (ed.), *Jane Austen: New Perspectives* (New York and London: Holmes and Meier, 1983), pp. 208–23, and Marilyn Butler, *War of Ideas*, pp. 248–9. Amis regards *MP* as 'the witness of [the] corruption' of Austen's 'judgement and moral sense'; Auerbach sees Fanny as a monster of spurious piety with whom the reader cannot identify; Butler describes the novel as well meant but 'an artistic failure' because of its attachment to 'old absolutes' which do not suit the novel form (pp. 248–9).

13 See, for example, Bernard Paris, *Character and Conflict in Jane Austen's Novels: A Psychological Approach* (Brighton: Harvester Press, 1978). He cites a number of incidents which reveal Fanny as anything but perfect; but he regards these as almost accidental on the part of the author. He suggests that 'the combination of mimetic characterization, comic action and moral theme poses artistic problems which may be insoluble' (p. 19). The implication is that Austen made Fanny more complex than she intended.

14 Sir Thomas's professed standards (and Edmund's and Fanny's initially) owe a good deal to the work of another Evangelical, Thomas Gisborne, especially his conduct-book *An Enquiry into the Duties of the Female Sex* (London, 1797). Bradbrook has pointed out how close his views on private theatricals come to those of Gisborne, who regarded them as 'almost certain ... to prove injurious to the female performers' (Gisborne, *Enquiry*, 2nd edn, p. 173, cited in Bradbrook, *Jane Austen and her Predecessors*, p. 36).

15 Said, *Culture and Materialism*, p. 104, sees 'the productivity and regulated discipline' of the Antigua plantation as reflected in the 'domestic harmony and attractive tranquillity' of the Mansfield household, and proceeds from there to establish to his satisfaction Austen's support for British commerce and colonialism. The attentive reader will find only the *appearance* of these things. The 'tranquillity' of Lady Bertram, for instance, is presented as irresponsible indolence, and the day at Sotherton should show how little actual harmony exists among the Mansfield family. Maria even loses her grip on basic good manners towards her host in her competition with Julia for the attention of Henry. 'Moral chaos' would better describe the situation, and *could* reflect a similar view of British commerce, but such an external reference seems unnecessary to explain the novel's dynamics.

16 *Cœlebs*, chapter 14, p. 66; chapter 17, p. 78.

17 Ibid., chapter 33, p. 163.

18 See Marilyn Butler, *War of Ideas*, p. 223, n. 2. Butler sees this as 'genuinely objective concern for the horse'; another reading suggests that, on the contrary, Fanny does not really know herself at this time.

19 See Garside and McDonald, 'Evangelicalism and *Mansfield Park*', p. 229, where attention is drawn to Fanny's impotence during this episode.

20 Paris, *Character and Conflict*, p. 53. Paris cites this point in evidence that

Austen failed in her task of combining 'mimetic characterization, comic action and moral theme'.

21 Bradbrook, *Jane Austen and her Predecessors*, p. 15, points out the similarity of the memory effusion to Johnson's remarks in *Idler* 74 and Hannah More's in *Strictures on the Present System of Female Education* (London: Cadell, 1799), p. 349. Lucilla is unwontedly communicative and enthusiastic about gardens in chapter 33, p. 165, of *Cœlebs*.

22 Hannah More, *Essays on Various Subjects, Principally designed for Young Ladies* (London: Cadell and Davies, 1777), 'True and False Meekness', p. 115. More modified her vocabulary in the later *Strictures*, but maintained this rather difficult combination of habitual meekness combined with sturdy assertiveness on appropriate occasions. It is what, above all, makes Lucilla so improbable.

23 *Cœlebs*, chapter 31, pp. 154–6.

24 MacDonagh, *Jane Austen: Real and Imagined Worlds*, pp. 8–9, seems to make Sir Thomas an authorial spokesman here. Much of the support for the supposed unreconstructed Evangelicalism of *Mansfield Park* proceeds from a tendency to regard the utterances of Sir Thomas and Edmund as echoes of the author's own opinion. This proceeds from a conviction that there must of necessity be an authority figure present. See also Marilyn Butler, 'History, Politics and Religion', p. 206.

25 Tanner, (ed.) *Mansfield Park*, p. 8.

26 Archbishop Whately made this point in 1821; see Southam, *Critical Heritage*, p. 101; Paris, *Character and Conflict*, p. 60, notes this inappropriate euphoria also occurring at the end of the novel, when Fanny returns to Mansfield from Portsmouth.

27 *Cœlebs*, chapter 31, p. 156.

28 A further instance of this is Fanny's communication concerning the part played by Tom's illness in Mary's final attempt at 'complete reconciliation' (*MP* 459); Fanny convinces herself that she must be cruel to be kind – but her motive is clearly to put an end, finally, to Edmund's wavering.

5 MEN OF SENSE AND SILLY WIVES – THE CONFUSIONS OF MR KNIGHTLEY

1 Austen-Leigh, *Memoir* p. 157.

2 Elizabeth Hamilton, *Memoirs of Modern Philosophers* (Bath, 1800).

3 Two of these works are available in modern editions – *The Female Quixote* (1752; reprinted World's Classics, Oxford University Press, 1989); *Discipline* (London: Pandora, 1986); 'Angelina, or l'Amie Inconnue' will be included in Marilyn Butler and Mitzi Myers (eds.), *The Works of Maria Edgeworth* (London: Chatto and Pickering, forthcoming 2000), vol. 10.

4 Laura G. Mooneyham, *Romance, Language and Education in Jane Austen's Novels* (London: Macmillan Press, 1988), p. 107. Many other critics uphold this view in one way or another: Tanner, *Jane Austen*, esp. p. 202

– 'Mr Knightley and his brother, who speak only sense'; Edward Neill, 'Between Defence and Destruction: "Situations" of Recent Critical Theory and Jane Austen's *Emma*', *Critical Quarterly* 29 (1987), 39–54, esp. p. 44; Alison Sulloway, *Jane Austen and the Province of Womanhood* (Philadelphia: University of Pennsylvania Press, 1989), esp. p. 39; Roger Gard, *Jane Austen's Art of Clarity* (New Haven and London: Yale University Press, 1992); and Beth Fowkes Tobin, *Superintending the Poor: Charitable Ladies and Paternal Landlords in British Fiction, 1770–1860* (New Haven and London: Yale University Press, 1993), where comment on *Emma* sees Austen upholding traditional patriarchal values through Knightley – see chapter 3, esp. pp. 69–70.

5 For example, J. F. Burrows, *Jane Austen's 'Emma'* (Sydney University Press, 1968), p. 13, questions his authoritative function in the novel, but stops short of denying it altogether. 'It is a matter', he says in his introduction, 'of accepting him as a leading but not oracular participant . . . a matter of heeding his words but not bowing to them.'

6 See Kirkham, *Jane Austen: Feminism and Fiction*, chapter 18, esp. p. 133 and also Claudia Johnson, *Jane Austen: Women, Politics and the Novel*, p. 140. See also Kirkham, *Jane Austen: Feminism and Fiction*, introduction, p. xxi: 'we can see that Austen's subject-matter is the central subject-matter of rational, or Enlightenment feminism and that her viewpoint . . . is strikingly similar to that shown by Mary Wollstonecraft in *A Vindication of the Rights of Woman*'.

7 *Letters*, 2 March 1814, p. 377.

8 Barrett, *Heroine*, chapter 49.

9 Gisborne, *Enquiry*; 'I am glad you recommended 'Gisborne,' for having begun, I am pleased with it, and I had quite determined not to read it.' *Letters*, 30 August 1805, p. 169.

10 My attention has been drawn to an unusual exploration of Mrs Goddard's point of view in a recent novel: Joan Austen-Leigh, *Mrs Goddard: Mistress of a School* (Victoria, B.C.: Room of One's Own Press, 1993).

11 Glenda A. Hudson, *Sibling Love and Incest in Jane Austen's Fiction* (London: Macmillan Press, 1992), p. 51.

12 Juliet McMaster, *Jane Austen in Love* (Victoria, B.C.: English Literary Studies, 1978), p. 61.

13 Gregory, *A Father's Legacy*, p. 13 (see chapter 1, n. 3 above) and Hannah More, *Essays*, pp. 37–8. 'It has been advised, and by very respectable authorities too, that in conversation women should carefully conceal any knowledge or learning they may happen to possess. I own, with submission, that I do not see either the necessity or propriety of this advice.' Nevertheless, More goes on to erode her own argument by asserting that a girl with 'discretion and modesty, without which all knowledge is of little worth . . . will never make an ostentatious display of it'. More's speciality was providing quotable phrases for all sides of the argument.

14 Gisborne, *Enquiry*, chapter 12, pp. 271–2: 'if we speak of intelligent and

well-informed women in general, of women, who, without becoming absorbed in the depths of erudition, and losing all esteem and relish for social duties, are distinguished by a cultivated understanding, a polished taste, and a memory stored with useful and elegant information; there appears no reason to dread from the possession of these endowments a neglect of the duties of the mistress of a family'.

6 RATIONALITY AND REBELLION: *PERSUASION* AND THE MODEL GIRL

1 *Letters*, 23 March 1817, to Fanny Knight, p. 487: 'You will not like it, so you need not be impatient. You may *perhaps* like the Heroine, as she is almost too good for me.'

2 *War of Ideas*, p. 284.

3 *British Critic* n.s. 9 (March 1818), 293–301; cited in Southam, *Critical Heritage*, p. 84.

4 Butler, *War of Ideas*, suggests that the novel falls apart in its effort to reconcile its approval for intensity of feeling with 'the old ethical certainties' (pp. 278–80). Mudrick, *Jane Austen: Irony as Defense and Discovery*, p. 219, feels that it founders on the harsh treatment of the unsympathetic characters, such as Sir Walter and Mrs Clay. He thinks Anne as she is written incapable of such judgements and the novel therefore in need of radical revision. Margaret Kirkham, assuming with other critics a feminist constituency for the novel, feels that it falls short of its own objectives (see Kirkham, *Jane Austen: Feminism and Fiction*, p. 152). A less prescriptive programme for the novel will better preserve its artistic integrity.

5 *Letters*, 23 March 1817, pp. 486–7.

6 Ibid., 5 September 1796, p. 13.

7 *The Wanderer; or, Female Difficulties* (London: Longman, Hurst, Rees, Orme and Brown, 1814; reprinted, Margaret Anne Doody, Robert L. Mack and Peter Sabor (eds.), Oxford University Press, 1991, with introduction by Margaret Anne Doody).

8 *Letters*, 8 February 1807, p. 180.

9 Butler, *War of Ideas*, p. 275, gives Wentworth's ideas a Godwinian edge of 'revolutionary optimism' which she feels the novel sets out to undermine. Again this presupposes its didacticism, and simplifies Wentworth's essentially confused reactions.

10 Tanner, *Jane Austen*, p. 235.

11 The acknowledgement and representation of sexual passion in a female, especially if she is not certain of a return, is almost always, in Burney and Edgeworth, associated with infection from radical theories about the rights of woman drawn from such writers as Wollstonecraft, Hays and Godwin (see for example Elinor Joddrell in *The Wanderer* and Harriet Freke in *Belinda*).

12 Many critics have, I think, laid too little emphasis on the reader's consciousness in an Austen novel. Irony enables Austen to dispense almost entirely with the authorial voice except for the barest essentials of the narrative chronology. She rarely steps in to tell the reader what to think.

13 'There is no greater sorrow than to remember a happy time in the midst of misery', *Divina commedia*, 'Inferno', v, 121–3.

14 Quotations from *The Giaour* and *The Corsair* are taken from Frederick Page (ed.), *Byrons's Poetical Works*, 3rd edn (Oxford University Press, 1970).

15 And Charlotte Smith, whose Sonnet 2 in *Elegiac Sonnets* (1797) reprinted with introduction by Caroline Franklin, *The Romantics: Women Poets, 1770–1830* (Bristol: Thoemmes Press, 1996), may be the source of the idea of a 'second spring' which recurs throughout the novel. See Loraine Fletcher, 'Time and Mourning in *Persuasion*', *Women's Writing* 5 (1998), 81–90.

16 Many critics have discussed Austen's use of Byron in *P*. See Peter Knox-Shaw's admirable summing up of such work up to 1993 in his article '*Persuasion*, Byron, and the Turkish Tale', *Review of English Studies* 44 (February 1993), 47–69.

17 *Letters*, 5 March 1814, p. 379. What she actually writes is '& have nothing else to do' except write to Cassandra.

18 Chesterfield, 18 November o.s., 1748, p. 85.

19 Ibid., 22 May, o.s., 1749, p. 103.

20 Mr Elliot follows Chesterfield closely here. Compare Chesterfield (12 October o.s., 1748, p. 70): 'Good company is not what respective sets of company are pleased either to call or think themselves, but is the company which all the people of the place call and acknowledge to be good company, notwithstanding some objections which they may form to some of the individuals who compose it … It consists chiefly … of people of considerable birth, rank, and character'; and Mr Elliot, who regards the Dalrymple connection ' "as good company, as those who would collect good company around them … Good company requires only birth, education and manners, and with regard to education is not very nice" ' (*P* 150).

21 '… they almost adore that man, who talks more seriously to them, and who seems to consult and trust them; I say, who seems, for weak men really do, but wise ones only seem to do it' (Chesterfield, 5 September o.s., 1748, p. 66).

22 There is an irresistible indication here that Austen had *The Wanderer* in mind during the composition of *P*. In chapter 27 (p. 267) of Fanny Burney's novel, Juliet is caught in the rain as she comes out of church. Sir Lyell Sycamore, the vile seducer, who regards the unprotected Juliet as his next victim, offers his services in much the same terms as Wentworth. Both parallel and contrast are striking.

23 Reprinted in Chapman (ed.), *Novels of Jane Austen* vol. v, pp. 253–63.
24 Ibid., p. 255.
25 Mooneyham (*Romance, Language and Education*, p. 174) also acknowledges Anne's positive role in forcing a response from Wentworth in this episode.
26 These are oft-repeated views; see, for example, Tobin, *Superintending the Poor*, p. 97; and Tanner, *Jane Austen*, p. 249.

7 SANDITION – CONCLUSION

1 *Blackwood's Edinburgh Magazine* 86 (July 1859), 90–113, cited in Southam, *Critical Heritage*, pp. 148–66.
2 Butler, *War of Ideas*, p. 287; Tanner, *Jane Austen*, p. 252.
3 *Letters*, 14 September 1804, p. 138.
4 Ibid., p. 143.
5 Butler, *War of Ideas*, p. 287.
6 Williams, *The Country and the City*, p. 115.
7 Southam, *Literary Manuscripts*, p. 104.
8 Mudrick, *Jane Austen: Irony as Defense and Discovery*, p. 256.
9 Wiltshire, in *The Cambridge Companion to Jane Austen*, has highlighted the importance of the outdoors in the three last completed novels, especially *MP*: 'Settings are never neutral backgrounds in *Mansfield Park*, and the gardens at Sotherton, famously, are made to play an integral, even determinative part in the action' (p. 65).
10 Fanny Burney, *Wanderer*, p. 676.
11 Ibid., pp. 801–2.
12 This parallel from a novel of 1752 suggests that Mudrick (*Jane Austen: Irony as Defense and Discovery*, p. 256) is wrong in asserting that Austen was departing from convention in presenting the idea of seduction comically.
13 Kirkham, *Jane Austen: Feminism and Fiction*, p. 156.
14 The influence of theatrical structures in the narrative of *Mansfield Park* is discussed by Paula Byrne in '"We Must Descend a Little": *Mansfield Park* and the Comic Theatre', *Women's Writing* 5 (1998), 91–102.
15 Maria Edgeworth, *Patronage* (London, 1814, reprinted London: Pandora Press, 1986).
16 Gary Kelly makes just this point in 'Religion and Politics' in *The Cambridge Companion to Jane Austen*, pp. 166–7: 'Austen's novels have indeed been found eminently rereadable, a fact which has made them into "classics", or literature.'

Bibliography

Amis, Kingsley, 'What Became of Jane Austen?', *Spectator* (4 October 1957), 33–40.

Armstrong, Isobel, *Jane Austen: 'Mansfield Park'*, Penguin Critical Studies, London: Penguin Books, 1988.

Armstrong, Nancy, *Desire and Domestic Fiction: A Political History of the Novel*, Oxford University Press, 1987.

Auerbach, Nina, 'Jane Austen's Dangerous Charm – Feeling as One Ought about Fanny Price' in Janet Todd (ed.), *Jane Austen: New Perspectives*, New York and London: Holmes and Meier, 1983, pp. 208–23.

Austen, Henry, 'Biographical Notice of the Author', 1817, reprinted R. W. Chapman (ed.), *The Novels of Jane Austen*, 3rd edn, 5 vols., Oxford University Press, 1959, v.

Austen-Leigh, J. E., *A Memoir of Jane Austen*, London, 1870, 1871, reprinted R. W. Chapman (ed.), Oxford University Press, 1926.

Austen-Leigh, Joan, *Mrs Goddard: Mistress of a School*, Victoria, B.C.: Room of One's Own Press, 1993.

Austen-Leigh, W. and R. A., *Jane Austen: Her Life and Letters*, London, 1913.

Barker, Gerard A., *Henry Mackenzie*, Boston: Twayne, 1975.

Barrett, Eaton Stannard, *The Heroine, or Adventures of a Fair Romance Reader*, London, 1813.

Bateson, F. W., *English Poetry and the English Language*, Oxford University Press, 1934.

Bator, Paul G., 'Rhetoric and the Novel in the Eighteenth-Century British University Curriculum', *Eighteenth-Century Studies* 30, number 2 (Winter 1996–7), 173–91.

Bradbrook, Frank W., *Jane Austen and her Predecessors*, Cambridge University Press, 1966.

Brooks, Cleanth, *The Well-wrought Urn*, New York: Reynal and Hitchcock, 1947.

Brown, Ford K., *Fathers of the Victorians*, Cambridge University Press, 1962.

Brown, Lloyd W., *Bits of Ivory: Narrative Technique in Jane Austen's Fiction*, Baton Rouge: Louisiana State University Press, 1973.

Brownstein, Rachel M., '*Northanger Abbey, Sense and Sensibility* and *Pride and Prejudice*' in Edward Copeland and Juliet McMaster (eds.), *The*

Cambridge Companion to Jane Austen, Cambridge University Press, 1997.

Brunton, Mary, *Discipline*, London, 1815, reprinted London: Pandora Press, 1986.

Self-control, London, 1810, reprinted London: Pandora Press, 1986.

Burney, Fanny, *Camilla, or a Picture of Youth*, (London: Strahan, 1796), reprinted, E. and L. Bloom (eds.), World's Classics, Oxford University Press, 1983.

Cecilia, London 1782, reprinted, World's Classics, Oxford University Press, 1996.

Evelina, or a Young Lady's Entrance into the World, London, 1778, reprinted London: Everyman, J. M. Dent, 1967.

The Wanderer; or, Female Difficulties, London: Longman, Hurst, Rees, Orme and Brown, 1814, reprinted, Margaret Anne Doody, Robert L. Mack and Peter Sabor (eds.), with introduction by Margaret Anne Doody, Oxford University Press, 1991.

Burney, Sarah, *Clarentine*, London, 1798.

Burrows, J. F., *Jane Austen's 'Emma'*, Sydney University Press, 1968.

Butler, Marilyn, 'History, Politics, and Religion' in J. David Grey (ed.), *The Jane Austen Handbook with a Dictionary of Jane Austen's Life and Works*, London: Athlone Press, 1986.

Jane Austen and the War of Ideas, Oxford: Clarendon Press, 1975, reprinted 1985.

Byrne, Paula, ' "We Must Descend a Little": *Mansfield Park* and the Comic Theatre', *Women's Writing* 5 (1998), 91–102.

Byron, Lord (George Gordon), *Byron's Poetical Works*, Frederick Page (ed.), 3rd edn, Oxford University Press, 1970.

Chapman, R. W. (ed.), *Jane Austen's Letters*, 2nd edn 1952, reprinted Oxford University Press, 1964.

Chesterfield, Lord, see Stanhope.

Copeland, Edward and Juliet McMaster (eds.), *The Cambridge Companion to Jane Austen*, Cambridge University Press, 1997.

Davidoff, Leonore and Catherine Hall, *Family Fortunes*, London: Hutchinson, 1987.

Drew, Philip, 'A Significant Incident in *Pride and Prejudice*', *Nineteenth-Century Fiction* 13 (1958), 356–68.

Duckworth, Alistair M., *The Improvement of the Estate*, Baltimore and London: Johns Hopkins University Press, 1971.

Edgeworth, Maria, *Angelina, or l'Amie Inconnue*, Marilyn Butler (ed.), Oxford University Press, forthcoming, 1999.

Belinda, London, 1801, reprinted, Kathryn J. Kirkpatrick (ed.), World's Classics, Oxford University Press, 1994.

Letters for Literary Ladies, London, 1795, reprinted, with an introduction by Claire Conolly, London: Everyman, J. M. Dent, 1993.

Patronage, London, 1814, reprinted, London: Pandora Press, 1986.

Emerson, R. W., *Journals*, 9 vols., Boston, 1913, vol. IX.

Farrer, Reginald, 'Jane Austen, ob. July 18 1817', *Quarterly Review* 228 (July 1917), 20–33.

Fergus, Jan, *Jane Austen and the Didactic Novel*, London: Macmillan, 1983.

Flammenburg, Lawrence, *The Necromancer; or the Tale of the Black Forest*, translated by Peter Teutold (1794), reprinted Devendra P. Varma (ed.), *The Northanger Novels*, London: Folio Press, 1968.

Fletcher, Loraine, 'Time and Mourning in *Persuasion*', *Women's Writing* 5 (1998), 81–90.

Franklin, Caroline (ed.), *The Romantics: Women Poets 1770–1830*, 12 vols., London: Routledge/Thoemmes Press, 1996.

Gard, Roger, *Jane Austen's Art of Clarity*, New Haven and London: Yale University Press, 1992.

Garrod, H. W., 'Jane Austen: a Depreciation' in *Essays by Divers Hands*, London, 1928.

Garside, Peter and Elizabeth McDonald, 'Evangelicalism and *Mansfield Park*', *Trivium* 10 (1975), 34–50.

Gisborne, Thomas, *An Enquiry into the Duties of the Female Sex*, London, 1797.

Gregory, John, et al., *The Young Lady's Pocket Library, or Parental Monitor*, London, 1790, reprinted, with introduction by Vivien Jones, Bristol: Thoemmes Press, 1995.

Grey, J. David (ed.), *The Jane Austen Handbook with a Dictionary of Jane Austen's Life and Works*, London: Athlone Press, 1986.

Grundy, Isobel, 'Jane Austen and Literary Traditions' in Edward Copeland and Juliet McMaster (eds.), *The Cambridge Companion to Jane Austen*, Cambridge University Press, 1997.

Hamilton, Elizabeth, *Memoirs of Modern Philosophers*, Bath, 1800.

Harding, D. W., 'Regulated Hatred: an Aspect of the Work of Jane Austen', *Scrutiny* 8 (March 1940), 346–62.

Hays, Mary, *Memoirs of Emma Courtney* (1796), reprinted Eleanor Ty (ed.), World's Classics, Oxford University Press, 1996.

Hudson, Glenda A., *Sibling Love and Incest in Jane Austen's Fiction*, London: Macmillan Press, 1992.

Johnson, Claudia L., *Jane Austen: Women, Politics and the Novel*, University of Chicago Press, 1988.

Johnson, R. Brimley, *The Women Novelists*, London, 1918.

Kaye-Smith, Sheila and G. B. Sterne, *Talking of Jane Austen*, London: Cassell, 1943.

Kelly, Gary, 'Religion and Politics' in Edward Copeland and Juliet McMaster (eds.), *The Cambridge Companion to Jane Austen*, Cambridge University Press, 1997.

Kettle, Arnold, *An Introduction to the English Novel*, 2 vols. London: Hutchinson, 1951, vol. I.

Kirkham, Margaret, *Jane Austen: Feminism and Fiction*, Hassocks, Sussex: Harvester Press, 1983, reprinted London: Athlone Press, 1997.

Knox-Shaw, Peter, '*Persuasion*, Byron, and the Turkish Tale', *Review of English Studies* 44, number 173 (February 1993), 47–69.

Lascelles, Mary, *Jane Austen and her Art*, Oxford University Press 1939, reprinted 1968.

Lathom, Francis, *The Midnight Bell*, London, 1798, reprinted, Devendra P. Varma (ed.), *The Northanger Novels*, London: Folio Press, 1968.

Leavis, Q. D., *Fiction and the Reading Public*, London: Chatto and Windus, 1932.

'A Critical Theory of Jane Austen's Writings', *Scrutiny* 10 (June 1941), 61–87; (October 1941), 114–42; (January 1942,) 272–94; and *Scrutiny* 12 (Spring 1944), 104–19.

Leavis, Q. D. (ed.), *Mansfield Park*, London: Macdonald, 1957.

Lennox, Charlotte, *The Female Quixote*, London, 1752, reprinted, World's Classics, Oxford University Press, 1989.

Lewes, George Henry, 'The Novels of Jane Austen', *Blackwood's Edinburgh Magazine* 86 (July 1859), 99–113, reprinted in B.C Southam, *Critical Heritage*.

Litz, A. Walton, *Jane Austen: A Study of her Artistic Development*, London: Chatto and Windus, 1965.

Locke, Joseph, *Essay on Human Understanding*, Raymond Wilburn (ed.), London: Everyman's Library, Dent and Sons, 1948.

Lodge, David, *The Language of Fiction: Essays in Criticism and Verbal Analysis of the English Novel*, London: Routledge and Kegan Paul, 1966.

MacDonagh, Oliver, *Jane Austen: Real and Imagined Worlds*, New Haven and London: Yale University Press, 1991.

Mackenzie, Henry, *Julia de Roubigné*, London, 1777.

The Man of Feeling (1773), London: G. Routledge, 1906.

McMaster, Juliet, *Jane Austen in Love*, Victoria, B.C.: English Literary Studies, 1978.

Miller, D. A., *Narrative and its Discontents: Problems of Closure in the Traditional Novel*, Princeton University Press, 1981.

Mitford, Mary Russell, Letter to Sir William Elford 20 December 1814 in A. G. L'Estrange (ed.), *Life of Mary Russell Mitford*, vol. 1, p. 300, reprinted in B. C. Southam, *Critical Heritage*..

Moler, Kenneth, *Jane Austen's Art of Allusion*, Lincoln: University of Nebraska Press, 1977.

Monaghan, David, '*Mansfield Park* and Evangelicalism: a Reassessment', *Nineteenth-Century Fiction* 3 (1978), 215–30.

Mooneyham, Laura G., *Romance, Language and Education in Jane Austen's Novels*, London: Macmillan Press, 1988.

More, Hannah, *Cœlebs in Search of a Wife*, London, 1808, reprinted, with introduction by Mary Waldron, Bristol: Thoemmes Press, 1995.

Essays on Various Subjects, Principally designed for Young Ladies, London: Cadell and Davies, 1777.

Poems, with an introduction by Caroline Franklin, *The Romantics: Women*

Poets 1770–1830, 12 vols., London: Routledge/Thoemmes Press, 1996.

Strictures on the Present System of Female Education, London: Cadell, 1799.

Mudrick, Marvin, *Jane Austen: Irony as Defense and Discovery*, Berkeley and Los Angeles: University of California Press, 1952.

Neill, Edward, 'Between Defence and Destruction: "Situations" of Recent Critical Theory and Jane Austen's *Emma*', *Critical Quarterly* 29 (1987), 39–54.

Newsom, Robert, *A Likely Story: Probability and Play in Fiction*, New Brunswick and London: Rutgers University Press, 1988.

Paris, Bernard, *Character and Conflict in Jane Austen's Novels: A Psychological Approach*, Brighton: Harvester Press, 1978.

Parsons, Eliza, *The Castle of Wolfenbach*, London, 1793, reprinted, with introduction by Devendra P. Varma (ed.), *The Northanger Novels*, London: Folio Press, 1968.

The Mysterious Warning, London, 1796, reprinted, Devendra P. Varma (ed.), *The Northanger Novels*, London: Folio Press, 1968.

Patey, Douglas Lane, *Probability and Literary Form*, Cambridge University Press, 1984.

Poovey, Mary, *The Proper Lady and the Woman Writer: Ideology as Style in the Works of Mary Wollstonecraft, Mary Shelley, and Jane Austen*, University of Chicago Press, 1984.

Radcliffe, Ann, *The Mysteries of Udolpho*, London, 1794, reprinted, with introduction by Bonamy Dobrée and explanatory notes by Frederick Garber, World's Classics, Oxford University Press, 1980.

Richards, I. A., *The Principles of Literary Criticism*, London, 1924.

Richardson, Samuel, *Clarissa*, London, 1747–8, reprinted Angus Ross (ed.), Harmondsworth: Viking, 1985.

Pamela, London, 1740, reprinted with introduction by Margaret Doody, Harmondsworth: Penguin Classics, 1980.

Sir Charles Grandison, London, 1753–4, reprinted Jocelyn Harris (ed.), 3 vols., Oxford University Press, 1980.

Roberts, William, *Memoirs of the Life and Correspondence of Mrs. Hannah More*, 3 vols., London: Seeley and Burnside, 1834.

Roche, Regina Maria, *Clermont*, London, 1798, reprinted, Devendra P. Varma (ed.), *The Northanger Novels*, London: Folio Press, 1968.

Sadleir, Michael, *The Northanger Novels: A Footnote to Jane Austen*, English Association Pamphlet 68, 1927.

Said, Edward, *Culture and Materialism*, London: Chatto and Windus, 1993, reprinted Vintage, 1994.

Scott, Walter, 'Review of "Emma"', *Quarterly Review* 14 (March 1816), 188–201.

Secker, Thomas, *Lectures on the Church Catechism*, 1769.

Simpson, Richard, 'Jane Austen', *North British Review* 52 (April 1870), 129–52, reprinted in Southam, *Critical Heritage*, pp. 241–265.

Sleath, Eleanor, *The Orphan of the Rhine*, London, 1798, reprinted Devendra P. Varma (ed.), *The Northanger Novels*, London: Folio Press, 1968.

Smith, Adam, *Theory of Moral Sentiments* (1759), 4th edn, London, 1774.

Smith, Charlotte, *Elegiac Sonnets* (1797), reprinted, with introduction by Caroline Franklin, *The Romantics: Women Poets, 1770–1830*, 12 vols., Bristol: Routledge/Thoemmes Press, 1996.

    Emmeline, or the Orphan of the Castle, London, 1788, reprinted London: Pandora Press, 1988.

    Ethelinde, London, 1789.

Southam B. C., *The Critical Heritage*, London: Routledge and Kegan Paul, 1968, revised and reprinted 1986.

    Jane Austen's Literary Manuscripts: A Study of the Novelist's Development Through the Surviving Papers, Oxford University Press, 1964.

    'The Silence of the Bertrams: Slavery and the Chronology of *Mansfield Park*', *Times Literary Supplement*, 17 February, 1995, 13–14.

Stanhope, Philip Dormer, 4th Earl of Chesterfield, *Letters to his Son and Others*, Robert K. Root (ed.), London: Everyman's Library, Dent and Sons, 1951.

Sulloway, Alison, *Jane Austen and the Province of Womanhood*, Philadelphia: University of Pennsylvania Press, 1989.

Tanner, Tony, *Jane Austen*, London: Macmillan, 1986.

Tanner, Tony (ed.), *Mansfield Park*, London: Penguin Books, 1966.

Tobin, Beth Fowkes, *Superintending the Poor: Charitable Ladies and Paternal Landlords in British Fiction, 1770–1860*, New Haven and London: Yale University Press, 1993.

Todd, Janet (ed.), *Jane Austen: New Perspectives*, New York and London: Holmes and Meier, 1983.

Tompkins, J. M. S., '"Elinor and Marianne": a Note on Jane Austen', *Review of English Studies* 16 (1940), 33–43.

Trilling, Lionel, *The Opposing Self*, New York: Viking Press, 1955.

Varma, Devendra P. (ed.), *The Northanger Novels*, 7 vols. London: Folio Press, 1968.

Waldron, Mary, 'Ann Yearsley and the Clifton Records', *Age of Johnson* 3 (1990).

    Lactilla, Milkwoman of Clifton: The Life and Writings of Ann Yearsley, 1753–1806, Athens, Ga.: University of Georgia Press, 1996.

Watson, Nicola J., *Revolution and the Form of the British Novel 1790–1825: Intercepted Letters, Interrupted Seductions*, Oxford: Clarendon Press, 1994.

West, Jane, *A Gossip's Story*, London, 1796.

    Letters addressed to a Young Man, London, 1801.

    Letters to a Young Lady, London, 1806.

    A Tale of the Times, London, 1799.

Whately, Richard, '*Northanger Abbey* and *Persuasion*', *Quarterly Review* 24 (January 1821), 352–76, reprinted in B. C. Southam, *Critical Heritage*.

Wilberforce, William, *Practical View of the Religious System of Professed Christians in the Higher and Middle Classes in this Country Contrasted with Real Christianity*, London: Cadell and Davies, 1797.

Wilde, Oscar, *The Importance of Being Earnest*, Harmondsworth: Penguin Books, 1970.

Will, P., *Horrid Mysteries*, London, 1796, reprinted, Devendra P. Varma (ed.), *The Northanger Novels*, London: Folio Press, 1968.

Williams, Raymond, *The Country and the City*, London: Chatto and Windus, 1973.

Wiltshire, John, '*Mansfield Park, Emma, Persuasion*' in Edward Copeland and Juliet McMaster (eds.), *The Cambridge Companion to Jane Austen*, Cambridge University Press, 1997.

Wimsatt, W. K., *The Verbal Icon: Studies in the Meaning of Poetry*, (1954), reprinted London: Methuen, 1970.

Wollstonecraft, Mary, *A Vindication of the Rights of Woman*, London, 1792, reprinted, with introduction by Miriam Brody Kramnick, London: Penguin Classics, 1985.

Maria, or the Wrongs of Woman, London: Joseph Johnson, 1798 reprinted, Janet Todd (ed.), London: Chatto and Pickering, 1991.

Index

Angelina, or l'Amie Inconnue, see
    Edgeworth
Amis, Kingsley, 'What Became of Jane
    Austen?' 176 n. 12
Armstrong, Isobel, *Jane Austen: 'Mansfield
    Park'*, Penguin Critical Studies, 89
Armstrong, Nancy, *Desire and Domestic Fiction:
    A Political History of the Novel*, 10, 169 n. 30
Auerbach, Nina, 'Jane Austen's Dangerous
    Charm – Feeling as One Ought about
    Fanny Price', 176 n. 12
Austen, Anna (afterwards Lefroy), 1, 13;
    unpublished novel, 65
Austen, Cassandra, 1, 3, 13; note on order of
    composition of the novels, 25; ideas
    about fiction, 60; see also Letters
Austen, Henry, 'Biographical Notice of the
    Author', 5
Austen, Jane, narrowness of range, 3, 4, 6
    Catharine or the Bower, 18, **19–25**, 39, 41, 48;
    critical opinion: Southam, 22
    'Elinor and Marianne', 25–6, 64
    Emma, review by Scott, 4; **112–34**; critical
    opinion: Burrows, Gard, Mooneyham,
    Neill, Sulloway, Tanner, Tobin, 178–9
    nn. 4, 5, Kirkham, 114–15; see also
    'Opinions of *Emma*'
    'First Impressions', original draft of *Pride
    and Prejudice*, 37, 39; rejected by Cadell,
    the publisher, 25, 39
    Jack and Alice, 16–17
    Juvenilia, 15, 16–18
    Lady Susan, 18, 25, 64
    Lesley Castle, 17
    Love and Freindship, 17–18
    Mansfield Park, 8, 9, **85–111**; evangelical
    influence, 8, 12, 85–6, 90, 95, 99, 105;
    and the slave trade, 12–13; critical
    opinion: Isobel Armstrong, 89, Butler,
    10, *Englishwoman's Domestic Magazine*, 88,
    Farrer, 6, 88–9, Litz, 9, Paris, 177 nn. 13,

20, Said, 169 n. 34, 177 n. 15, Southam,
    169 n. 34, Tanner, 89, 105; see also
    'Opinions of *Mansfield Park*
Northanger Abbey, 1, 24, **26–36**; early
    version, 'Susan', 25–6; reference to
    Gregory, 18–19
Persuasion, 9, **135–56**; critical opinion:
    British Critic, 135, Butler, 135, Mudrick, 9,
    Tanner, 141; the cancelled chapter, 154
Plan of a Novel, 13, 79, 137–8, 150–1
Pride and Prejudice, 9, 37, 39, **41–61**,
    inheritance and money, 39; critical
    opinion: Austen's own critique, 'light,
    and bright, and sparkling', 13, 60, 62;
    Butler, 37, 51, Litz 9, Mudrick 9
Sanditon, 9, 15, **157–65**; critical opinion:
    Butler, 158, 159, Mudrick, 9, Southam,
    160, Tanner, 158
Sense and Sensibility, 9, 37, **62–83**, 162;
    publication, 26, 39; inheritance and
    money, 37, 62; probable date of
    composition, 62; critical opinion: Butler,
    10, Farrer, 6, Mudrick, 9
The Watsons, 18, 38–41, 43–4, 49; influence
    on *Pride and Prejudice*, 39–41; time of
    composition, 25–6
Austen-Leigh, James Edward, letter to, 16
    December 1816, 'little bit … of Ivory', 5;
    Memoir, 5, 13, 14, 169 n. 35

Barrett, Eaton Stannard, *The Heroine, or
    Adventures of a Fair Romance Reader*, 33, 113,
    114, 121
Bator, Paul G., 'Rhetoric and the Novel in
    the Eighteenth Century British
    University Curriculum', 167 n. 5
Belinda, see Edgeworth
'Biographical Notice of the Author', see
    Austen, Henry
Bronte, Charlotte, opinion of Austen, 168
    n. 24